Reluctant Crusaders

Reluctant Crusaders

POWER, CULTURE, AND CHANGE
IN AMERICAN GRAND STRATEGY

Colin Dueck

PRINCETON UNIVERSITY PRESS
PRINCETON AND OXFORD

Library of Congress Cataloging-in-Publication Data

Dueck, Colin, 1969–

Reluctant crusaders : power, culture, and change in American grand strategy / Colin Dueck

p. cm.

Includes bibliographical references and index.

ISBN-13: 978-0-691-12463-6 (cloth : alk. paper)

ISBN-10: 0-691-12463-9 (cloth : alk. paper)

1. United States—Foreign relations. 2. International relations. 3. Internationalism. I. Title.

E183.7.D74 2006

327.73′009′0511—dc22   2005051470

British Library Cataloging-in-Publication Data is available

This book has been composed in Sabon

Printed on acid-free paper. ∞

pup.princeton.edu

Printed in the United States of America

3 5 7 9 10 8 6 4 2

Without the controlling principle that the nation must maintain its objectives and its power in equilibrium, its purposes within its means and its means equal to its purposes, its commitments related to its resources and its resources adequate to its commitments, it is impossible to think at all about foreign affairs. ... An agreement has eventually to be reached when men admit that they must pay for what they want and that they must want only what they are willing to pay for.

—Walter Lippmann, *U.S. Foreign Policy: Shield of the Republic* (1943)

CONTENTS

ACKNOWLEDGMENTS

I AM GRATEFUL for the support that I have received in writing this book, which began as a Ph.D. thesis, and has since gone through repeated changes. My mentor at Princeton, Aaron Friedberg, encouraged an interest in American grand strategy, and followed it up with trenchant advice and help over a period of several years. George Downs, Michael Doyle, and Robert Gilpin provided very useful, early thoughts and recommendations. Fred Greenstein, Kathleen McNamara, and Gideon Rose offered invaluable constructive criticisms. The Society of Fellows of the Woodrow Wilson Foundation at Princeton University gave me financial support in 1999–2000. And the Institute for Humane Studies provided crucial financial as well as intellectual support as I completed my dissertation. Since moving to the University of Colorado, I have continued to benefit from the assistance offered by a wide variety of individuals and organizations. The following people all read and provided incisive suggestions regarding earlier versions or elements of this book: Robert Art, Theo Farrell, Richard Ned Lebow, Jeffrey Legro, Daniel Markey, Kevin Narizny, Henry Nau, John Owen, Edward Rhodes, Randall Schweller, Wallace Thies, and William Wohlforth. Michael Brown, John Ikenberry, Charles Kupchan, James Kurth, and Robert Pastor also offered helpful commentary regarding my central argument. A year spent as a postdoctoral fellow at Harvard's John M. Olin Institute for Strategic Studies was critical in allowing me the time to revise the manuscript. It also provided an exceptionally stimulating intellectual environment, surrounded by talented scholars with similar interests and under the capable headship of Stephen Rosen. I thank Charles Myers of Princeton University Press for his encouragement and support throughout this process. Sections of the concluding chapter are drawn from my article "Ideas and Alternatives in American Grand Strategy, 2000–2004," *Review of International Studies* 30 (October 2004). I thank the editors of that journal as well as its publisher, Cambridge University Press, for permission to reprint these sections. The Department of Political Science at the University of Colorado, Boulder, has proven to be a remarkably supportive and congenial environment in which to teach, write, and research. Vanessa Baird, Steve Chan and Roland Paris offered particularly useful comments on elements of this manuscript. I thank my colleagues at Boulder, as well as my students, for their help, input, and friendship over the years. Finally, my deepest gratitude is to my wife, Kirsten. This book is dedicated to her.

Reluctant Crusaders

Grand Strategy
 prioritization of foreign policy goals
 id existing/potential resources
 reconcile goals w/ resources

Wilsonian Liberal Tradition
 ↳ democratic govts, open markets
impacts Bush strategy

 do not match available resources

Goals resources have been in disconnect
    tend to
domestic cultural forces limit activism abroad
int'l conditions tend to stimulate US involvement

Goals + Resources (handwritten, top margin)

Introduction

CHANGE AND CONTINUITY IN
AMERICAN GRAND STRATEGY

interests (handwritten, right margin)
threats
resources

EVER SINCE THE terrorist attacks of September 2001, a wide-ranging debate has opened up regarding the proper course of American national security policy. Some critics have advocated a retrenchment of America's international commitments, while others have called for a more multilateral approach; still others, including the Bush administration itself, have embraced the aggressive promotion of American primacy overseas. The immediate focus has been on counterterrorism. But the broader question at stake has been the future of American "grand strategy."

Def. (handwritten, left margin)
✳ (handwritten, left margin)

Grand strategy involves the prioritization of foreign policy goals, the identification of existing and potential resources, and the selection of a plan or road map that uses those resources to meet those goals. Whenever foreign policy officials are faced with the task of reconciling foreign policy goals with limited resources, under the prospect of potential armed conflict, they are engaging in grand strategy. Levels of defense spending, foreign aid, alliance behavior, troop deployments, and diplomatic activity are all influenced by grand strategic assumptions. Whether implicitly or explicitly, leading officials in every nation-state have a sense of their country's interests, of the threats that exist to those interests, and of the resources that can be brought to bear against those threats. Grand strategy is the inevitable process of ranking and assessing those interests, threats, and resources. And any nation's grand strategy can sometimes change dramatically.

One of the conventional criticisms of the Bush administration's grand strategy is that it is excessively and even disastrously unilateralist in approach. According to the critics, the Bush administration has turned its back on a long-standing and admirable American tradition of liberal internationalism in foreign affairs, and in doing so has provoked resentment worldwide. But these criticisms misinterpret both the foreign policy of George W. Bush, as well as America's liberal internationalist tradition. In reality, Bush's foreign policies since 9/11 have been heavily influenced by traditional liberal internationalist, or Wilsonian, assumptions—assumptions that all along have had a troubling impact on U.S. foreign policy behavior and have fed into the current situation in Iraq.

The conduct of American grand strategy has long been shaped, to a greater or lesser extent, by a set of beliefs that can only be called "liberal." These assumptions specify that the United States should promote, wherever practical and possible, an international system characterized by democratic governments and open markets. President Bush reiterated these classical liberal assumptions in his November 6, 2003, speech to the National Endowment for Democracy, when he outlined what he called "a forward strategy of freedom in the Middle East." In that speech, Bush argued that "as long as the Middle East remains a place where freedom does not flourish, it will remain a place of stagnation, resentment, and violence ready for export." In this sense, he suggested, the United States has a vital strategic interest in the democratization of that region. But Bush also added that "the advance of freedom leads to peace," and that democracy is "the only path to national success and dignity," providing as it does certain "essential principles common to every successful society, in every culture." These words could just as easily have been spoken by Woodrow Wilson, Franklin Roosevelt—or Bill Clinton. They are well within the mainstream American tradition of liberal internationalism. Of course, U.S. foreign policy officials have never promoted a liberal world order simply out of altruism. They have done so out of the belief that such a system would serve American interests, by making the United States more prosperous, influential, and secure. Americans have also frequently disagreed over how to best promote liberal goals overseas. Nevertheless, it is fair to say that liberal goals and liberal assumptions, broadly conceived, have had a powerful impact on American foreign policy, especially since the presidency of Woodrow Wilson.

Wilsonian Goals ≠ Resources

The problem with the liberal, or Wilsonian, approach, however, has been that it tends to encourage very ambitious goals and commitments abroad, while assuming that these goals can be met without commensurate cost or expenditure on the part of the United States. Liberal internationalists, that is, tend to define American interests in broad, expansive, and idealistic terms, without always admitting the necessary costs and risks of such an expansive vision. The result is that sweeping and ambitious goals are announced, but then pursued by disproportionately limited means, thus creating an outright invitation to failure. Indeed, this pattern of disjuncture between ends and means has been so common in the history of American twentieth-century diplomacy that it seems to be a direct consequence of the nation's distinctly liberal approach to international relations.

Americans have often been "crusaders"—crusaders in the promotion of a more liberal international order. But Americans have also frequently been "reluctant"—reluctant to admit the full costs of promoting this liberal international vision. These two strains within the American foreign policy tradition have not only operated cyclically; they have operated simultaneously. In this sense, the history of American grand strategy is a history of "reluctant crusaders."

The Bush administration's present difficulties in Iraq are therefore not an isolated event. Nor are they really the result of the president's supposed preference for unilateralism. On the contrary, the administration's difficulties in Iraq are actually the result of an excessive reliance on classically liberal or Wilsonian assumptions regarding foreign affairs. The administration willed the end—and a very ambitious end—in Iraq, but it did not, initially, will the necessary means. In this sense, the Bush administration is heir to a long liberal internationalist tradition that runs from Woodrow Wilson through Franklin Roosevelt and Harry Truman to William Jefferson Clinton. And Bush inherits not only the strengths of that tradition, but also its weaknesses and flaws.

When and why might we expect further changes in American grand strategy? When and why does grand strategy change? Are the causes of change in U.S. grand strategy the same as in other countries, or are there patterns of strategic adjustment that are distinctly American? In all of the recommendations for one policy course or another, these are questions that are rarely asked. Yet the United States has been through such periods of strategic adjustment before—notably, in the immediate aftermath of each world war. By examining and comparing these historical periods, together with the post—Cold War period, we can begin to answer the question of how and why grand strategy actually changes. Those insights can then be applied to current conditions, allowing us to predict future changes in American strategic behavior.

POWER AND CULTURE: EXPLAINING CHANGE AND CONTINUITY IN AMERICAN GRAND STRATEGY

The study of grand strategy—and of international relations—has undergone dramatic changes over time. The "classical" realist authors of the 1940s, such as Walter Lippmann (from whose writings this book's epigraph is drawn) and George Kennan, understood that cultural factors can have a profound effect on the strategic behavior of nations. Indeed, in the case of the United States, these same classical realists pointed to the impact of a liberal and idealistic political culture precisely to condemn its impact on American foreign policy. At the same time, classical realists took it for granted that any country's grand strategy must eventually reflect international pressures. Authors like Lippmann and Kennan were as much interested in history, policy, and prescription as in scientific explanation. Contemporary realism, on the other hand—known as "structural" realism, for its emphasis on the structure of the international system—in its search for theoretical rigor and parsimony tends to downplay, ignore, or even deny the influence upon grand strategy of nationally distinctive cultural factors. This tendency in contemporary realism has only encouraged the creation and growth of an alternative, "constructivist" school of thought, which in turn emphasizes culture at the expense of international pressures.

International relations theory today is therefore characterized by a dichotomy between realist approaches, which emphasize international pressures, and constructivist approaches that emphasize the importance of norms, ideas, and culture. Much of the work from both perspectives is written as if the two approaches were entirely incompatible. In this book, I try to bridge that gap, and advance the realist-constructivist debate, by showing exactly how international pressures and American "strategic culture" have acted together to push and pull U.S. grand strategy in opposite directions over time.

I examine in depth three major turning points in America's role in the world: the first, after World War One, the second, after World War Two, and the third, after the end of the Cold War. I argue that in each case international conditions were a crucial influence on U.S. strategic behavior. But I also show that certain cultural legacies, unique to the United States, have had a powerful impact on patterns of change and continuity in American grand strategy.

First, I will contend that classical liberal assumptions have acted as a filter on potential policy options in the United States, allowing certain strategic alternatives while rendering others unthinkable. U.S. foreign policy officials have tended to rule out strategic concepts that do not resonate with America's liberal political culture, both because they anticipate public rejections of such concepts, and because they do not themselves believe in such "illiberal" approaches. So, for example, after World War One, certain senators, such as Henry Cabot Lodge, favored a simple balance-of-power alliance with France in order to check any future German aggression. Similarly, a number of credible foreign policy experts such as Walter Lippmann advocated a pure "sphere-of-influence" arrangement in 1945, whereby the United States and the USSR would explicitly agree to a straightforward partition of influence in Europe and Asia. Both concepts were feasible in material, structural terms. But both alternatives were ruled out of consideration by leading officials, because they could not be framed in terms that suited the predominantly liberal discourse characteristic of American foreign policy debates.

Second, I will argue that a tradition of "limited liability" in matters of grand strategy has encouraged Americans to limit the costs of overseas commitments, to an extent greater than realists would have predicted.

And while this tradition was strongest before World War Two, it remains an important constraint on American strategic behavior.

To a large extent, as will be seen, these two cultural legacies contradict one another. Liberal assumptions encourage American officials to define American goals in unusually idealistic, expansive, and global terms. At the same time, the tradition of limited liability discourages Americans from making concrete sacrifices toward that liberal vision. The result tends to be that expansive goals are pursued by quite limited means.

These twin cultural legacies also incline American grand strategy in opposite directions from international pressures. Whereas domestic cultural forces tend to constrain U.S. strategic behavior abroad, and pull it in a more "liberal" direction, international conditions tend to stimulate American involvement overseas, while forcing unwanted compromise on liberal principles. The result is a persistent tug of war between international pressures and U.S. strategic culture: a cyclical tension that drives the story of American strategic adjustment over time.

I use historical counterfactuals, extensive archival research, and competitive theory testing to show exactly how and why cultural legacies, in tension with international conditions, have shaped and will continue to shape American grand strategy. The result is a study that seeks to recover some of the strengths of classical realist thinking in international relations by combining an appreciation for the role of both culture and power in international affairs.

ORGANIZATION OF THE BOOK

In chapters 1 and 2, I look at some potential sources of U.S. strategic adjustment. I begin by defining the term "grand strategy," and indicate the ways in which such a strategy can change. I examine two common explanations for changes in grand strategy: first, a realist explanation, emphasizing international conditions, and second, a domestic cultural explanation. Then I outline my own neoclassical realist model, showing exactly how realist and cultural factors interrelate in the formation of strategic choice. The first chapter is meant as a starting point for a theory of change and continuity in grand strategy, potentially applicable to any country. Readers who are strictly interested in the history and causes of American grand strategy, but not in general theories of strategic adjustment, may wish to move directly to the second chapter.

In chapter two, I analyze and describe American strategic culture, and provide a typology of four distinct strategic "subcultures" within the United States: nationalist, realist, progressive, and internationalist. I discuss the factors and forces that allow one subculture to win out over the others at a given point in time. I pay special attention in this chapter to the precise way in which culture and ideas have an impact on American grand strategy, through processes of agenda setting and coalition building. Finally, I discuss my use of cases, theory testing, and historical counterfactuals.

In chapter 3, I address the empirical puzzle of why the United States returned to isolationism after World War One. I show that there were not two, but three plausible alternatives for U.S. grand strategy after that war: a League of Nations, disengagement, or a simple military alliance with France and Great Britain. I demonstrate that international conditions could not have predicted the return to disengagement, given America's immense power by 1918. From a structural realist perspective, any of the three options were viable, and in fact, a Western alliance would have been preferable. I then show how domestic patterns of agenda setting and coalition building by Woodrow Wilson, conditioned by cultural considerations, shaped and directed the process of strategic choice. A simple balance-of-power alliance with Western European countries was ruled out by Wilson and many other Americans, because it seemed to represent a violation of liberal foreign policy goals; but membership in a strong League was ruled out by the Senate, because it violated the U.S. tradition of limited liability in strategic affairs. The culturally influenced result was a return to the default option of disengagement, in spite of the fact that America was materially ready to assume a larger role in world affairs.

In chapter 4, I address the puzzle of why the United States adopted the strategy of containment after 1945. I show that four major alternatives were discussed at the time: first, the isolationist option of strategic disengagement; second, the alternative of rolling back the Soviet sphere by military means; third, an explicit sphere-of-influence arrangement with the USSR; and fourth, the containment of Soviet influence worldwide. I show that international conditions, while ruling out isolationism, cannot explain why American officials selected containment. Specifically, from a realist perspective, a sphere-of-influence strategy was feasible and even preferable to containment. Containment was selected not because it was the only strategy that matched international conditions, but because it was the only strategy that matched international conditions as well as domestic cultural concerns. I then show how American classical liberal assumptions regarding international affairs worked against a sphere-of-influence strategy, and in favor of containment. I also show how the American tradition of limited liability continued to exert pressure on U.S. officials, even after 1945, leading them to select a strategy that was extremely ambitious but relatively inexpensive—a combination that could not last, and indeed broke down after 1950.

In chapter 5, I address the puzzle of why the United States followed a broadly liberal internationalist strategy after the collapse of the Soviet Union. I outline four major alternatives that were open to U.S. foreign policy officials after the end of the Cold War: neoisolationism; a pure balance-of-power strategy; liberal internationalism; and a strategy of American primacy. I show that international material conditions, while rendering isolationism unlikely, did not rule out any of the other three strategies. The pursuit of an essentially liberal internationalist strategy by the Clinton administration was as much a response to domestic cultural assumptions and expectations, especially at the elite level, as it was a response to international conditions. American liberal foreign policy assumptions continued to make a pure balance-of-power strategy problematic from a domestic political point of view, while the more ambitious strategy of international primacy was incompatible with the desire for limited liability in strategic affairs. The result during the 1990s was a paradoxical combination of liberal foreign policy goals pursued worldwide, but by strictly limited means.

In the sixth and concluding chapter, I use the same analytical approach as in previous chapters to explain patterns of U.S. strategic adjustment since the inauguration of George W. Bush. I also summarize my findings: first, pointing to a neoclassical realist framework as the best way of understanding the real relationship between domestic cultural factors and international material conditions; second, noting how American strategic adjustment has always been driven by a tug of war between international pressures and domestic cultural concerns; and third, suggesting how this tension will continue to drive future changes in U.S. grand strategy.

One of the central findings of this work is that certain cultural legacies, unique to the United States, have had and will probably continue to have a powerful effect on change and continuity in American grand strategy. Classical liberal ideas, in particular, have shaped and molded U.S. strategic assumptions and behavior in ways that no structural realist or materialist could have predicted. This is not to say that liberal ideas have been the only force behind American grand strategy, or that the United States has been selfless in its promotion of a liberal international order. Obviously, American foreign policymakers have often pursued nominally liberal goals in a manner that was largely rhetorical, self-interested, and/or hypocritical. But the basic liberal vision of an international system characterized by democratic governments and open markets has also been a genuine animating force behind the making of American foreign policy. After all, there would be little point in making rhetorical gestures toward liberal ideas if these ideas did not have real power. And even when leading decision-makers are skeptical of this broad liberal vision, they are still constrained by it for domestic political reasons. The overall effect is that on questions of grand strategy, the United States often behaves in a surprising way—or at least, in a way that must be surprising from a realist perspective. Realists tell us that in the end, all states are basically alike, because they are forced to act alike, and to play the balance-of-power game, in order to survive. That may be true, up to a certain point. But U.S. foreign policymakers have often refused to engage in simple or straightforward balance-of-power behavior, and the cause of their refusal can be traced to the influence of America's liberal strategic culture.

Chapter One

POWER, CULTURE, AND GRAND STRATEGY

THE FOLLOWING TWO CHAPTERS provide a conceptual basis for understanding patterns of U.S. strategic adjustment. In this first chapter I examine some of the most important potential sources of change and continuity in American grand strategy. I begin by defining the term "grand strategy," and indicate the ways in which strategies can vary. Then I examine two potential explanations for changes in grand strategy: first, a domestic cultural explanation, and second, a power-based explanation, emphasizing international conditions. Finally, I outline an alternative "neoclassical realist" model of strategic adjustment, showing how cultural and power-based variables interrelate in the formation of strategic choice.

GRAND STRATEGY

What exactly is "grand strategy"? The phrase was first used by British military theorist B. H. Liddell Hart to describe the "higher level" of wartime strategy above the strictly military, by which the nation's policymakers coordinate all of the resources at their disposal—military, economic, diplomatic—toward the political ends of any given war.[1] As such, grand strategy was considered by Liddell Hart to be an essentially political exercise, conducted by the highest state officials, and involving a broad range of policy instruments besides the military. Still, he thought of it as a wartime phenomenon.[2] In recent years, there has been renewed interest in the concept of grand strategy, but the definition of it has been stretched to include periods of peace as well as war. In this new conception, not only the means of grand strategy, but also the ends have been expanded to include a broad range of peacetime goals—political, economic, and diplomatic. Recent definitions of grand strategy include the following:

> Any broad-based policies that a state may adopt for the preservation and enhancement of its security.[3]
>
> A political-military "means-ends" chain, a state's theory about how it can best "cause" security for itself.[4]
>
> A state's overall plan for providing national security by keeping national resources and external commitments in balance.[5]

The full package of domestic and international policies designed to increase national power and security.[6]

All of these definitions have certain key features in common, and point toward a new conception of grand strategy; that said, a number of them are rather broad. The danger with too general a definition of grand strategy is that it leaves the term without any distinct meaning or utility. If, for example, it is used to refer to the pursuit of all national ends in international relations by all available means, it is difficult to see what distinguishes grand strategy from foreign policy in general. In that case, the phrase is no longer of any particular use.[7] What precise limits can we bring to the definition of grand strategy?

First, like all strategy, grand strategy is (1) a calculated relationship of ends and means, (2) in the face of one or more potential opponents. The task of identifying and reconciling goals and resources—of making difficult trade-offs and setting priorities in the face of potential resistance—is the essence of strategy.[8] In a world of unlimited resources, without the possibility of conflict, there is no need for strategy. But in a world of scarce resources, in which leading actors may or may not cooperate, strategic decisions are inevitable. In this sense, not all foreign policy is "strategic." But insofar as international relations involve scarcity and potential conflict, it is a realm of strategic interaction.

Second, it seems reasonable to suggest that grand strategy only exists when there is the possibility of the use of force internationally.[9] This restriction conforms to common usage. Generally, we do not refer to any nation's grand strategy, on a given issue or in a given region, when there is absolutely no possibility of armed conflict. If strategy refers to the balancing of ends and means in the face of potential resistance, then grand strategy refers to the same balancing act on the part of states, in the face of potential armed conflict with other international entities: states, terrorists, and so on. This means that military policy instruments will always be central to grand strategy—not exclusively so, but centrally. Foreign aid, diplomatic activity, even trade policy ought, under certain circumstances, to be considered crucial elements in a nation's grand strategy. But they are elements of a grand strategy only insofar as they are meant to serve the overall pursuit of national goals in the face of potential armed conflict with potential opponents.

Having narrowed down our definition of grand strategy somewhat, let us specify what it still includes. It includes the pursuit of a wide variety of nonmilitary interests, ends, and objectives, whether political, economic, or ideological. It includes the use of nonmilitary means, subject to the restrictions already specified. It includes peacetime as well as wartime policymaking—in fact, this study will focus primarily on peacetime grand strategy. It thus conforms in many respects to calls for a more expansive definition of the subject.[10] Grand strategy is a branch of foreign policy, and grand strategic outcomes are a subset of foreign policy outcomes. This means that the actors, causes, and processes involved in strategic adjustment will be similar to those of foreign policy decisionmaking. But grand strategy is not synonymous with foreign policy in general.

Any grand strategy involves the identification and prioritization of (1) national interests, goals, and objectives; (2) potential threats to such interests; and (3) resources and/or means with which to meet these threats and protect these interests.[11] A grand strategy is both a conceptual road map, describing how to match identified resources to the promotion of identified interests, and a set of policy prescriptions. The road map addresses the crucial question of how to rank interests, assess threats, and adapt resources; its essence is the attempted reconciliation of ends and means.[12] The specific policy prescriptions follow from the road map. In the final analysis, any grand strategy must provide concrete guidelines on the use of policy instruments such as: the form and level of defense spending; the nature and extent of strategic commitments abroad; the deployment of military forces abroad, peacefully or not; the use of foreign aid; the use of diplomacy with real or potential allies; and the diplomatic stance taken toward real or potential adversaries.

It might be asked whether or not most governments actually follow any sort of conscious, coherent, and intentional strategic "plan" over time. The United States, in particular, seems unlikely to do so, given its fragmented and decentralized political system.[13] The short answer is that, for our purposes, it does not really matter. Whether or not national governments actually design and follow through on any overarching grand strategy, they act as if they do. Whether or not a strategic plan literally exists, nations must make difficult choices on matters of defense spending, alliance diplomacy, and military intervention. Decisions regarding trade-offs between ends and means are inevitable, even if they are neither coherent nor coordinated. This is as true for the United States as for any other country. We cannot assume the existence of a premeditated strategic design on the part of any administration, but it is not unreasonable to speak of governments being forced to make strategic decisions, whenever political and military ends and means must be reconciled amidst the possibility of armed conflict.

How, then, should we define change in grand strategy? There are a number of strategic typologies already in existence. Edward Luttwak contrasts "expansionist" strategies with "status quo" strategies.[14] Charles Kupchan offers a slightly more refined typology, distinguishing between "compellent," "deterrent," and "accommodationist" strategies.[15] Alastair Iain Johnston points out that states can follow defensive ends by aggressive means, and vice versa; he therefore leaves political ends out of his typology, but creates three categories of grand strategy otherwise similar to those of Kupchan: "accommodationist," "defensive," and "expansionist."[16] It is not difficult to imagine a number of dimensions along which we might categorize grand strategies: conflictual as opposed to cooperative, realist as opposed to idealist, unilateral as opposed to multilateral, and so on.

While the typologies offered by Luttwak, Kupchan, and Johnston do provide useful guidelines, it seems unlikely that most states follow either a purely defensive-status quo, offensive-compellent, or accommodationist strategy.[17] Nor is it likely that these three broad categories capture the subtle changes that characterize shifts between strategies, even at times of great upheaval. Presumably, it is quite rare that American grand strategy moves from one of these three categories to another, even assuming that it can be fitted into these three strategic archetypes.

A more fruitful approach might be to simply ask whether the United States has expanded, contracted, or in any way significantly changed its overall strategic capabilities and commitments: a process known as "strategic adjustment."[18] Referring back to the policy instruments typically associated with strategic decision making, we could measure such change along the following dimensions:

1. Is military spending raised or lowered?*
2. Are alliance commitments extended or withdrawn?
3. Are military deployments overseas expanded or reduced?
4. Is foreign aid increased or decreased?
5. Does the state engage in significant new diplomatic initiatives, or does it disengage from existing diplomatic activities?
6. Does the state adopt a more aggressive and confrontational stance toward its adversaries, or does it adopt a less confrontational stance?

Note that the United States might expand its commitments in one area while reducing them in another: for example, by extending new alliance commitments while reducing defense spending. It is nevertheless useful to ask whether the nation has expanded or contracted its strategic commitments as a whole, while keeping in mind the possibility of variation within each of these six categories. It is also useful to distinguish between major change and minor change in U.S. grand strategy. A massive shift in the extent of strategic commitments—as in the case of the adoption of containment—can be described as a *first-order* change. A less fundamental alteration—for example, Eisenhower's introduction of the "New Look"—can be described as a *second-order* change. Most strategic adjustments are of the second order. And of course, a great deal of minor tinkering goes on within the framework of any given strategic approach, without qualifying as either a first- or second-order alteration.

In sum, variation in American grand strategy will be defined as a significant overall change in the nature and levels of: military spending, alliance commitments, foreign aid, diplomatic activism, and/or foreign policy stands toward potential adversaries. This gives us a concrete set of strategic outcomes that vary in a precise and observable manner. We now know what must be explained when we ask how and why grand strategy changes. What are some potential explanations for such change?

EXPLAINING STRATEGIC ADJUSTMENT

It is quite probable that both the causes and the processes of strategic adjustment differ from one country to the next. The concept of grand strategy can and has been fruitfully applied to a variety of countries.[19] Our main concern in this book, however, is with the sources of *American* grand strategy. What theories and approaches might be helpful in focusing specifically on the sources of strategic adjustment within the United States?

Whenever attempting to explain the grand strategy of any country, it is always useful to begin with its position in the international system. The international system is a good place to start because it constitutes a powerful, generalizable influence on any country's grand strategy.[20] The further we get with this sort of "structural" explanation, in terms of testing its causal power, the further we have gone in developing a theory that may have cross-national applications. The same may be said for cultural theories. An appropriate method, then, in developing a model of U.S. strategic adjustment is to begin by considering the potential weight of broad, general causes, such as power and culture, and subsequently to focus in on those elements of the decision-making process that are distinctive to the United States. This ought to provide us with a model of strategic choice unique to the United States, but with potential applications to other countries.

I will therefore begin with those factors and theories that possess the broadest potential for explaining strategic adjustment in comparative terms: specifically, international pressures (structural realist theory), and culture (constructivist theory).[21] After investigating the relative importance and interaction of these general factors, I will start to "fill in the blanks" in chapter 2 by outlining and discussing the precise nature of *American* strategic culture. Then I will focus on the distinctive processes of strategic adjustment as they occur within the United States. By walking through the sources of strategic adjustment in this manner, we should end up with a model that is potentially generalizable, but also especially useful and accurate with reference to the United States. Finally, I should clarify that my purpose in these first two chapters is not to analyze or discuss *every* potential cause of strategic adjustment, but rather to examine the relative weight of two very important general causes—power and culture—while adding some additional insight into the making of grand strategy as it occurs in the United States.

Power and Culture: The Debate

One potential explanation for strategic adjustment would refer to international pressures, such as the global distribution of power. Alternatively, one could refer to country-specific strategic cultures. In international relations theory, realists refer primarily to international ("systemic" or "structural") pressures, while constructivists refer primarily to culture. Realist theories and cultural-constructivist theories are both leading candidates for explaining changes in grand strategy. Thus far, however, constructivists and realists have tended to talk past one another, dismissing each other's claims without a serious, competitive testing of alternative approaches.[22] How do culture and international pressures "fit" together, if at all, in causing strategic outcomes? What is their exact relationship? What are the limits on each type of explanation? These are the kinds of questions that have yet to be satisfactorily answered.

We can at least begin to answer these questions by framing several potential theories of strategic adjustment in a clear, competitive fashion, and then testing each of them against the evidence. Only then can we gain a sense of how much cultural, as opposed to international-structural or power-based, factors actually explain, and how they may interrelate.[23] What follows is a brief summary of three potential explanations of strategic choice: cultural, structural or power-based, and neoclassical realist.

Cultural Explanations

Cultural explanations of strategic adjustment start from the premise that international pressures are essentially indeterminate. For cultural theorists, such as Thomas Berger, Elizabeth Kier, and Edward Rhodes, international pressures—like the "national interest"—must be interpreted and represented subjectively, through a cultural process, in order to have any effect on strategic choice.[24] This cultural process operates as follows. In formulating grand strategy, as in foreign policy generally, leading officials are forced to rely upon preconceived beliefs and assumptions in order to interpret and act upon a mass of incoming information.[25] These beliefs and assumptions may be held either by individuals or by groups of policymakers as a whole. "Culture," as a general term, simply refers to any set of interlocking values, beliefs, and assumptions that are held collectively by a given group and passed on through socialization.[26] In the context of grand strategy, then, the relevant cultural values and beliefs are those that relate to the legitimate and efficient conduct of political-military affairs, while the relevant cultural unit or group is the citizenry of a given nation-state, and particularly its foreign policy elite.[27] Consequently, cultural theorists of grand strategy posit the existence of an interlocking set of values and beliefs held by the politically interested people of each nation-state that relate to strategic affairs; a set of beliefs that can be referred to as a nation's "strategic culture."[28]

Cultural theorists go on to suggest that culture shapes strategic choice in several ways. First, culture influences the manner in which international events, pressures, and conditions are perceived.[29] Second, it provides a set of causal beliefs regarding the efficient pursuit of national interests.[30] Third, it helps determine the actual definition of those interests, by providing prescriptive foreign policy goals.[31] In this last sense, it should be noted, political-military culture is normative as well as descriptive, and constitutive as well as cognitive.[32] Strategic culture not only provides a set of analytical tools; it also meshes with a sense of national self-image, or sense of identity, which is itself a ground for action.[33] For example, one constitutive effect of political-military culture may be that policymakers are held to certain norms, or rules of behavior, not for consequentialist reasons, but simply because the violation of such rules is viewed as illegitimate and inappropriate.[34] The seeming violation of accepted norms, or the abandonment of culturally prescribed national goals, is likely to trigger domestic opposition that is not only strong, but emotional, since such norms and/or goals are closely linked to a basic and constitutive sense of national identity.[35]

Perhaps the most striking characteristic of cultural explanations is their claim that strategic culture can prevent meaningful choices by rendering certain plausible strategic alternatives unacceptable or even unthinkable. Culture is said to delimit a set range of acceptable options, tactics, and policies as legitimate and/or efficacious; any alternatives that fall outside this range will not even be seriously considered.[36] Cultural scholars would further suggest that the influence of strategic culture is entrenched through formal and/or informal institutionalization.[37] Formally, a particular culture can be institutionalized within bureaucratic agencies. Informally, it can be institutionalized through regular discourse.[38] The informal process of institutionalization is the less direct of the two but arguably the more powerful. As the assumptions of a given strategic culture are iterated again and again, the language itself takes on real power. It becomes difficult to discuss or even conceive, much less to consider, strategic alternatives that are not culturally sanctioned. Strategic assumptions that might otherwise be open to debate are instead taken for granted. As a result of this process of institutionalization, political-military culture tends to persist, independent of material changes; consequently, policymakers tend to resist strategic adjustment, and adhere to existing grand strategies, in spite of changing international conditions.[39]

In sum, cultural theorists suggest that any state's grand strategy is best explained by the existence of distinct strategic cultures rather than by international material pressures. Culture determines strategic behavior by shaping the preferences, perceptions, and beliefs of a given nation's citizens. It predisposes each state toward certain strategic choices, in keeping with unique, deep-rooted cultural assumptions, which necessarily vary from state to state. When culture is taken as a variable, then a change in strategic culture is said to explain variation in grand strategy. When culture is taken as a constant, then each nation's strategic culture is said to limit and influence policy choices, without directly "causing" strategic adjustment.[40]

Power-Based Explanations

A second approach to explaining strategic adjustment is to emphasize international pressures, by pointing to conditions like the international distribution of power. This is the approach taken by structural realists of various types. Realists suggest that patterns of strategic adjustment are ultimately shaped by material or "structural" pressures at the international level.[41] The realist premise is that because the international system is an anarchic system, in which violent conflict is always a possibility, states are forced to rely upon their own material capabilities—along with those of their allies—in order to survive. Consequently, international pressures are the primary cause of the strategic behavior of individual states.[42] Realists do not deny that each nation-state within the international system may have peculiar historical, cultural, and/or domestic political legacies, but they do insist that these domestic-level differences tend to be washed out by the pervasive pressures of international competition. As a result, realists suggest that all states tend eventually to act in the same manner, they pay close attention to their relative position in the international system, try to promote their own power and security, and act to check potential threats. They become "undifferentiated" or alike in their strategic behavior, regardless of cultural differences, due to the overriding pressures of international competition.[43]

Realists, like cultural theorists, however, are often vague as to the exact causal significance of international as opposed to domestic-level pressures when attempting to explain patterns of strategic adjustment. For "structural" realists, the problem of causal underspecification is particularly severe; the leading structural realist of the last thirty years, Kenneth Waltz, has stated quite consistently that his theory cannot be used to explain foreign policy outcomes.[44] But many international relations theorists remain unconvinced that structural realism does not or cannot make foreign policy predictions.[45] In practice, structural realism both requires and implies a theory of state behavior. This is hardly an insuperable obstacle for realists. But it does mean that realist theories of foreign policy must fill in the blanks left by Waltz; they must specify how far and to what extent systemic or structural pressures actually determine the foreign policy behavior of individual states. And on this question, realists divide into several distinct camps.

"Offensive" realists, such as John Mearsheimer, maintain that international systemic pressures and constraints exert an all-powerful influence on grand strategy. According to offensive realists, the fiercely competitive nature of the international system forces states to adopt aggressive strategies, and to expand their relative power, whenever possible.[46] As states grow in relative capabilities, they adopt more expansive grand strategies. According to Mearsheimer, such expansion is not necessarily intentional. Pervasive uncertainty over the intentions of other states forces policymakers to seek a margin of safety internationally. Powerful states therefore end up acting as if they sought dominion, even if self-consciously they only seek security. The key point for offensive realists is that powerful states adopt more expansive grand strategies, because they have both the opportunity and the incentive to do so.[47]

Offensive realists also provide clear predictions regarding the relationship between international material pressures, distinct national cultures, and strategic adjustment. According to the logic of offensive realism, culture is essentially epiphenomenal or irrelevant to strategic choice.[48] Distinct strategic cultures may exist, but they have little or no independent impact on grand strategy. International pressures not only determine strategic choice; they also override cultural concerns. Cultural rhetoric may be used to justify chosen strategies, but the actual explanation for those strategies lies in the international system.[49] Finally, cultural beliefs may change, and these new beliefs may be coincident with the selection of new policies, but offensive realists suggest that, in such cases, both the new strategy—and the new cultural beliefs—can be best explained by referring to international pressures.

Offensive realism has the virtue of conceptual clarity and parsimony; it claims to explain a great deal by referring to only a few simple variables. But this parsimony comes at a very heavy price. By suggesting that domestic-level variables are essentially irrelevant to strategic choice, offensive realism rests upon a dubious theoretical assumption. It is precisely for this reason that Kenneth Waltz never made any such claim.[50] The fact is, as even many realists admit, that domestic-level motives and intentions vary from state to state, and that such intentions often have a dramatic and independent impact upon foreign policy behavior.[51] Simply put, some states maximize power; others do not.[52] In reality, the grand strategies of states are regularly and significantly influenced by domestic-level factors, including cultural assumptions. By arguing the opposite, offensive realists inadvertantly demonstrate the limits of systemic influences on state behavior. Such pressures may be the most important cause of foreign policy behavior without being entirely determinate. The challenge, for realists, is to create an internally consistent and empirically plausible theory that preserves an appreciation for the importance of systemic pressures alongside an appreciation of their limits.[53]

A Neoclassical Realist Model of Strategic Adjustment

An alternative to both offensive realist and cultural theories of strategic adjustment can be found in neoclassical realism. In recent years, there has been a striking tendency among many realists to "layer in" domestic-level factors when explaining foreign policy behavior. Authors such as Thomas Christensen, Aaron Friedberg, Randall Schweller, Stephen Walt, William Wohlforth, and Fareed Zakaria have all produced research that is recognizably realist in inspiration, but that admits a certain causal significance to domestic-level variables.[54] Gideon Rose has identified this trend as a revival of classical realist assumptions, albeit with a greater concern for theoretical rigor—hence the term "neoclassical realism."[55] According to Rose, neoclassical realists are united by certain common assumptions. First, they seek to explain particular foreign policy behaviors and not simply broad international outcomes. Second, they take the international system—understood in material terms—as the most important long-term cause of changes in any nation's foreign policy behavior. This is what makes them "realists." Third, they layer domestic-level factors into their explanatory models in order to achieve greater predictive and empirical precision. Simply put, they tend to be sensitive to the cultural legacies and domestic politics of specific countries. This is what makes them "neoclassical."[56]

How would neoclassical realism explain changes in grand strategy? First, it would look to the international system as the single most important overall cause of strategic behavior. It would suggest that strategic adjustment is encouraged by changes in the international distribution of power and/or changes in the level of external threat faced by the state.[57] When a given state becomes more powerful, or when it faces greater threats from abroad, it tends to adopt a more costly and expansive grand strategy. Conversely, when a state becomes less powerful, or when it faces fewer foreign threats, it tends to adopt a less costly and less expansive grand strategy. At the same time, neoclassical realists would agree that there is generally some indeterminacy in international conditions, some range of strategic options that might plausibly serve the national interest, and that within this limited range, culture—along with other domestic factors—can have an impact upon strategic choice.[58] Neoclassical realists would agree, for example, with cultural theorists that country-specific cultural variables can influence the preferences and perceptions of a state's foreign policymakers; that culture can predispose a state toward certain strategic choices rather than others; and that culture can delimit the range of acceptable alternatives in a given situation. In other words, from a neoclassical realist perspective, cultural factors can help to specify and explain the final choices made by foreign policymakers.

What exactly is the process by which strategic culture influences strategic choice? A neoclassical realist theory would suggest that the process is twofold. First, foreign policy officials need domestic support for any new departure in grand strategy.[59] This is particularly true in a democracy like the United States. Changes in grand strategy are often costly, involving the extraction and mobilization of considerable national resources. Such changes must be politically feasible at home before they can be implemented; they must be viewed as legitimate. Officials that violate cultural preferences and expectations in formulating grand strategy risk their own political support, as well as the success of their chosen policies. Consequently, there are strong political incentives to frame strategic choices in terms that are culturally acceptable, and to modify grand strategy in accordance with cultural preferences, in order to maintain domestic political support for new strategic initiatives. In fact, political officials frequently anticipate such domestic cultural constraints beforehand, and adapt their policies to them, precisely to avoid political controversy.[60] In this way, through the need for domestic support, strategic culture can have an impact on strategic choice, even when state officials employ cultural symbols instrumentally. But the causal influence of culture is not necessarily limited to the need for domestic political support. Foreign policy officials themselves may actually share, or come to share, or even shape the cultural preferences and perceptions held by their constituents. That is to say, to a greater extent than is generally recognized by international relations theorists, the cultural assumptions voiced by elite foreign policy officials may be internalized and genuine.[61] And if national cultural assumptions regarding grand strategy are either shared or shaped by elite officials, then the beliefs of those officials are a second means by which culture can act as an important influence on patterns of strategic choice.

When applied to the subject of grand strategy, a distinct contribution of neoclassical realist theory is that it provides us with a more precise and subtle understanding of the ways in which international and cultural variables typically interact to shape and determine patterns of strategic choice. Neoclassical realists would concede that cultural factors influence the manner in which states respond to systemic conditions. Strategic adjustment is neither easy nor automatic, particularly when international pressures run up against deeply held cultural beliefs. For this very reason, the existence of nationally distinct strategic cultures often creates significant "lags" or discontinuities between international changes and national responses.[62] At the same time, however, neoclassical realists would argue that it is ultimately international conditions that drive the process of both strategic adjustment and cultural change. That is to say, when national strategic cultures come under intense international pressure, in the end they adjust and adapt.[63] New state strategies are adopted and state officials respond to international pressures by reframing cultural arguments in order to minimize the appearance of discontinuity; those nations that refuse to adapt or respond to systemic conditions are punished in the international arena.[64] Culture is thus best understood as a supplement to, and not a substitute for, realist theories of strategic choice.[65] Strategic culture can certainly help to explain "deviations" from balancing behavior, but since the very concept of such deviations presumes some sort of appropriate or expected response to international conditions, it is only within a realist framework that such explanations make any sense.[66]

A neoclassical realist model of strategic adjustments promises to be useful in bridging domestic and international factors, and in better understanding patterns of adjustment under a variety of circumstances. It sets the parameters for strategic choice more convincingly than either a purely cultural or a purely power-based approach. But even this neoclassical realist model cannot claim to completely explain specific policy decisions at the most detailed level. It still leaves room for other factors, such as domestic politics, as well as for choice on the part of individual policymakers. We now turn to an examination of U.S. strategic culture, and to processes of strategic choice that are distinctly American, and in doing so, develop a more detailed understanding of strategic adjustment as it occurs within the United States.

Chapter Two

STRATEGIC CULTURE AND STRATEGIC ADJUSTMENT IN THE UNITED STATES

AMERICAN STRATEGIC CULTURE

Any model of strategic adjustment that incorporates cultural factors requires specifying the cultural traits of the country in question. In the case of the United States, we can identify two dominant and persistent features of the nation's traditional strategic culture. The first persistent feature is the relative weight of *classical liberal* assumptions within American strategic thinking; the second is an historical and intense preference for *limited liability* in strategic affairs. These two characteristics of American strategic culture, in turn, give rise to several distinct strategic "subcultures" that wax and wane over time: namely, *internationalists, nationalists, progressives*, and *realists*.

Liberalism

To an extent that is unusual compared to other countries, Americans define their national identity according to a classical liberal creed, or set of beliefs.[1] In the United States, and unlike the situation in most other advanced democracies, Lockean liberal assumptions are so widespread as to be taken for granted. The classical liberal or "American" creed emphasizes individual freedom, equality of right, majority rule, progress, enterprise, the rule of law, and the strict limits of the state. The power of the liberal creed within the United States over time probably has much to do with material conditions, such as plentiful land, a predominant middle class, and the recurrent need to integrate new immigrants from a variety of backgrounds. In any case, this creed was locked in, so to speak, by the justifications offered for rebellion against Britain, it has persisted over time, and there are really no significant ideological rivals to it within American society. Needless to say, it has not been monolithic or unchanging. There has been intense, sometimes violent conflict over the precise meaning and application of America's classical liberal creed.[2] Within its boundaries, there are competing versions: left, right, moralistic, nationalistic, egalitarian, capitalist, democratic, individualistic, and so on. A powerful civic republican tradition has existed alongside it and also within it.[3] And it has been reinterpreted over time to include races, ethnicities, religions, and women who were originally excluded from its full promise. Nevertheless, the American liberal tradition, broadly defined, is a very big tent, and it has had remarkable success in integrating and defusing potential opponents. Rather than really questioning its fundamental premises, Americans tend to argue over its precise definition. Consequently, if there is such a thing as a distinctly American approach to grand strategy—one that is due to cultural factors— then it ought to flow in large part from this classical liberal creed, and the power that it has over U.S. strategic culture.

The American liberal creed is an outgrowth and extension of a broader, transnational classical liberal tradition, represented historically by authors such as Thomas Paine, Immanuel Kant, Richard Cobden, and Woodrow Wilson. This liberal tradition assumes that progress in international affairs is possible—that we are not necessarily stuck in an endless cycle of conflict, war, and balance-of-power politics.[4] According to classical liberals, democratic governments are inherently less warlike than authoritarian ones; democracy encourages trade; and trade, in turn, encourages peace.[5] The result is a virtuous cycle, by which popular governments, commercial exchange, and peaceful international relations feed off one another. The United States, for its part, was founded on the hope of building a "new order," specifically, a more liberal order in world affairs.[6] This new order was to be characterized by peace, progress, republican forms of government, trade, freedom, and the rule of law. It represented a self-conscious rejection of Europe's "old order," supposedly characterized by militarism, autocracy, war, secret alliances, corruption, and balance-of-power politics. Many Americans thought of—and continue to think of— the United States as morally and politically distinct from, and superior to, the Old World. Beyond that, Americans have long taken it for granted that their experiment in republican government has implications for the rest of the world. The United States has a special mission or destiny in world affairs; classical liberal ideals will ripple and spread worldwide from the United States; the result will be a more open and peaceful international system, characterized by democratic governments and open exchange—all of these are common American assumptions, and have been since the very founding of the Republic.[7]

The promotion of a more liberal international order, broadly speaking, has always been a central goal of American grand strategy. It is of course only one of many such goals. But the United States is remarkable for the extent to which classical liberal assumptions have actually informed the nation's international behavior. A more liberal international system, characterized by democratic governments and open markets, is seen by U.S. foreign policymakers as a worthy end in itself. More importantly, such an international system is seen as serving American interests, in that it will make the United States more influential, prosperous, and secure. Consequently, there is fairly wide agreement, in the abstract, within the United States over the principle of promoting a more liberal world order. The real question has always been *how* to promote such a system. And on this question, two competing answers have traditionally been given.

One school of thought—call its adherents "crusaders"—has argued that the United States must promote democracy and freedom abroad, by force if necessary. This school of thought is interventionist, but to classical liberal ends. Crusaders believe that the United States should root out authoritarianism overseas, and remake the international system in order to preserve the American experiment at home. This is a school of thought that had a particular impact on American strategic thinking during the Cold War, as well as during both world wars, and it has had a significant impact again ever since the terrorist attacks of 2001.[8]

The alternative school of thought—comprising "exemplarists"—has argued that the United States best promotes liberal ideals overseas by example.[9] According to exemplarists, the United States should remain somewhat detached from the messiness of international politics; it should provide a sanctuary for freedom, but it should follow a strategy of nonintervention with respect to military conflict overseas. This is a school that had particular influence in the years prior to 1941, but which resurfaces from time to time, as it did during and after the Vietnam War.

The debate between crusaders and exemplarists recurs again and again in American history. The two sides seem like opposites, but actually they have much in common: namely, the desire to see democratic values and systems of government spread overseas. They differ on tactics, but both contain a strong element of idealism, and both reject older traditions of balance-of-power politics. Both crusaders and exemplarists, in other words, work from classical liberal assumptions. Americans can and often have been quite realistic in promoting their national interests abroad, but nineteenth-century European-style "realism" or "realpolitik" as a self-conscious school of thought has never had a very broad domestic audience among America's opinion elites.[10] In the United States, at least, grand strategy is seen as legitimate to the extent that it helps promote classical liberal goals overseas.

The obvious potential counter to this argument is to say that liberal ideals have little real impact on U.S. strategic behavior. Skeptics suggest that American officials may talk about promoting democracy overseas, but in actuality this is simply to build domestic political support at home. In fact—so say the skeptics—the United States pursues its own narrow strategic and economic interests overseas while using liberal rhetoric to rationalize any given course of action.

For our purposes, a second problem with the prior argument is that it
cannot explain variation in the degree of America's strategic commitments abroad. Since America's liberal political culture is taken as a constant, it cannot explain changes in grand strategy. A cultural variable that
does not vary cannot predict or explain policy change.

How, then, to answer these criticisms? Certainly, there is no doubt that
the United States pursues liberal international goals in a manner that is
often hypocritical, rhetorical, or self-serving. Idealistic ends are not as
important in U.S. policy as most presidents publicly suggest; after all, such
goals are only one factor among many in the decision-making process.
No doubt, there is an important distinction to be made between symbolic
or rhetorical idealism, on the one hand, and operational pragmatism, on
the other.[11] If that were the whole story, then the only real impact of liberal
ideas upon strategic outcomes would be that policymakers phrase their
decisions in terms of America's liberal creed. Other than that, the actual
policies would be entirely "illiberal." Strategic culture would explain very
little. But there is another possibility: that genuine belief in liberal ideas,
either on the part of the public or on the part of policymakers, has at
least a constraining effect on American grand strategy, ruling out certain
options that might have made sense from a "realpolitik" perspective.

In truth, public and presidential references to liberal foreign policy
goals within the United States are not inconsequential. Such language is
used for a reason. At a minimum, policymakers appeal to cultural symbols
in order to legitimize their authority as well as their chosen policies. References to common ideals function as a form of communication between
policymakers and the public, so that grand strategy takes on a meaning
that is intelligible in terms of the national creed.[12] More to the point, the
cultural content of policy framing has practical consequences for policy
outcomes, in that decision-makers (1) have to tailor their policies to fit
their rhetoric in order to maintain public support, and/or (2) actually
come to believe their own public statements and therefore follow a different policy than they would have otherwise.[13]

When U.S. grand strategy is framed with public reference to liberal
goals, presidents frequently find themselves politically constrained later
on, simply out of concern for their own credibility. The liberal content of
policy statements, in other words, can come to have a real impact on
American grand strategy, even if such framing is used instrumentally at
first. But this by itself is still an inadequate basis for understanding how
and why presidents employ liberal foreign policy rhetoric. In fact, it would
be absurd to deny that in many cases U.S. officials actually believe in the
liberal goals to which they refer. Classical liberal assumptions have a kind
of filtering effect upon the process by which foreign policy officials within
the United States formulate national goals and perceive international con-

ditions. This notion of culture as a filter, or permissive cause, rather than an "independent variable," is actually quite close to the approach favored by culturally minded political scientists.[14] According to such an approach, culture is somewhat indeterminate, but it narrows down the range of acceptable policy options by specifying which policy courses are legitimate. In this sense, culture really does help explain foreign policy outcomes. As we shall see in the following chapters, it is simply historically inaccurate to suggest that classical liberal cultural assumptions have had no impact on American grand strategy. The more interesting question is: what sort of impact have they had?

Here, it turns out, the answer is actually mixed. The liberal tradition has had many welcome and positive effects upon the conduct of American grand strategy, but it has had unintended and negative consequences, as well. One obvious negative consequence is that it tends to encourage an all-or-nothing approach. The crusading liberal tradition implies that if we could just defeat and reform our opponents overseas once and for all, then we could achieve the long-awaited new order in world affairs. The problem, of course, is that there is never any such thing as permanent victory in international relations. Whatever the momentary triumph, some new foreign policy problem arises. Inevitably, euphoric expectations are disappointed, and frustration ensues, tempting Americans to retreat back into an exemplarist or noninterventionist stance. These periods of disengagement typically leave the United States unprepared for the next external challenge, and so the unfortunate cycle of underreaction and overreaction begins anew.[15]

In a sense, the classical liberal tradition sees the entire enterprise of grand strategy as somewhat suspect. Secret diplomacy, tiny elites, Machiavellian ethics, powerful executives, standing armies, security precautions, intelligence services and covert operations—all of these are common features of national security policies, and all of them seem suspicious or even sinister from a liberal perspective. The liberal tendency is to want to keep a very tight lid on such practices. At the same time, such practices are sometimes necessary in order to protect a liberal society from external dangers. Consequently, there is a natural and inevitable tension between the classical liberal worldview, on the one hand, and the effective conduct of national security policy, on the other.[16] Can the United States play the role of a major power and still be true to its own republican and democratic traditions? Can it play the role of a major power and still preserve its freedoms at home?[17] This is a debate that recurs in U.S. history, reflecting a distinctly American set of concerns. It is hardly surprising that liberal ideals sometimes give way to national security concerns. What is interesting, from both an historical and a comparative perspective, is that this debate occurs at all.

In sum, classical liberal cultural assumptions have certain distinct implications for U.S. grand strategy. Americans tend to assume that their system of government is, at a minimum, a model for other countries to follow—an example that will eventually lead to the spread of liberal and democratic institutions worldwide. This belief in the United States as an exemplar can be used to justify both strategic disengagement and active American intervention overseas. The defining feature of America's liberal foreign policy worldview, however, is resistance to "realpolitik." That is, when the issue is not one of seeming self-defense, Americans tend to favor military intervention overseas either for liberal reasons, or not at all. The result is a distinctly liberal pattern of oscillation in matters of grand strategy: first intervention, which turns into a crusade, followed by disappointment, then retreat back into disengagement, which leaves the United States unprepared for the next challenge. The tendency toward moralistic crusading; a conception of war as atavistic and unnatural; the disconnection between the use of force and the use of diplomacy; a reluctance to consider limited aims in wartime—all of these are implications of America's liberal strategic culture.[18] Of course, the existence of a set of liberal assumptions cannot explain variation in grand strategy, since in this case, America's liberal strategic culture is generally taken as a constant. It can still act as a filter or permissive cause, however, making some grand strategies more likely than others. Specifically, we can say that American leaders and foreign policy officials will tend to gravitate toward strategic options that are consistent with classical liberal assumptions, even in spite of international pressures to the contrary.

Limited Liability

American strategic culture is also characterized by assumptions of "limited liability," the strength of which varies over time.[19] Limited liability can be defined as a culturally shaped preference for avoiding costs and commitments in grand strategy, to an extent that is actually inconsistent with stated and established international goals. Of course, every state seeks to reduce the costs and risks of foreign policy. A strategy of nonintervention or nonentanglement can be perfectly rational under a wide variety of circumstances. But when a state fails to promote its own influence, prosperity, or security in the optimal manner, or when it lays out certain ambitious goals and then fails to provide the resources to meet those goals, we are entitled to ask why. In the case of the United States, a strong preference for limited liability in strategic affairs goes a long way toward providing the answer.

The tradition of limited liability has historically influenced American grand strategy in two ways. First, it has meant that the United States often plays less of a role in world affairs than one would expect given America's considerable material power.[20] For example, the United States already had immense material capabilities by the beginning of the twentieth century, yet it was extremely reluctant to employ those resources on behalf of promoting U.S. economic and strategic interests in Europe and East Asia. This intense preference for nonentanglement went well beyond the rational pursuit of the nation's self-interest. It is surprising that such a powerful country failed to promote its own leading role in the world for as long as it did; the source of this surprising behavior was in a deeply rooted cultural preference for limited liability. Second, assumptions of limited liability have encouraged the pursuit of foreign policy aims by disproportionately limited means. Indeed, the disjuncture between ends and means has been so common in American diplomatic and military history that it appears to be culturally determined. This is *not* to deny that Americans have paid a heavy price over the years for sustaining a leading role in the world; obviously, they have. It is to say that the United States has generally been unwilling to pay the costs that would be fully commensurate with the goals and policies articulated by U.S. foreign policy officials. Historically, the United States has tended to prefer limited liability in strategic affairs *relative* to the goals laid out by U.S. officials, and *relative* to America's actual material power. In this sense, we can say that a preference for limited liability is an important part of American strategic culture.

The inclination toward limited liability was especially powerful prior to World War Two. This meant that the first preference of Americans was for a strategy of military and political disengagement from other powers, not simply on utilitarian grounds but on the basis of stubborn and deeply held cultural beliefs and assumptions. George Washington best articulated these common American assumptions in his 1796 Farewell Address, in which he argued that "the great rule of conduct for us in regard to foreign nations is, in extending our commercial relations to have with them as little political connection as possible."[21] Of course, Americans never rejected trade or economic opportunities abroad—far from it. Nor did they reject U.S. expansion within the Western Hemisphere. They certainly hoped that the example of American democracy would spread overseas. Outside of Latin America and the Pacific, however, and well into the twentieth century, Americans were generally very reluctant to make strategic commitments, to engage in alliance diplomacy with other major powers, or to make concrete material sacrifices in order to support broad foreign policy goals. The words of Washington's Farewell Address, warning against international commitments, attained an almost religious stature, and a strategy of nonentanglement became deeply tied up with symbols of American nationhood.[22] The practical implications of this included an inordinate resistance to any alliance commitments, resistance to involvement in European wars, resistance to the creation of a large standing army, and resistance to any constraints on America's freedom of action in international affairs.

Needless to say, a grand strategy based upon limited liability was hard to maintain. America's involvement in World War One attested to that. The striking thing about the U.S. preference for limited liability, however, is how it has persisted in spite of international pressures to the contrary. Certainly, the United States had long possessed the power to intervene and tilt the European balance one way or the other through military commitments and economic aid, but, prior to 1917, the U.S. government hardly even considered committing American lives or taxpayers' money to upholding the balance in Europe: this, in spite of the fact that American exporters and financiers had a significant and growing interest in keeping European markets open. The preference for limited liability, then, was just that: a preference, and a culturally sanctioned one, particularly before 1941.[23] This preference could be overridden by international pressures, but it also had a strong and independent effect on U.S. strategic behavior.

The Japanese attack on Pearl Harbor led to a new era in American foreign policy, one in which strict nonentanglement would be laid aside for good. The tradition of strategic disengagement has never been as strong as it was prior to World War Two. But assumptions of limited liability continued to inform U.S. grand strategy after 1941, and they still do to this day. Immediately after Pearl Harbor, for example, the United States followed a wartime strategy that was relatively capital-intensive rather than manpower-intensive; with a population as large as Russia's and much greater than Germany's, the United States produced far fewer divisions than either.[24] During the Cold War, the United States tended to pursue national security strategies that de-emphasized conventional military power, preferring instead to stress America's long-term economic and technological strengths.[25] During the 1990s the United States was often remarkably reluctant to sustain any significant costs on behalf of stated national interests in locations such as Somalia and the Balkans. And even after the terrorist attacks of 2001, the Bush administration proved quite unwilling to plan or prepare for the inevitable "nation-building" or postwar reconstruction efforts in Afghanistan and Iraq. Again, the point is not that Americans are averse to the costs of grand strategy. The point is that in every one of these cases, U.S. officials first determined and said publicly that significant national interests existed, but then failed to pursue the stated interests with the requisite level of effort, thus robbing the United States of considerable influence over political or military outcomes.

As to *why* this tradition of limited liability has been so strong within the United States, the answer seems to lie in a combination of historical, geopolitical, institutional, and cultural factors. Historically, as previously noted, a precedent was set early on in favor of an overarching strategy of nonentanglement with regard to European wars and alliances; the long-term outcome was path-dependent. Americans grew used to following a strategy of disengagement from European affairs; alternative policies were not seriously considered; the country's general prosperity seemed to justify the traditional strategy; and it was only in the face of repeated and overpowering external pressures that this strategy was eventually questioned and overturned. Geopolitically, the existence of two great oceans separating the United States from any other major military power has also encouraged a somewhat insular strategic mentality. America's relative distance and security from conventional military threats have frequently fed into a mindset that denies the need for costly, long-term commitments overseas.[26]

U.S. domestic political institutions have reinforced the tendency toward limited liability in strategic affairs. The American political system was created to resist dramatic policy changes, and it performs this function as intended. The challenge of mobilizing public and legislative support for costly new initiatives in the United States is as great as in any democratic country. Indeed, the U.S. federal government is fragmented, decentralized, and constrained to an extent unusual among advanced democracies.[27] The most important constraint on executive power lies in the division of authority between the president and Congress—a division instituted deliberately so as to check the power of state actors. Neither the Constitution nor historical practice has conclusively settled the issue of congressional authority in foreign affairs. While presidents generally take the leading role, and while some of them have enjoyed considerable dominance in matters of foreign policy, Congress has never fully relinquished its place as a powerful check on executive decision making; its role in relation to the president has varied from that of merely subtle constraint to outright obstacle. Presidents are also partially constrained by the power of public opinion, and, ultimately, by the prospects for successful re-election. Public opinion in the U.S. grants considerable leeway to presidential activism in foreign affairs, but there are limits to this deference. The American public tends to be unenthusiastic, for example, about military intervention overseas, and presidents are less likely to use force during election season than at other times, in part for this very reason.[28] While the evidence is mixed, on balance it suggests that within the United States, public opinion, elections, and Congress typically act, more often than not, as a *constraint* on costly strategic initiatives, rather than as a stimulus toward them.[29] In this way, the American political system tends to pull U.S. grand strategy back in the direction of limited liability.

Finally, in an important sense, assumptions of limited liability are implicit within the classical liberal tradition that informs American strategic culture. Liberal ideas can certainly encourage a militant, crusading approach to strategic affairs. Fundamentally, however, the liberal assumption is that such crusades are not "normal"—and neither, for that matter, is military competition between states. For liberals, the tendency of history is toward a peaceful, democratic international system. Military intervention may sometimes be necessary, albeit temporarily, to stave off threats. But the baseline liberal assumption is that a more peaceful international order can and will evolve through economic exchange, interdependence, and social interaction, without the need for regular military interventions on the part of any nation-state. Indeed, for much of U.S. history, assumptions of limited liability were seen as being entirely compatible with the most ambitious visions for a new and progressive world order. The American liberal tradition has therefore played into long-term assumptions of limited liability, even when liberals are in "crusader" mode.[30]

The impact of limited-liability assumptions can be measured by looking at the extent to which the United States has historically converted, or failed to convert, its material potential into usable forms of military, political, and economic leverage over other nations. The relevant metrics include: a readiness to engage in costly military interventions overseas; peacetime alliance commitments; levels and forms of defense spending; levels of foreign economic and military aid; expenditures on international affairs, including postwar reconstruction efforts; peacetime troop deployments overseas; and potentially costly commitments to international and/ or multilateral organizations. A willingness to deploy these various forms of usable power can certainly be disaggregated, and often is, from one administration to the next. In recent years, conservatives in the United States have been willing to sustain relatively high levels of defense spending, while being unenthusiastic about new multilateral commitments overseas. Liberals have preferred the opposite course. In part, this particular pattern is the result of a bifurcation of American internationalism that dates back to the Vietnam War era.[31] Viewed from a longer historical perspective, however, it is best to keep in mind that this pattern has not always existed. In the early 1950s, for example, conservatives were opposed to high levels of defense spending *and* to multilateral commitments, while mainstream liberals supported both. As a result, it is useful to rely upon a metric of limited liability that is applicable across periods in American history, without forgetting that different political coalitions may apply elements of limited liability selectively at various points in time.

Strategic Subcultures

Undoubtedly, various U.S. foreign policy officials may place greater or lesser emphasis upon assumptions of limited liability, depending on their own personal preferences, just as they may place greater or lesser emphasis on liberal assumptions of international progress. One can imagine, for instance, a given administration that is, in relative terms, "strongly" committed to democracy promotion, but only "weakly" committed to limited liability: Roosevelt during World War Two comes to mind in this context. One can even imagine an administration that is strongly committed to both, as, for example, Herbert Hoover appears to have been.[32] The degree of commitment to liberal assumptions—"strong" versus "weak"—can be defined by how easily decision-makers allow other considerations to trump the pursuit of classical liberal goals: namely, democratic government, open markets, multilateral institutions, and national self-determination overseas. The degree of commitment to limited liability can be defined by how easily decision-makers allow other considerations to trump the maintenance of low levels among the following: foreign aid, military spending, overseas deployments, military interventions, and alliance or international commitments.[33]

It is important to point out that a strong commitment to liberal or limited liability assumptions does not imply that such considerations will be the only ones shaping grand strategy. Similarly, a weak commitment to either set of assumptions does not mean that such ideas will be completely insignificant in the decision-making process; the question is one of emphasis. One can further imagine a range of possibilities, encompassing a variety of inclinations such as "moderate," "very weak," or "very strong" along either dimension. The exact location of any given official's preferences will always be a matter of degree. Nevertheless, the various permutations allow for four basic types, usefully thought of as American strategic "subcultures": internationalist, nationalist, progressive, and realist.[34]

Internationalists are strongly liberal but only weakly committed to limited liability. This has been the single most common and influential strain of thought among U.S. foreign policy officials since World War Two. Internationalists believe in the promotion of a liberalized world order characterized by open markets, strong international institutions, and democratic governments. They are sensitive to the costs of an ambitious grand strategy but ultimately see such costs as manageable. They are willing to promote liberal goals through the use of force if necessary. Internationalists have no intense aversion to new commitments abroad, and they are more willing than many of their compatriots to spend money on national defense and foreign aid. Their readiness and/or ability to create usable forms of international leverage is, however, often outstripped by their very ambitious foreign policy goals. Examples of internationalist American leaders include Woodrow Wilson, Franklin Roosevelt after 1938, Harry Truman, John F. Kennedy, and, to some extent, Bill Clinton.

Nationalists are weakly liberal but strongly committed to limited liability. This is a school of thought with a long tradition in the United States and considerable popular appeal. Nationalists are rather dubious about the possibilities of an easy or rapid liberalization of the international system. They consider a keen attention to American interests, narrowly conceived, to be entirely legitimate. Nationalists are very reluctant to cede any part of U.S. sovereignty to international organizations, or to make diplomatic concessions to potential adversaries. They are skeptical of new commitments overseas and foreign aid. Having said that, they can be the most hawkish and uncompromising of all foreign policy schools once they believe the United States has been insulted or attacked.[35] Over the past century, nationalists have exercised a pronounced, if secondary, influence on American grand strategy. Powerful senators such as Robert Taft and Jesse Helms have spoken out on behalf of nationalist assumptions. And under the administration of George W. Bush, foreign policy nationalists have had a greater influence on U.S. grand strategy than at any time since the 1920s.

Progressives are strongly committed to both liberalism and limited liability in strategic affairs. Like nationalists, they have an ancient lineage in U.S. diplomatic history. Progressives are dedicated to the promotion of a more liberal international order, but they would pursue that goal through peaceful means rather than through U.S. military intervention overseas. Traditionally, progressives in the United States were often wary of formal international entanglements; in recent years, however, they have become much more enamored of multilateral institution building. They remain skeptical about the need for and uses of military power, and they are reluctant to associate with illiberal or undemocratic regimes. Prior to World War Two, this school of thought was often a dominant strain in American foreign policy thinking, and it remains so on the political Left. Progressive assumptions also had a powerful impact on the strategies of both the Carter and Clinton administrations. Leading American political figures over the years such as Henry Wallace, George McGovern, and Ralph Nader have articulated progressive foreign policy assumptions. And while progressivism is today associated with the Democratic Party, this was not always the case; both the Taft (1909–1913) and Hoover (1929–1933) Republican administrations operated under essentially progressive strategic assumptions.

Realists, the last of the four subcultures, are weakly committed to both liberalism and limited liability. Like nationalists, they are somewhat skeptical about the possibilities for democracy-promotion overseas, and view the pursuit of America's economic and strategic interests as entirely legitimate. Unlike nationalists, however, but like internationalists, they are not fixated on the preservation of limited liability in strategic affairs. They are willing to consider the careful use of military, political, and economic instruments—diplomacy, foreign aid, armed force—to meet stated strategic goals. In their case, this willingness flows not so much from a commitment to a more liberal international system as from an attempt to promote the national interest in a balanced manner. It is worth noting, however, that even foreign policy "realists" within the United States typically share a certain measured commitment to broad liberal goals in world politics— the promotion of democracy and the pursuit of an open international economic order. This is what makes them *American* realists, rather than simply advocates of unmitigated realpolitik.[36] The outstanding example in recent decades of American realism in action was the Nixon-Kissinger team. The policies of George H. W. Bush (1989–1993) were also strongly influenced by realist assumptions. One major weakness of realism, in political terms, is its poor fit with America's liberal political culture. But there have been numerous articulate and influential foreign policy realists in American history, such as Senator Henry Cabot Lodge, George Kennan, and Walter Lippmann, and realist assumptions have often had more of a policy impact than one would think from the public pronouncements of American leaders.

Since these are each ideal types, it is worth reiterating that a given administration may combine two or more of these subcultures within itself. Truman's foreign policy, for example, was internationalist with a strong dose of realism. Carter's, on the other hand, was internationalist with a heavy progressive bent. Even *within* an administration, there will of course be shades of opinion, and the overall tenor of a single president's foreign policy can certainly alter or change with time.

WHY ONE SUBCULTURE OVER ANOTHER?

The preceding discussion gives rise to an obvious question: if these four subcultures characterize foreign policy debate within the United States, how does one subculture win out over the others at any particular moment? How does one school of thought establish and maintain its ascendancy, however temporarily, over the conduct of American grand strategy? The answer lies in the intersecting pressures of four distinct factors:

international conditions, dominant strategic cultures, domestic politics, and political leadership.[37]

International conditions are the most important long-term influence on patterns of strategic adjustment, and such conditions can work for or against the influence of a particular strategic subculture. Whenever the United States gains in relative power internationally, this tends to work in favor of subcultures that advocate more assertive grand strategies. Conversely, whenever the United States loses relative power, or is forced to consolidate its position from sheer necessity, this naturally works in favor of subcultures that advocate a less interventionist strategic approach. Changes in the level of external threat can also trigger the rise or fall of particular subcultures. The appearance of sudden or dramatic threats tends to favor those schools of thought that advocate a vigorous response to such threats. The disappearance of threats tends to favor subcultures that downplay the need for costly or interventionist strategies. Each individual outcome depends upon the specific demands of a given strategic subculture at a certain point in time, in combination with international conditions, but the basic trends are predictable. For example, progressives tend to benefit from nonthreatening international conditions, and from losses or low points in America's relative power. Internationalists benefit from increases in American power, and realists benefit from difficult or constraining international conditions. The international power shifts of the 1940s greatly benefited internationalists, helped realists, and substantially undermined the other two subcultures. The fallout from America's war in Vietnam created new political opportunities for progressives as well as for realists. The end of the Cold War had a different effect, making the need for realism less obvious, and opening up opportunities for each of the other three schools of thought. International pressures, however, are only that—pressures. By themselves, they are rarely completely constraining or determinant.

The *dominant strategic culture* helps determine the relative domestic political appeal of a given school of thought. The crucial insight here is that realism, of the four alternatives, has the worst "fit" with America's nationally dominant strategic culture. Internationalism appeals to the liberal strain in U.S. culture, while nationalism appeals to the preference for limited liability. The arguments of progressives appeal to both. Realists, on the other hand, seem uncommitted to either liberal or limited-liability assumptions, and for this reason, are always suspect to an American audience. The result is that realists will tend to come under attack within the United States, simply on principle, and regardless of their actual foreign policy successes—a pattern that occurred, for example, in the case of Henry Kissinger.[38] It should also be noted that if the nationally dominant strategic culture changes—a rare occurrence—then this will subsequently favor some subcultures over others. The one great example of this, again, was in the 1940s, when strict assumptions of limited liability were likely permanently weakened. It has since then been easier for internationalists to win the strategic debate when, to a certain extent, the nation's dominant strategic culture changed.

Domestic politics are often crucial in determining which strategic subculture will win out at any given point in time. This is true in two senses. First, electoral turnover creates new administrations and new governing coalitions with both the inclination and the incentive to make changes in grand strategy. The inclination toward change comes from conceptions of the national interest that differ from one administration to the next; the incentive for change comes from the desire to differentiate oneself from previous presidents, and from the particular combinations of interests represented by incoming administrations. Actual and subsequent policy changes are sometimes more superficial or secondary than one might expect from the overheated rhetoric of election campaigns; international pressures continue to operate on succeeding administrations in a strong and consistent manner. Nevertheless, there is room for interpretation and adjustment, and the election and inauguration of a new president is therefore one of the developments most likely to produce significant changes in American grand strategy.[39]

Second, presidents seek to win re-election, and to build winning coalitions across a variety of issue areas, including foreign policy. The president's challengers also seek electoral success. Grand strategy is therefore not immune from political considerations. Narrow electoral incentives are not necessarily uppermost in decisions to make war or peace, but they can hardly be absent, even if only as a constraint on executive decision making. Domestic political factors influence strategic choice insofar as political constraints can force presidents to accept policy outcomes that would not have been their first preference. The arguments offered by one strategic subculture or another may carry greater or lesser political weight with key interest groups, Congress, or public opinion, at a particular moment in time; and this political weight is bound to have an impact on the process of strategic adjustment. For domestic reasons, nationalists, internationalists, realists, or progressives may be politically weak or politically strong, regardless of international pressures in one direction or the other. In fact, it is sometimes the case that domestic political factors intrude on the process of U.S. strategic adjustment for reasons that have nothing to do with international conditions. Since political party coalitions come together in the United States on a variety of issues, of which foreign policy is only one, electoral turnover will typically reflect a popular expression of preferences along several policy dimensions: economic and social, as well as international. Election results in the United States often have little to do with international conditions, per se. But elections frequently have a major impact on American grand strategy, when a new president first campaigns upon and subsequently implements significant strategic adjustments. In this sense, the temporary triumph of one strategic subculture over another sometimes has more to do with domestic politics than with any other factor.[40]

Finally, *political leadership* is vital in determining the relative influence of the four strategic subcultures. This is particularly true with regard to the White House. Presidents build support from a great variety of interests, and across a wide range of issues; they are positioned at the head of broad political coalitions. They are also positioned at the point where international pressures intersect with the American political system. The president is the single most important figure in the decision-making process. For all these reasons, presidents have a certain amount of latitude when it comes to the formation of American grand strategy. The specific policy assumptions and preferences of a particular president can make a great deal of difference in the process of strategic choice. The precise political strategies they employ to build support for themselves can make a difference, too. Beyond the president, key political or policy officials sometimes have a dramatic impact on American grand strategy: leading senators, cabinet officials, and bureaucratic entrepreneurs can all help to shape strategic choice. In sum, international, domestic cultural, and political pressures together explain a great deal, but they do not explain everything when it comes to strategic outcomes. There is still a role for choice, agency, and leadership. The case studies examined within this book will illustrate the considerable impact that political leadership can have upon processes of strategic choice within the United States.

All of the above factors intersect and interact in determining the relative influence of America's strategic subcultures; all four factors operate in conjunction. International shocks create opportunities for new grand strategies, and, in the long run, international conditions are most important in determining the broad contours of American strategic adjustment—but, again, this is only true in the long run, and at a very broad level. As we focus in on the process of decision making, factors such as leadership and domestic politics become crucial in helping to determine specific strategic outcomes. Strategic culture at the national level tends to act as a constraint, and a filter, rather than a determinant "cause" of grand strategy in and of itself, but cultural factors often push or pull strategic choice in one direction or another. Culturally shaped preferences for liberalism and limited liability in strategic affairs often have an independent and striking impact upon the success or failure of specific strategic subcultures within the United States.

THE PROCESS OF STRATEGIC ADJUSTMENT:
AGENDA SETTING AND COALITION BUILDING

The question of why one subculture wins out over another is intimately related to the question of how strategic adjustments are made. First, it is analytically useful at this point to distinguish between "strategic cultures" or "subcultures," which are nationally distinct and persistent, from the particular grand strategies chosen by leading decision-makers at a given moment in time. For example, Germany and Japan may have had antimilitaristic strategic cultures since 1945, but that still leaves open the more precise question of the exact grand strategies followed by these two countries. Similarly, the United States may possess a "liberal" strategic culture, but that culture allows for a number of strategic options: containment, disengagement, and so forth. In the following section, I will argue that domestic political processes of agenda setting and coalition building within the United States allow for nationally distinct strategic cultures and subcultures to influence strategic behavior through the conception and implementation of specific strategic ideas. These same political processes of agenda setting and coalition building permit—indeed, require—leading state officials to formulate and effect particular strategies with a certain amount of freedom, because of perennial uncertainties over international conditions.

The existence of uncertainty over exactly how to pursue national interests, and the limited time and information available to policymakers, forces leaders to rely not only upon broad cultural assumptions but also upon specific mental shortcuts or preconceived beliefs variously described by international relations theorists as "belief systems," "operational codes," "policy paradigms," or simply "policy ideas."[41] These beliefs or assumptions offer policymakers specific guidance under conditions of uncertainty, and therefore have an independent impact on foreign policy decisions. For our purposes, ideas or beliefs regarding the value and efficacy of particular grand strategies will be called "strategic concepts" or "strategic ideas."

Strategic ideas tend to persist—in spite of changing material conditions—until they are perceived to have "failed."[42] In the United States, this sense of policy failure typically occurs in one of two ways: either through electoral turnover, or because of severe external shocks. Both kinds of developments cause existing policies to be questioned regardless of their inherent merits. Especially severe shocks can even bring broadly held cultural assumptions into question. The most obvious sources of such shock are major wars or international crises. But a dramatic new threat, or significant changes within the international distribution of power, can also act as a shock to existing strategies, even in the absence of war.[43] Consequently, the pattern of U.S. strategic adjustment, according to a neoclassical realist approach, is predicted to be one of "punctuated equilibrium"—somewhat uneven and episodic.[44] Existing grand strategies will tend to persist until shaken by some dramatic international or domestic political change.

Given that the expectation with a neoclassical realist approach is that change in American grand strategy will be uneven, how can such an approach explain or predict which direction such change will take? How exactly does strategic culture matter at moments of upheaval, and why does one strategic idea or concept win out over another? These are questions that have received comparatively little attention in the literature on culture and foreign policy. I suggest that at moments of change, international pressures and electoral turnovers determine the basic direction of American grand strategy. But I also suggest that in the wake of such developments, strategic culture continues to have a significant impact on strategic outcomes, through two domestic political mechanisms: (1) agenda setting, and (2) coalition building.

External shocks and electoral turnover both create unusual degrees of uncertainty over questions of grand strategy. At such moments of flux and crisis, a window of opportunity is opened for new strategic concepts.[45] Any one of a number of alternative grand strategies might plausibly serve the national interest. Of course, international constraints do set real limits on the feasibility of any potential strategy. Some may be more feasible than others. But there is almost always more than one grand strategy that might be viable internationally. International conditions do not usually leave only one possible option to policymakers. This is where agenda setting and coalition building come in.

Once some international shock or electoral turnover has opened up a window of opportunity for new strategic ideas, the exact nature of those ideas—and the nature of the one that finally wins out—is crucially influenced by a process of agenda setting. However feasible a given strategic concept might be, it must be put on the agenda of leading policymakers before it can have any real impact. In this initial stage of agenda setting, strategic ideas may come to the attention of policymakers because of the efforts of interest groups, bureaucratic actors, or elected officials.[46] Within the United States, pluralistic as it is, any number of political actors may play a role in this process.[47] But the key point is that a strategic idea not put on the agenda by some credible messenger or policy entrepreneur has no chance of success, regardless of its merits. Just as there are ideas whose time has come, so there are moments when the time is right but new or potentially good ideas are unavailable.[48]

In the latter stage of agenda setting, the process of strategic adjustment within the United States takes on a very different dynamic, and the number of politically relevant actors narrows considerably. In this second stage, leading state officials become the key agenda-setters, the crucial link between new ideas and policy outcomes. Leading officials—including eventually, and most importantly, the president—use their influence to determine which strategic ideas will be put forward for consideration. They shape the nature of the choices facing Congress and the public.[49] They can do this because they are given considerable leeway on national security policy, and because international pressures are somewhat indeterminate. This is especially true at moments of crisis and upheaval.[50] Particularly at such moments, on questions of grand strategy, there is room for choice, for advocacy, and for creativity on the part of chief executives, if, that is, they elect to use it. They cannot always secure their preferred result, but they can certainly determine which options will be considered, and this in itself helps shape the final outcome. At the same time, any strategies that seem to violate the nation's dominant culture are unlikely to be forwarded in the first place. In this way, cultural legacies act as a filter on strategic options, tilting the process in favor of cultural and historical continuity.

If agenda setting determines which strategic ideas receive a hearing, the process of coalition building determines whether the ideas put forward by state officials can be put into action without being changed beyond all recognition. Here again, the president is the single most important actor, positioned as he is at the fulcrum of domestic and international pressures. It is up to the president to win support for his preferred strategy through persuasion, pressure, and/or negotiation. This inevitably involves compromise, both at home and abroad, but beyond a certain point such compromise must come to mean that an entirely different grand strategy has been adopted. Any proposed strategic adjustment must be capable of winning at least minimal necessary support both domestically and internationally; coalition building thus involves trade-offs between these two levels, and between the both of them and the preferences of the executive.[51] A further constraint is that any new strategic concept must pass this crucial domestic hurdle—it must be framed in terms that resonate with the nation's strategic culture. This constraint is overlooked in much of the literature on foreign policy and domestic coalition building, which tends to focus more narrowly on the material interests of political actors. In sum, for any new strategic idea to be put into practice, it must be capable of winning a certain amount of support on two broad fronts, international and domestic, and it is incumbent upon the president to win that support through a process of coalition building. And again, if new strategic ideas seem to run against the nation's strategic culture, then these new ideas will be unlikely to pass the hurdle of domestic coalition building, regardless of their international feasibility.

Strategic ideas can play a key role in helping to cement political coalitions together. That is, while the executive is obliged to build support for any new strategic concept, the strategy can itself serve as a focal point for coalition building, attracting support and/or creating divisions on its own merits. Since political coalitions within the United States typically come together on a variety of social, economic, and foreign policy issues, strategic ideas are likely to be only one of many issues that hold together a given coalition. But when questions of grand strategy are at the forefront of public debate, new strategic ideas can play an important part in rearranging political alignments and reshaping the political landscape—one more way in which ideas have an impact at moments of strategic adjustment and uncertainty.

A neoclassical realist approach recognizes that on questions of grand strategy, especially at moments of change and uncertainty, leading state officials have considerable autonomy to react to external pressures in the manner they see fit. In the United States, executive officials typically react to such pressures—at least partially—on the basis of their perception of the national interest, perceptions that often differ from one person and one administration to the next, even apart from questions of political self-interest. Ultimately, it is through leading state officials that new strategic ideas have a concrete impact on policy outcomes; and it is because of their relative autonomy on questions of national security that such officials can put these ideas into practice. Contrary to the views of structural theorists, there is a surprising degree of room for creativity on the part of the executive to shape and develop grand strategy. The power of ideas is both a cause and a consequence of that freedom. Once any period of strategic adjustment has passed, however, and a new strategic idea is implemented with reasonable success, resistance to innovation once again comes to the fore until the next international shock, or the next electoral turnover. New strategic ideas are locked in and institutionalized, both formally and informally, and the bias toward policy continuity resumes. Moreover, the only strategic ideas that are likely to survive this process are those that seem consistent with past policies, and those that resonate with the country's strategic culture.

To recapitulate the argument thus far: culture and ideas have a role in the making of grand strategy because they help specify the interests of political actors and of the nation as a whole amidst conditions of uncertainty. International pressures are to a certain extent indeterminate, and leading state officials are given considerable autonomy to interpret and act upon their conceptions of the national interest; these conceptions necessarily have a major impact on policy outcomes. In times of relative stability and continuity, strategic culture and strategic ideas have an impact primarily through their institutionalization or entrenchment in positions of power, both formal and informal. In the wake of international shocks and electoral turnovers, culture and ideas still have a great impact on American strategic adjustment, but in a very different way: through the twin processes of agenda setting and coalition building. While a variety of political actors can play a role in the early stages of agenda setting, leading state officials are the key figures in both processes. Concretely, it is only through the advocacy of such officials—including, ultimately, the president—that new ideas can have an impact on strategic outcomes. The typical process or "life cycle" of strategic adjustment within the United States therefore includes the following predictable phases:

1. Existing grand strategies tend to persist until (a) the occurrence of an international shock or series of shocks, which reveal(s) changes in the international distribution of power and/or threats, or (b) periods of electoral turnover.

2. International shocks and electoral turnovers increase policy uncertainty and open a window of opportunity for alternative strategic ideas.

3. The adoption of a given strategic idea depends crucially upon a process of agenda setting. This process has two stages. In the first stage, new ideas are brought to the attention of leading state officials. Interest groups, bureaucratic actors, and legislators can each play a role in developing alternatives during this first stage. In the second stage, the president puts forward new ideas for public and/or legislative consideration. Executive officials play the key role in narrowing down the available options during this second stage.

4. The adoption of a given strategic idea also depends upon a process of coalition building. Any strategic alternative must be minimally feasible internationally and domestically before it can be adopted. Such constraints may require the modification or elimination of certain strategic alternatives. But new ideas can also be used creatively as the cement for new coalitions. Again, the executive plays the key role in this process.

5. The strategic ideas that are most likely to be put forward by state officials for public consideration are those most consistent with the nation's strategic culture.

6. After adoption, new strategic ideas act as a powerful, independent, and persistent influence on grand strategic behavior, shaping the direction, nature, and extent of strategic adjustment.

In sum, any new strategic idea within the United States needs to meet four key conditions in order to win out over the alternatives. First, it needs the right moment. Some international shock or election result must have discredited existing policy. Second, it needs to be minimally feasible internationally.[52] Third, it needs a series of influential advocates or supporters, including the president. And fourth, it needs to be culturally resonant. Without all of these four conditions, no new strategic concept will be put into practice, however deserving. Conversely, in the wake of an international shock or electoral turnover, the first internationally and politically feasible strategic idea put forward by leading executive officials will typically become state policy, regardless of its merits.

RESEARCH METHOD AND DESIGN

How, then, to test this model of strategic adjustment? A quantitative method, one that uses a large number of cases, has the advantages of a large sample size, but it carries with it certain disadvantages. With a large number of cases, we gain little sense of the actual process or causal mechanism involved in strategic adjustment. A quantitative method can confirm or deny correlations between variables, but it cannot provide us with a theory as to why such correlation holds. Such a method inevitably sacrifices on the details of any given case; and it is precisely such detail that allows us to establish whether or not our model is accurate. Given our focus on the process of grand strategic change, then, a large-N method is inappropriate. At the same time, those who favor a quantitative approach are right in saying that a single case study in itself is of limited use in theory building. The solution is to use more than one case, and then to compare and contrast each case through the comparative method. A few useful methods will serve to effectively increase our sample size, and to gain some of the benefits of a large-N study, while retaining the contextual richness of a case study approach.

First, the exact process of strategic adjustment will be scrutinized in detail. Such "process-tracing" allows us a greater number of effective observations, in spite of a small number of case studies involving multiple variables.[53] Second, the number of observations will effectively be increased through the controlled comparison of relevant variables, matching and/or contrasting them where necessary. This kind of controlled comparison insures variance between cases and allows us to draw causal inferences from a smaller number of cases.[54] Third, we will increase the number of effective observations through the use of counterfactuals. Each case study will be framed in terms of broad strategic options or alternatives: not only those that were in fact chosen, but also those that could have been. For example, after 1945 the United States adopted a strategy of containment, and most of the literature on the period has tried to explain why that alternative was chosen. But any attempt to explain the adoption of containment is at least implicitly a claim as to why another alternative—such as neoisolationism—was rejected. Counterfactuals simply make explicit the causal claims that are already implicit in any such study. There is, of course, good reason to be skeptical of farfetched counterfactuals; this is a method that must be used with care and precision. One way to ensure such precision is to refer only to policy alternatives that were credible or plausible at the time. Another is to apply generalizable theories to the historical case, and then deduce what sort of outcomes each theory would predict. These two restrictions bring both historical plausibility and theoretical rigor to our investigation. With these restrictions, the careful and theoretically informed use of counterfactuals actually adds to our search for a generalizable theory, and to the effective number of observations in a given case study.[55]

The cases under investigation here have been selected to fit a number of important criteria. Together, they provide a range of variance in terms of both causal forces and outcomes. They each involve a key turning point or potential turning point in the history of American grand strategy. And finally, they form a natural combination, since together they tell the story of America's rise to its current global predominance. The three central cases are:

Chapter Three: 1918–1921, the defeat of the League of Nations
Chapter Four: 1945–1951, the origins and consolidation of containment
Chapter Five: 1992–2000, the immediate post–Cold War era

Within each case, the explanatory power of international pressures, culture, leadership, and domestic politics will be tested, weighed, and compared. My theoretical findings will be summarized in the concluding chapter, and applied to the most recent case of American strategic adjustment under the George W. Bush administration. Finally, at the end of that chapter, predictions will be drawn regarding the future of U.S. grand strategy.

A final word on method. Politics is a complex and human world of contingency, choice, and chance. It is unrealistic to think that pure "covering laws" can be discovered in political life, along the lines of Newtonian physics. But this is no reason to abandon the search for general patterns in politics. Rather, it is all the more reason to be precise and explicit about our causal assumptions, and to continue to look for possible patterns in the knowledge that they are likely to be less deterministic and more probabilistic than in the natural sciences. With that in mind, we turn now to an examination of several major turning points in American grand strategy.

Chapter Three

THE LOST ALLIANCE: IDEAS AND ALTERNATIVES

IN AMERICAN GRAND STRATEGY, 1918–1921

THE PERIOD IMMEDIATELY following the Allied victory over the Kaiser's Germany was one of intense public debate and upheaval regarding the issue of American grand strategy. For the first time, Americans had made great sacrifices of men and material to serve foreign policy goals overseas. The question of what new strategic commitments the United States ought to undertake, if any, was wide open. The outcome is well known: Woodrow Wilson's proposal of American entry into a League of Nations was defeated in the Senate, and shortly thereafter a new Republican administration confirmed that the United States would remain aloof from any sort of new security arrangements in Europe. The United States reduced its army to less than two hundred thousand men, and refused to make any material commitments to European states, whether in the form of military guarantees or economic aid. This outcome had an historic impact on eventual prospects for international peace and stability. Had the United States made a genuine, long-term commitment in 1919 to some sort of European security system, at the very least it would have posed a powerful counterweight to Hitler's expansionist ambitions twenty years later. The significance of America's strategic withdrawal from Europe by 1921 is plain. Most accounts of these events, however, emphasize their idiosyncratic, and even supposedly irrational, causes, due to factors such as Wilson's personal inflexibility, the provincialism and parochialism of Congress, or a general mood of disillusionment in the country by the fall of 1919.[1] There have been few attempts to study this episode rigorously and systematically as one example of the larger phenomenon of change in U.S. grand strategy.[2]

In the chapter that follows, I show that there were not two, but three plausible alternatives for U.S. grand strategy after World War One: a League of Nations, disengagement, or a straightforward military alliance with France and Great Britain. I demonstrate that international conditions could not have predicted the return to disengagement, given America's immense power by 1918. I then show how cultural assumptions—through, and in conjunction with, domestic patterns of agenda setting and coalition building—shaped and influenced the process of strategic choice.

As we will see, domestic politics, presidential leadership, and sheer chance all had a dramatic effect on the eventual outcome of the League debate. In particular, there is good reason to believe—and most historians of the period now agree—that a more narrowly circumscribed set of League commitments would have passed through the Senate, if Wilson had significantly moderated his demands. But this simply begs the question: why was Wilson's vision so ambitious? And why was resistance to it from within the Senate so intense? Why were American officials unable to come up with or agree upon any limited and realistic strategic commitment to European security and stability? In order to answer these fundamental questions we need to look to the subtle but powerful impact of American strategic culture in all its varieties.

Briefly put, common assumptions of limited liability, together with a heritage of classical liberal thought, acted as a sharp constraint on new strategic ideas within the United States. These cultural assumptions operated *through* processes of political leadership, and also *in spite* of them. In the end, certain plausible strategic choices were removed from consideration for what were essentially cultural reasons. A simple "balance-of-power" alliance with France was ruled out by Wilson, and by many other Americans, because it seemed to represent a violation of liberal foreign policy goals. Membership in a strong League of Nations, however, was ruled out by the Senate, because it violated the U.S. tradition of limited liability in strategic affairs. Cultural factors interacted with leadership and domestic politics to determine the final result: a return to the default strategy of disengagement, in spite of the fact that the United States was materially ready to assume a larger role in world affairs.

ALTERNATIVE STRATEGIC IDEAS, 1918–1920

In the years before World War One, American grand strategy was heavily informed by classical liberal ideas and by assumptions of limited liability. This did not mean that the United States was literally "isolated" from the rest of the world. U.S. policymakers sought foreign markets for American products, and expected that under conditions of equal treatment American commerce would outsell the competition—the so-called "Open Door" approach. They likewise expected that the expansion of international trade would encourage the development of liberal and democratic institutions overseas.[3] The United States was held up as a model for worldwide emulation; American popular culture was promoted abroad as a means of increasing American influence, and as a supposedly liberalizing and pacifying force internationally.[4] From the 1890s onward, a powerful battleship fleet was constructed to support U.S. interests abroad. Pacific islands such as Hawaii and Samoa were forcibly annexed. The independence and integrity of China was proclaimed as a major foreign policy goal. An informal sphere of influence was asserted over the Caribbean, involving repeated military interventions. And Spain was defeated in a brief war, leading to American control over Cuba, Puerto Rico, and the Philippines. Such an expansionist list of activities can hardly be captured by the term "isolationist." But there were still strict limits on the use of American power overseas. Outside of Latin American and the Pacific, before 1917 the United States was unwilling to make any strategic commitments, to engage in alliance diplomacy, or to make concrete national sacrifices to support broad foreign policy goals such as the "Open Door." This legacy of nonentanglement, informed by liberal assumptions, would have a major impact on Woodrow Wilson, as well as on his opponents.

The strategy of nonentanglement began to break down only after a series of major international shocks. Even the German invasion of France in 1914 was insufficient to seriously dent America's commitment to an insular strategy. But Berlin's declaration of unrestricted submarine warfare early in 1917 highlighted the German threat to U.S. interests and led to an American declaration of war against Germany. Wilson took the opportunity to lead Congress and the nation into war, but he did so on grounds that differed significantly from those favored by Britain, France, and leading Republicans within the United States. Many Republicans favored American entry into a straightforward alliance designed to force Germany into complete surrender.[5] Wilson, on the other hand, viewed war against Germany as a necessary first step in promoting an international order, led by the United States, entailing collective security, democratization, disarmament, and open markets worldwide: a strategy about which the Allies were bound to be skeptical.[6] These differences over war aims carried into the postwar era. In this sense, the seeds of later disagreements were planted in 1917. But as long as war continued, debate over grand strategy was subordinated to the immediate priority of military victory.

The war itself was a severe shock to old strategic assumptions and ideas. It revealed the United States as a great power not only in economic but in military terms, capable of projecting its forces across the Atlantic and having a decisive impact on European affairs. Over four million men were mobilized into the U.S. armed forces: 1.3 million served on the western front; over 300,000 were killed or wounded.[7] The war also led to a much greater role for the federal government in the nation's economy. In spite of demobilization after 1918, there was no return to the very limited federal government of the prewar era. It was conceivable that this newfound government power might be used toward a more permanent set of military commitments overseas. The costs, upheavals, and lives lost during the war all shocked longstanding assumptions of insularity. The majority of Americans were temporarily prepared to consider some limited modification or alternative to the old concept of nonentanglement.[8] But which alternative?

Three broad strategic alternatives existed for the United States after World War One: first, the assertion of American leadership through a League of Nations; second, a more traditional and limited alliance with France and Britain; and third, a return to insularity and nonentanglement.

Wilson's League of Nations

Wilson's proposed alternative in 1918–1920 was American membership in a League of Nations—the ultimate "internationalist" option. In public addresses and private letters, from the winter of 1915–1916 until the very end of his presidency, Wilson's conception of the League was remarkably consistent. It was to be an "association of nations"—preferably democratic—providing a "virtual guarantee of territorial integrity and political independence" to all member states.[9] This mutual guarantee—eventually enshrined in Article 10 of the League Covenant—was regarded by Wilson as the key to the whole enterprise. It meant that member states were obliged to act against territorial aggression from any quarter. Wilson hoped that an American military response would prove to be unnecessary in the vast majority of such cases. He believed that the combination of arbitration, economic sanctions, public opinion, and the deterrent effect of overwhelming military power on the part of other states would usually be enough to prevent or defeat aggression. But if all of this proved insufficient, Wilson recognized that force might have to be used against aggressors; otherwise, the League guarantees meant nothing. As Wilson put it when presenting the newly drafted League Covenant to a plenary session at the Versailles conference, "armed force is in the background of this programme, but it is in the background, and if the moral force of the world will not suffice, the physical force of the world shall."[10] Membership in the League represented a general commitment to act against aggression, a commitment that might entail concrete sacrifices, and Wilson meant it as such.

Wilson hoped to use these new League commitments, together with America's considerable financial, political, and military leverage, to pressure allies and enemies alike into disbanding their protectionist spheres of influence, their exclusive military alliances, and their swollen stacks of armaments. The other great powers were to be pressed into an international order characterized by collective security, democratic government, self-determination, freedom of the seas, and peaceful settlement of disputes. Britain, for example, was asked to participate in naval disarmament efforts, under the threat of an arms race with the United States.[11] Both Britain and France were pressured to open their colonial markets to American products. Japan, similarly, was asked to abandon its claims to an exclusive sphere of influence in Manchuria, and to respect the integrity and independence of China under an Open Door system.[12] Germany was to be disarmed, punished, supervised, and in effect placed on probation until it had earned its credentials as a democracy. At the same time, Wilson was determined to protect the right of the German people to self-determination, to prevent prohibitive reparations, and eventually to integrate a democratic and chastened Germany into a liberal international order through the League.[13] The one major power that had no place in a Wilsonian League was the Soviet Union. The fact that the USSR openly called for worldwide revolutionary upheaval meant that it could not be a partner in any liberal League of Nations; it had to be cordoned off and contained. But apart from a limited and half-hearted intervention in 1918, there would be no sweeping military crusades against Lenin's regime on the part of the United States or within Wilson's strategic design.[14]

Wilson's grand strategy was to promote a liberal international order, with the United States in the lead, through a League of Nations, and to coopt other great powers into playing a role in the new order. This was essentially an attempt to assert American hegemony over the international system at minimal cost. An end to formal spheres of influence on the part of other major powers meant that Wilson was in effect asserting an *informal* sphere of influence, on the part of the United States, over much of the surface of the globe. The price of American leadership would be a sweeping new commitment to uphold the integrity and independence of fellow League members—a commitment that undoubtedly represented a sharp departure from the prewar doctrine of nonentanglement, in that it could easily involve the United States in military efforts against aggression in both Europe and mainland Asia.

A Western Alliance

The second strategic alternative after World War One was to form a straightforward peacetime alliance with France and Britain under the cover of a nominal commitment to the League of Nations. This was the option favored by Republican realists in the party establishment: Senate Foreign Relations Committee Chairman Henry Cabot Lodge, onetime presidential nominee Charles Evans Hughes, former Secretaries of State Elihu Root and Philander Knox, Republican National Committee Chairman Will Hays, and of course ex-president and perennial troublemaker Theodore Roosevelt.

Lodge, Roosevelt, and their colleagues were not altogether opposed to some sort of League of Nations commitment. Roosevelt expressed the feeling of many Republicans when he said that "we ought to join the other civilized nations of the world in some scheme that in times of great stress would offer a likelihood of obtaining settlements that will avert war."[15] But the League that Republicans wanted was a modest one, one that would soften international conflict at the edges through mediation and consultation, rather than one that committed the United States to a global system of collective security. Republicans were troubled by the notion that the United States might commit itself under Article 10 of the League Covenant to literally defend the independence and integrity of all other League members; this seemed to tie the hands of the president, of Congress, and of the United States, and to deny Americans the ability to judge case by case whether such efforts were in the national interest. As Lodge put it, it was "easy to talk about a league of nations and the beauty and necessity of peace, but the hard practical demand is, are you ready to put your soldiers and sailors at the disposition of other nations?"[16] Worse yet, the concept of collective security seemed to undercut the Monroe Doctrine, and the special place of the United States within the Western Hemisphere, since Monroe had denied Europeans the right to intervene militarily in Latin America, but had never denied that right to the United States. Article 10 was therefore anathema to Lodge and his supporters, even if the idea of a League of Nations was not.

Republican realists believed that Wilson had his strategic priorities backwards: a strong peacetime alliance with France and Britain ought to be the first priority, and a weak commitment to the League of Nations second, since the United States had no concrete interest in the independence and integrity of all nations, but a very keen interest in Western Europe. And the best guarantee of peace in Western Europe was to curb and check German power. As Lodge put it, "the first and controlling purpose of the peace must be to put Germany in such a position that it will be physically impossible for her to break out again upon other nations with a war for world conquest."[17] In the view of the realists, the crucial element in making such aggression "physically impossible" was a clear-cut military commitment from the United States and Britain to come to the aid of France in case of another German invasion. Philander Knox called this a "new American doctrine": if any power or coalition threatened European peace and freedom, the United States would intervene militarily against that power, as it had in 1917. As Knox put it, "If it prove wise for the United States to enter into some definite entente, well and good, provided it be a small and natural one, bringing only limited and appropriate obligations."[18] This was indeed a new doctrine, and a dramatic departure from the tradition of nonentanglement, since in effect it meant that the United States would commit itself to upholding the European balance of power. But this is exactly what many leading Republicans favored. After forming an alliance with France, then the United States could join in a League of Nations, so long as the League involved no additional military commitments, and so long as it reflected the underlying reality of close cooperation between France, Britain, and the United States.

Disengagement from Europe

The third alternative was for the United States to disengage militarily from Europe and return to a strategy of nonentanglement. This was the option favored by a small but important group of nationalist and progressive Republican senators such as William Borah and Hiram Johnson—"irreconcilables," as they were commonly known, because they opposed any form of League membership whatsoever. Nonentanglement did not entail "isolation" from the outside world, per se. Most irreconcilables shared the common American interest in open markets overseas, an active foreign policy in Latin America and the Pacific, and the promotion of a liberal international order. With the exception of two or three senators, such as Wisconsin's Robert LaFollette, most irreconcilables also favored a strong national defense, and specifically a strong navy.[19] The real difference of opinion between Borah, Johnson, and their opponents was over the nature and extent of America's strategic commitments in the Eastern Hemisphere, and especially in Europe.

Like Republican internationalists, such as Lodge and Roosevelt, irreconcilables did not believe that the United States had any concrete interest in upholding the independence and integrity of all other states under Article 10 of the League Covenant. Where irreconcilables went further was in denying that the United States had any interest in a peacetime military commitment to France. Borah and Johnson saw very clearly that the League, if it meant anything, meant an alliance with Britain and France, and they opposed it precisely on those grounds. First of all, they saw the United States as having very limited economic interests in Europe. American prosperity, they argued, did not rely upon European markets, but on the home market, and on trade and investment in the Americas. Second, they argued, those economic interests that did exist in favor of League membership were largely the interests of Wall Street financiers, not the interests of the nation as a whole. Third, any such interests were no longer under threat from Germany. Fourth, even if some power, such as Germany, were to achieve dominance in Europe, this would not pose a deadly threat to America, since the United States was immensely secure geographically and immune from invasion. As Albert Beveridge put it, "we are now in a perfectly wonderful position of power—we sit on the throne of the world—the world's two greatest oceans on either side of us. Why surrender such a position which nature and providence has given us?"[20] Finally, according to the irreconcilables, the real threat to U.S. interests around the world came not from Germany, but from Britain, America's erstwhile ally. Britain and America did not have a common interest in the maintenance of the British Empire, or in British naval supremacy, or in British commercial and financial success. Any partnership with Britain via the League was in fact a partnership to uphold Britain's interests, at the expense of America's. As Borah put it in his typically embroidered manner, "the League of Nations makes it necessary for America to give back to George V what it took from George III."[21]

In sum, the strategy of disengagement was one of limits: limited interests, limited threats, and limited costs. The irreconcilables did not dispute the value of a growing liberal international order, or an Open Door abroad, or a balance of power among the great nations of Europe and Asia. They simply argued that any new military commitments to these ends were costly and unnecessary given the interests at stake.

REALISM AND INTERNATIONAL CONDITIONS, 1918–1921

Having outlined the various strategic alternatives in 1918–1921, the question is: why did the United States select disengagement? Why not a League of Nations, or an alliance with France? And what role did international conditions, as opposed to ideational and cultural ones, play in this process of strategic adjustment?

The fact that Americans chose disengagement from Europe after World War One poses a serious puzzle for structural realism.[22] By almost any standard, the power of the United States reached unprecedented heights in those years. The United States had mobilized over four million men into its armed forces, and outspent any other belligerent in the last years of the war. It had become the largest creditor in the global economy, as financial power shifted from London to New York. It was set to challenge Great Britain as the leading commercial and naval power in the world. It produced more industrial goods than all of the great powers of Europe combined. By playing a critical role in the Allied victory, the United States had revealed its ability to translate its great wealth into military strength. Structural realists would expect a state with such considerable and growing material power to play a greater role overseas, and engage in a more expansive grand strategy. Yet U.S. policymakers did just the opposite: they brought American troops home, demobilized, rejected membership in the very League of Nations their own president had proposed, and withdrew from any material commitments to Europe, robbing themselves of much potential influence over the postwar international order. As Paul Kennedy admits, the American retreat from Europe after Versailles seemed to be in "contradiction" to "world power trends."[23] In the long run, of course, by the 1940s, the diplomatic and military role of the United States in the world did "catch up" with its economic power. But this lag of a quarter century, which included and may have even permitted a second world war, ought to be of some interest to us, since it demonstrates quite vividly the limited ability of structural realism to predict grand strategic change.

As we have established, the return to disengagement was, from a realist perspective, surprising. But what about Wilson's proposed alternative of U.S. membership in a strong League of Nations? How feasible was this particular strategy internationally? The realist response, of course, is and always has been that it was totally infeasible, particularly insofar as it relied on the idea of collective security.[24] Even sympathetic authors have been forced to admit that there are profound questions as to the inherent viability of *any* collective security system.[25] The idea that states in fact share a common interest in such a system, that they will cede substantive powers to an organization like the League of Nations, or that this organization will have any practical effect unless states do cede such power, have all proven to be deeply flawed assumptions, both in theory and in practice. Neither British, nor Japanese, nor American policymakers—including Wilson—actually thought of all cases of international aggression as worth contesting militarily, and no League could make them think differently. What, then, was the point of having a League?

The answer lies in the extent to which the League reflected Wilson's willingness to commit American resources to peace and stability in Europe and East Asia. Granted, the League was flawed from its very beginning if it was intended to be a "pure" collective security system. But it had a chance to work, insofar as it reflected the common interests of a dominant, American-led coalition of status quo powers. Wilson's statements regarding the balance-of-power system are instructive on this point. Wilson of course denounced the balance of power on a regular basis, and these statements have always been taken by realists as indicative of a utopian idealism. But Wilson did not reject the necessity of military power in enforcing the peace. On the contrary, he made constant reference to the need for such power, since, as he put it, "in the final analysis the peace of society is obtained by force." Wilson's comments on the balance-of-power system actually included a practical and intriguing criticism: that it was necessarily an "unstable thing," since it did not stay "balanced inside itself."[26] In other words, the balance of power was too precarious, too prone to miscalculation and war. In its place, Wilson insisted that "it will be absolutely necessary that a force be created as guarantor of the permanency of the settlement so much greater than the force of any nation now engaged or any alliance hitherto formed . . . that no nation, no probable combination of nations could face or withstand it."[27]

Wilson did not reject the balance of power in favor of pacifism or indifference to power; he rejected it in favor of a preponderance of power on the part of democratic nations. "There must now be," he affirmed, "not a balance of power, not one powerful group of nations set off against another, but a single overwhelming, powerful group of nations who shall be the trustee of the peace of the world."[28] In 1919, that kind of power could only be exercised by Britain, France, and the United States working in combination. Insofar as the League reflected a kind of oligopoly of power on the part of these three states, it was neither impractical nor unrealistic.[29] In fact, it was unrealistic only if it did *not* reflect such an oligopoly. Nor was it implausible that Britain and France would make certain concrete concessions to U.S. interests, and cooperate with Wilson to some extent, in exchange for an American commitment to Europe. The real question, then, was not whether collective security would work; that question was bound to have a disappointing answer. The real question regarding the feasibility of the League, and the feasibility of Wilson's strategic ideas, was whether they reflected a real willingness on the part of the United States to work with Britain and France in meeting new strategic commitments outside of the Western Hemisphere. And of course this was a question only Americans could answer.

Wilson no doubt understood American leadership in the League as involving concrete sacrifices. He admitted to a group of Republican senators that under the League, the United States "would willingly relinquish some of its sovereignty."[30] Such statements were politically risky and would have been unnecessary had Wilson not believed in making a material commitment to the new international order. But the vague and sweeping nature of these new commitments was bound to raise questions about where, when, and how, exactly, Americans would be expected to fight any given aggressor. If the United States was actually obliged to uphold the integrity and independence of other member states, then this would involve real costs. What sort of sacrifices, precisely, were Americans expected to make under this new League? None, in terms of economic aid or the assumption of war debts; U.S. policymakers were uniformly hostile to such measures.[31] But would not a commitment to collective security necessitate a larger standing army, and higher taxes to pay for it, in order to respond to aggression overseas? Here, Wilson refused to admit any dilemma, insisting that the League would *prevent* the United States from having to maintain such forces. Such a low-maintenance hegemony was a contradiction in terms. Either the United States paid the price to secure a preponderant influence in the new international order, or it did not; it could not expect the benefits without the cost. Wilson seems to have expected that a hegemonic role would devolve to the United States automatically by virtue of its economic power. Under the League, he asserted, "the financial leadership will be ours. The industrial primacy will be ours. The commercial advantage will be ours. The other countries of the world are looking to us for leadership and direction."[32] Perhaps so, but the other countries were not about to surrender vital economic or political interests—tariff walls, military strength—without a struggle. Wilson would often be unable to force concessions from the other great powers at Versailles precisely because America's immense economic power did not entirely translate into military or political leverage.

International conditions immediately after World War One—specifically, the rise of American power—suggested that the United States would adopt a more expansive grand strategy, and remain engaged in European security affairs. Wilson's League was indeed an expansive strategy, but it entailed a general collective security obligation, without any clear and specific commitment to France. Lodge's concept, on the other hand, of the League as a Western alliance, without any universal collective security obligation, did not suffer from the same contradictions. It went to the heart of the dilemma over collective security: namely, that either the obligations are unreal, and therefore ineffective, or real, and therefore excessive. It also recognized that any strength the League might have could only come from individual nation-states with the power and the interest to uphold international order. In 1919 the only such nations were France, Britain, and the United States. France and Britain were eager to secure a lasting U.S. commitment to Europe; they accepted Wilson's League because it seemed to promise such a commitment. Germany, Japan, and the USSR could do nothing, as of yet, to prevent close cooperation between the three North Atlantic powers. So from a realist perspective, a peacetime Western alliance through a nominal League commitment was an entirely feasible alternative—in fact, it was the optimal one. It is the alternative that a realist would have expected the United States to adopt, given America's dramatic rise in relative power, its strong interest in European stability, and its continuing uneasiness over Germany. Structural realists can demonstrate the difficulty with any collective security system, such as the one Wilson proposed. But they cannot actually explain why the United States ultimately rejected the League. Even less can they explain why the United States rejected the more practical and plausible alternative of a peacetime alliance with France and Britain. These decisions can only be explained by referring to American strategic culture, and to the way in which crucial elements of that culture were managed, mismanaged, and ultimately defied by President Woodrow Wilson.

Domestic Agenda Setting, 1915–1919

The process of agenda setting began as early as 1915, as America's traditional strategic concept of nonentanglement came under increasing strain. The shock of World War One opened up an opportunity for advocates of new strategic ideas to make their case. A variety of political actors within the United States—notably, pro-League lobbies such as the League to Enforce Peace (LEP)—played a part in putting the idea of a League of Nations on the political agenda. But the most important such actor was President Wilson himself. Drawing on the suggestions of other advocates, and on the liberal tradition of thought in American diplomacy more generally, Wilson fashioned his own particular concept of a League—including a firm commitment to collective security—and championed it in public from 1916 onward. Through Wilson, the idea of a League of Nations achieved political power. In effect, he presented his own country with two strategic possibilities for the postwar era: his League, or a return to disengagement. This subtle but powerful pattern of presidential agenda setting removed other options from active consideration by the U.S. government—notably, the option of a Western alliance and a more modest League. Common American liberal assumptions regarding strategic affairs thereby had a major impact on the process of agenda setting, both through Wilson and upon him.

Needless to say, Wilson did not come up with the idea of a League of Nations out of thin air. A variety of political actors had been pushing for such a League since the beginning of the war. Theodore Roosevelt, for example, argued in the fall of 1914 for the creation of a "world league for the peace of righteousness"—a condominium of great powers to enforce international peace, order and morality.[33] Roosevelt believed that the existence of such a League would convince Americans to take up what he considered to be their international duties in cooperation with Britain. Membership would necessarily require strong armed forces on the part of the United States; otherwise, it would be in no position to enforce the peace. But Roosevelt soon cooled on the idea of a League, and increasingly he emphasized military preparedness and a straightforward alliance with Britain. Wilson's conception of the League was both too abstract for Roosevelt's liking, and insufficiently muscular, since Wilson offered a universal guarantee against aggression, but balked at maintaining the peacetime forces needed to enforce such a guarantee.[34]

"Colonel" Edward House, Wilson's closest advisor, also favored some sort of great power condominium, in which the United States would assume a leading role. Before the war, in fact, House had written a curious book about an administrative genius, Philip Dru, who takes power in

Washington and subsequently engineers an Anglo-American world order of peace and free trade.[35] Apart from Dru's establishment of clear spheres of influence for each of the great powers, the hero's plan bore a striking resemblance to Wilson's own hopes. But House, while certainly influential with Wilson, was not one of the most active or important proponents within the United States of a League of Nations. That role fell to a number of progressive and internationalist interest groups, which as the war continued came out strongly in favor of a postwar League of Nations. Feminists, liberals, pacifists, socialists, and social reformers joined in calling for a new international order based upon disarmament, collective security, and self-determination against the imperialism, militarism, and power politics of the past. The League of Free Nations Association, the Socialist Party, and the Women's Peace Party were three leading examples of groups advocating such an approach.[36] The most influential pro-League lobby, however, was the League to Enforce Peace (LEP), formed in June 1915. The LEP was led by respected establishment figures, notably former President Taft. Its leaders were well connected and well financed, and its membership numbered in the hundreds of thousands. While the LEP voiced the general desire for a postwar association of nations, its specific proposals were modest enough to forestall vigorous opposition from government officials. Indeed, the LEP's emphasis on arbitration and conciliation, rather than collective security, and its conservatism on disarmament and self-determination, left it closer to the British cabinet's view than to Woodrow Wilson's.[37]

Wilson was aware of these various ideas for a League, and he listened to all of them. In the end, he drew elements from each that he found most convincing. In essence, there were two broad versions of the League idea in public debate after 1915. The first was the more conservative or "establishment" version, the version in which the League functioned mostly as a forum for discussion, mediation, and conciliation between the great powers. This was the version favored by Republican elder statesmen, by many of the leaders of the LEP, and, incidentally, by the majority of British policymakers. It was a version that still allowed for—indeed, demanded—a strong national defense on the part of the United States, in alliance with Britain and France. The second version in widespread discussion was the "progressive" one, the version in which the League functioned as the capstone of a new international order based upon liberal democracy, collective security, disarmament, self-determination, open diplomacy, and domestic reform. This was the version favored by the liberal Left, and by lobby groups such as the Women's Peace Party. Wilson did not fully accept either of these two versions. He viewed the establishment version as toothless, and insufficiently bold to introduce real change into the international system. The Left-liberal version of the League, on the other hand, Wilson considered impractical in its pure form. On issues like disarmament and self-determination, its proponents refused to compromise with political necessities, or to settle for anything less than total victory. Beyond that, the Left-liberal version of the League was logically incoherent: how would collective security be enforced if the great powers were disarmed?[38]

Wilson's version of the League combined elements of both the conservative version and the progressive one. Unlike most establishment figures, he wanted a true collective security system—a firm commitment to act against aggression, anywhere. He did not accept the conservatives' pessimism with regard to the inevitability of alliance politics; his heart lay with the progressives, in their hopes for a new international system. At the same time, his conception of the League was very different from the progressive, Left-liberal version. First, Wilson was willing (necessarily, as a head of state) to compromise with the other great powers on the precise workings of the League, since he hoped to coopt these powers into supporting the new international order. Progressives, unlike the president, opposed such compromises in every case where liberal principles of national self-determination, open diplomacy, or disarmament came into conflict with the territorial, strategic, or economic interests of particular states. Second, Wilson saw the League as a means of achieving an effective American hegemony over the international system; progressives were either uninterested in such hegemony or appalled by the prospect of it. Third, Wilson saw, more clearly than most progressives, that a certain amount of military power would ultimately be necessary to enforce a collective security system; for this reason, he viewed their advocacy of disarmament as premature. Finally, many progressives and Left-liberals were sympathetic to communism, and to the new USSR, while Wilson was implacably opposed to socialist revolution. This opposition to communism, both domestically and internationally, gave Wilson's League a different coloration than many progressives and Left-liberals would have preferred.

In the final analysis, it seems fair to say that the most important influence on Wilson's conception of the League was not any specific lobby or pressure group. Rather, the most important intellectual influence on Wilson, in general, was the crusading liberal tradition within U.S. strategic culture. Specific interest groups had influence with Wilson to the extent that they embodied this tradition. Wilson was a brilliant exponent and embodiment of American liberal assumptions, but as we have already seen, he did not invent them. U.S. foreign policymakers had long assumed, in the words of historian Frank Ninkovich, that "the future would not bring a global version of power politics; on the contrary, progress would bring peace, growing prosperity, and an integration of the world along democratic lines."[39] These were mainstream assumptions within elite U.S. foreign policy circles at the turn of the century. What Wilson did, better than any U.S. president before or since, was to articulate a new, internationalist school of thought—a school strongly committed to liberal goals, but relatively unconcerned about the loss of limited liability in strategic affairs. The strategy was new; the goals were not.

The idea of a League of Nations was newly credible and popular as a result of the war; these circumstances surely influenced the president. But the specific version of the League that he eventually forwarded was essentially his own. Indeed, if interest groups like the LEP had limited influence on Wilson, U.S. government officials had even less. Apart from Colonel House, there is no evidence that any bureaucratic actor or elected official had a crucial impact on Wilson's conception of the League. Congress played no major role in the origins of the League idea, nor did the State Department. In 1915 the most credible advocate of a League of Nations within the United States was probably former President Taft. But by the following year, the most important advocate by far was President Wilson himself.

Wilson's first step in taking on this advocacy role—on Christmas Eve, 1915—was to respond favorably to Sir Edward Grey's queries about the possibility of American membership in a postwar League of Nations. Even at this early date, Wilson made it clear that the purpose of a "league of nations" would be to "secure each nation against aggression," and not simply to provide a forum for mediation and discussion.[40] Discussions between Wilson and Grey continued into the next year, with Colonel House acting as intermediary. On May 16, 1916, Wilson again indicated interest in a "universal alliance," offering a "virtual guarantee of territorial integrity and political independence" to all nations.[41] This universal alliance was to go hand in hand with a program of universal disarmament, on land and sea. Naturally, this was not quite what the British had in mind, since their main concern was in securing concrete American aid against Germany. But Wilson pressed forward with his own separate program. Less than two weeks later, he made his first public statement on the matter. Speaking to the members of the LEP, he offered his support for the idea of a "universal association of nations" to provide "a virtual guarantee of territorial integrity and political independence"—the very words he had used in private with Colonel House.[42] The speech was well received within the United States; it also received favorable attention from many liberals and socialists in Great Britain. In the fall of 1916, facing re-election, Wilson again called on Americans to lend the "full force of this nation—moral and physical—to a league of nations."[43] The very fact that a strong and popular president had taken a definite stand on the issue gave it a new political force. By staking out a public position in favor of the League idea, Wilson secured for himself the leadership of the League of Nations movement.

Once the United States entered the war against Germany, in April of 1917, Wilson took advantage of the opportunity to build support for U.S. membership in a postwar League. Wilson argued that the purpose of the war was not simply to check German expansion, but to establish a new international order. A collective security system under the League would be the guarantor of that order. No other alternative was seriously discussed by the president: not a return to disengagement, not a limited alliance with France and Britain, not a modest League with a limited mandate. Only a sweeping departure from the old diplomacy, insisted Wilson, could justify the sacrifices of the war effort. The shock of war had opened up a window of opportunity for new strategic ideas, and Wilson used it to good effect, building support for the concept of a League.

While Wilson put the idea of a League at the top of his agenda, he delayed offering any detailed proposals for as long as possible.[44] This delay served to gain support for the League without committing the president to any particular scheme. In fact, his central demand regarding the League's design was already obvious from public and private statements: a positive guarantee of the independence of member states, supported by force if necessary. There was little to be gained in belaboring this point, since a number of other powerful political actors—most British cabinet members, for example—were likely to oppose such a guarantee.[45] Therefore, as long as the war continued, Wilson said little regarding the specific architecture of any postwar League. But since support for the idea of a League was growing by 1918, in Britain as well as the United States, and since America was actively in the fight against Germany by that time, British cabinet members felt compelled to make a general commitment to the idea of a League of Nations. The Phillimore committee was set up early in 1918 to study the subject, and Lord Robert Cecil, the cabinet's most enthusiastic advocate of a League, was permitted to run with the idea.[46] In this way, Wilson set the agenda for postwar strategic planning not only within the U.S. government, but, to some extent, within the British government, as well.

In a series of historic speeches, Wilson made the case for his particular strategic idea with great energy, eloquence, and skill. His request to Congress for a declaration of war in April 1917, his famous "Fourteen Points" speech of January 1918, his Liberty Loan address in September of that year—all of them held out the promise of a liberal international order, characterized by peace, disarmament, open markets, public diplomacy, national self-determination, and collective security.[47] This new order was to be supported and led by America. The League was its keystone. International peace would be enforced by arbitration, by economic sanctions, and, ultimately, by the combined military strength of the democratic powers. As Wilson put it:

I am proposing, as it were, that the nations of the world should with one accord adopt the doctrine of President Monroe as the doctrine of the world: that no nation should seek to extend its polity over any other nation or people, but that every people should be left free to determine its own polity, its own way of development, unhindered, unthreatened, unafraid, the little along with the great and powerful.[48]

Coming as it did from a man who had used the very same Monroe Doctrine to justify repeated military interventions into other "polities," this message must have seemed disingenuous to many foreign observers. Nevertheless, Wilson's soaring rhetoric encouraged the hopes of liberal-minded supporters abroad, and was extremely well received at home.[49] It became almost sacrilegious within elite circles in the United States to question Wilson's premise of a liberal international order buttressed by a universal association of nations. Skeptics such as Senator Lodge had to frame their criticisms in technical, rather than philosophical, terms so as to not alienate potential allies. By the end of 1918, Wilson's program of public education had done its work: the idea of a League of Nations was extremely popular. Americans were determined to either enter into such a League, or return to a policy of disengagement.[50]

One of the little-noted effects of this process of presidential agenda setting was to remove from public consideration the idea of a firm but limited U.S. alliance commitment to certain European countries, such as France and Britain. Also removed from consideration was the idea of a more modest League, along the lines favored by most British policymakers—a League that would serve as a forum for mediation and conciliation, without committing the United States to a universal system of collective security. As noted earlier, leading Republicans such as Henry Cabot Lodge, Elihu Root, and Theodore Roosevelt favored this very alternative: a Western alliance together with a more modest League commitment. But confined to the Senate, without the pulpit of the presidency, Republican realists and internationalists found it very difficult to gain a hearing for their preferred grand strategy. Moreover, Wilson was so successful in setting the agenda that it seemed politically suicidal to challenge the idea of a League outright. Republicans were reduced to a reactive stance. They responded to Wilson and nipped at his heels with minor criticisms, but offered no fundamental critique of his program. They had little choice, since the president had effectively removed their favorite alternative from active consideration.[51]

Wilson understood that if Americans were to be won over to any new strategic commitment toward Europe, then that commitment would have to be framed in terms that resonated with America's traditional aversion to "entangling," "balance-of-power" alliances. The political advantage of the League idea was that it might succeed in winning over liberal opinion at home, where a straight military alliance with France and Britain would not. As Wilson told a British audience in 1918:

> You know that the United States has always felt from the very beginning of her history that she must keep herself separate from any kind of connection with European politics. . . . If the future had nothing for us but a new attempt to keep the world at right poise by a balance of power, the United States would take no interest, because she will join in combination of power which is not the combination of all of us.[52]

In other words, Wilson argued that the only way to preserve America's sense of moral detachment, while simultaneously lending its power to the preservation of international peace and stability, was through a universal League of Nations. Only through such a League would Americans be willing to abandon strict nonentanglement in Europe's military and political affairs. The League represented a liberal alternative to nonintervention; as Wilson was perfectly aware, this was what gave it much of its political appeal within the United States. But there is no evidence that Wilson would actually have preferred a less idealistic or less universal approach. On the contrary, he shared the common American assumption that a simple military alliance with any major European powers, by itself, would represent a betrayal of America's traditional ideals.

INTERNATIONAL PRESSURES, 1919

At the height of his international prestige, Wilson arrived in Paris in December 1919 to negotiate a peace treaty. He embodied the hopes of European progressives for a new international order; he also represented the nation that had tipped the military balance against Germany. But Wilson's attempt to win international support for his League idea was marked in the end by hard bargaining with former allies. Most such bargaining took place early in 1919 at the Versailles peace conference, where the President's popularity with European liberals and democratic socialists turned out to count for little. Rather than being able to dictate his own terms, Wilson was forced to make a number of substantive concessions in order to win support for the League of Nations from Britain, France, and Japan.[53] These concessions were widely viewed as scandalous back in the United States, but they were necessary given the fact that Wilson had limited negotiating power and that he chose to make the League his highest priority. Wilson's chief goal at Versailles was actually breathtakingly ambitious: to coopt the other great powers—including, eventually, Germany—into a liberal international order embodied in the League of Nations. Given the scope of his vision, and the fact that no other national leader really shared it, it is perhaps surprising that Wilson achieved as much success as he did in getting the other victorious powers to sign on to the League.

British support for the League came first, both chronologically and in terms of U.S. diplomatic priorities. Given the temporarily weakened condition of Germany and Russia, Great Britain was one of the two most powerful nations in the international system in 1919, a global power, a naval power, and a great commercial and financial power. It was also a country that shared many interests with the United States: notably, the revival of the German economy. There were, however, certain key differences between Britain and the United States over the terms of the peace settlement. These were: first, the nature of any new League commitments; second, the preservation of British naval supremacy; and third, the disposal of German colonies in Africa and the Pacific. In essence, Wilson secured Britain's approval for his version of the League by making major concessions on naval and colonial matters.

As has been noted, mainstream opinion in British policymaking circles was in favor of a modest or conservative League of Nations, one that did not commit Britain outright to any firm system of collective security. The British hoped to win an American commitment to European peace and stability, while keeping their own continental obligations limited. For this reason, the British cabinet was very skeptical of any sweeping commitments of the kind—to uphold the territorial integrity and political independence of all member states—envisioned by Wilson under Article 10. As late as January 1919, Prime Minister Lloyd George voiced his opposition to such commitments, arguing that "the attempt to impose obligations of this kind will either end in their being nugatory or in the destruction of the League itself."[54] While this was a prescient view, and one shared by Republicans within the United States, Lloyd George eventually conceded Article 10 to Wilson in order to win support on other matters. The prime minister knew that the League was Wilson's way of making a new commitment to European stability, and he accepted Article 10 in part for that reason. He also accepted it because Wilson made important concessions on naval and imperial matters.

Beginning in 1916, and again in 1918, the U.S. Congress had passed bills initiating naval construction of unprecedented scope and size. The British viewed this American naval buildup with considerable alarm, as they did Wilson's talk of naval disarmament. Maritime supremacy was a central British interest, and London was unwilling to see any power— even a nominally friendly one—threaten that supremacy.[55] Wilson had initially hoped to simply outbuild the British navy, but the strength of Britain's opposition forced him to change tactics. Congressional support for naval construction was waning by 1919 in any case, and Wilson's highest priority was the League, not naval power. The obvious alternative was to use naval power as a bargaining chip to win British support for the League. In a series of informal meetings between November 1918 and April 1919, British and American officials agreed to "suspend" the issues of naval disarmament and freedom of the seas.[56] In practical terms, this meant that the United States accepted the British position. Freedom of the seas (one of Wilson's original "Fourteen Points") was abandoned, and America's 1918 naval building program was never put into effect. As early as December 1918, Wilson began to speak glowingly of the Royal Navy's potential role in "the marine policing of the world."[57] By 1919 Wilson had accepted the fact of British naval power, and hoped that it could be turned into an instrument of a new liberal international order under a League of Nations.

The other significant concession to Britain was on the question of Germany's ex-colonies. Wilson's preference, in accord with liberal principles of self-determination, was to place these territories under the direct control of the League, rather than handing them over to the victorious powers. Britain's dominions, on the other hand, pressed for outright annexation. South Africans sought control of Namibia, while Australians and New Zealanders hoped to take over Germany's islands in the Pacific. The compromise engineered by General Smuts, and agreed to by Wilson, was the creation of a mandate system, whereby the League retained formal authority over Germany's former colonies. In substance, however, South Africa, Australia, and New Zealand exercised real control over these territories. The same was true of British and French annexations in the Middle East: their status as mandates belied the reality of imperial control. As with "freedom of the seas," Wilson retained a pleasing legal fiction, but ceded the substance of the dispute to Britain and its dominions.[58]

Having secured key concessions on naval and colonial matters, Lloyd George accepted Wilson's version of the League of Nations, with its Article 10 obligation to act against aggression. By the opening weeks of the Versailles conference in February 1919, Britain and America were largely in agreement on the nature of any League commitments. They then used this agreement to force Wilson's version of the League on their most important ally: France. As sweeping as Wilson's conception of the League was, it was still insufficiently strong to satisfy French policymakers. Having suffered two invasions within fifty years, and fearing another, the French insisted—understandably—on what they called "physical guarantees" against German aggression. By this they meant the disarmament of Germany; the return of Alsace-Lorraine; the creation of an independent Rhineland; the maintenance of French military power; and the peacetime continuation of the alliance with Britain and America.[59] If there was to be a League of Nations, instead of a traditional military guarantee from Washington, French negotiators at Versailles insisted the League possess independent enforcement capabilities, with an international military force under the command of a League general staff, and that Germany be excluded from League membership indefinitely.[60] Needless to say, this is not what Wilson had in mind. Like his British colleagues, Wilson wanted Germany disarmed, and Alsace-Lorraine returned to France; but he balked at carving out an independent Rhineland from German territory, or placing American troops directly under the command of an international police force. The American interest, in Wilson's eyes, was to constrain Germany, not to crush it.

This Franco-American difference with regard to Germany caused the most serious impasse of the Versailles conference. At one point, both Wilson and French Premier Georges Clemenceau threatened to abandon the proceedings altogether. In March and April, however, a compromise was reached. At the suggestion of Lloyd George, Britain and the United States agreed to offer a military guarantee to France in case of any future German attack. The Rhineland was also to be demilitarized and occupied by Allied troops for fifteen years. In exchange, Clemenceau abandoned French demands for an independent Rhineland, and accepted the League as it stood.[61] The French premier continued to insist that any German violation of the Treaty of Versailles would count as an act of aggression, but Wilson refused to consider making any promises under conditions other than an overt attack on France by Germany.[62]

It is worth pausing here for a moment to consider how dramatic a concession this U.S. guarantee of French security actually was. Remember that the essence of Wilson's vision of collective security was that there be an end to special, preferential, or "entangling" alliances between particular powers. In this little-noted concession, Wilson violated the entire spirit of that universalistic vision, and committed America to a postwar defense alliance with France. Here was a concrete, exclusive military commitment, signed by Wilson, directed against Germany and only Germany. Many observers, including Wilson's close advisor Edward House, noted and criticized the discrepancy. As House put it in his diary: "I thought I ought to call the President's attention to the perils of such a treaty. Among other things, it would be looked upon as a direct blow at the League of Nations. The League is supposed to do just what this treaty proposed, and if it were necessary for the nations to make such treaties, then why the League of Nations?"[63]

This was an excellent observation on House's part, and an excellent argument against the League—unintentionally no doubt. The alliance with France became one of the many features of Wilson's League that drew criticism from across the political spectrum. It ran against the liberal idealism that informed the League concept in the first place. This is not to say that Wilson's reluctant commitment to France was not a worthwhile step. Republican internationalists had been arguing all along that this was exactly the right course for the United States to take. Rather, it is simply to note that the logic for such an alliance was so strong that Wilson was forced to go along with it in the end, in spite of his bitter opposition to the supposed evils of a balance-of-power system. A Western alliance was thus folded in to the general structure of the new League of Nations, at the risk of watering down the League's purity in liberal eyes.

One final area of disagreement between the United States and its former European allies was over postwar economic reconstruction. The British and French hoped that wartime economic cooperation between the allies would continue into the postwar era. They also hoped that the United States would forgive their massive war debts. This option was not quite as one-sided as it seemed; arguably, the United States had an interest in encouraging the revitalization of European trade and industry through some sort of program of debt cancellation and/or economic aid.[64] But Americans were very reluctant to foot any part of the bill for Europe's wartime efforts. Not only would such an aid program have involved great costs to U.S. taxpayers; it also went against the entire American philosophy of minimal governmental interference in matters of international finance. Wilson agreed with his leading advisors that such debt cancellation was neither politically possible nor desirable in its own right.[65] The president's approach to postwar reconstruction, shared by Republicans, was instead to encourage other great powers to lower their tariff barriers, and, if necessary, to borrow from private lenders at the going rate. U.S. policymakers expected that such a laissez-faire approach would offer new opportunities for American exports, stimulate European economic recovery, liberalize the politics of formerly autocratic powers, and encourage peaceful trade rather than military competition. Government loans were therefore phased out over the course of 1919.[66] In the end, neither the United States nor Britain nor France actually lowered tariffs in the years immediately following World War One.[67]

America's reluctance to provide any economic aid to Britain and France, whether in the form of debt cancellation, government credit, or reduced tariff barriers, left those two powers with only one alternative: reparations from Germany. If the United States would not subsidize the costs of the war, then Germany would. The need for capital was felt especially keenly in France, parts of which had been devastated by the war. If the United States would not forgive French war debts, it seemed only fitting that Berlin pay to rebuild the French countryside. Wilson, of course, opposed large reparations on the grounds that they would hobble Germany's economic recovery. But having failed to offer Britain or France any economic relief from America, he could not resist Allied claims for reparations indefinitely. In the end, he was forced to agree to considerable reparations on the part of Germany—the quid pro quo for his refusal to have the U.S. government assume the burden of Europe's war debts.[68]

Japan had limited claims at Versailles, but as with Britain and France, these claims ran into resistance from Wilson, since they violated his vision of the new international order. Japan had made considerable territorial and political gains during the war, largely at the expense of China. The Japanese sought to consolidate these gains, to secure recognition of Japan's new sphere of influence in Shantung, and also to introduce a clause into the League covenant affirming racial equality. The racial-equality clause was unacceptable to Wilson.[69] But he had to make some concrete concessions to Japan in order to keep it reasonably satisfied within the League of Nations. The concession that he made was over China. In effect, he recognized the transfer of Shantung from Germany to Japan. He had little choice, since the Japanese had military control of that region. In the long run, Wilson hoped that Japan could be coopted into playing the role of regional leaders within a liberal international order. As he said to journalist Ray Stannard Baker in explaining the Shantung concessions: "the only hope was to keep the world together, get the League of Nations with Japan in it and then try to secure justice for the Chinese not only as regarding Japan but England, France, Russia, all of whom had concessions in China. If Japan went home there was the danger of a Japanese-German-Russian alliance, and a return to the old 'balance of power' system in the world, on a greater scale than ever before."[70] In practical terms, however, the Japanese left Versailles with an exclusive sphere of influence over significant parts of northeastern China in exchange for signing on to Wilson's League.

Having secured international acceptance of his League idea, Wilson returned to the United States in June 1919 to win the Senate's approval. Idealistic critics immediately characterized Wilson's efforts at Versailles as a sellout to Old World realpolitik, and the charge has stuck ever since. But none of these critics ever made it clear how Wilson was supposed to compel universal acceptance of his scheme with the limited powers he possessed. Wilson replied to such criticisms sensibly: "it is undoubtedly true that many of the results arrived at are far from ideal, but I think that on the whole we have been able to keep tolerably close to the lines laid down at the outset."[71] Certainly the settlement that emerged from the Versailles conference was not as consistently liberal as Wilson would have hoped. The principles of national self-determination, disarmament, and open markets had been seriously compromised in order to win the acceptance of the other powers. Britain refused to disarm at sea; France refused to disarm on land. The principle of self-determination had been applied somewhat selectively, and at the expense of the defeated powers. Tariff barriers had not been lowered significantly. The victor's imperial and protectionist spheres of influence had not been dismantled. Still, Wilson could justifiably claim that liberal principles had had a profound effect on the precise terms of the Versailles settlement. The president had succeeded, above all, in his chief goal of gaining international acceptance of a budding collective security system. The covenant of the League conformed to Wilson's own design: arbitration, economic sanctions, and, ultimately, a promise to uphold the integrity and independence of member states, by force if necessary. Whether this system turned out to be effective would depend primarily upon the state of cooperation between Britain, France, and the United States. But this diplomatic trio could be viewed, quite reasonably, as the core of a new, preponderant, and essentially liberal coalition of powers.

DOMESTIC COALITION BUILDING, 1919–1920

In the abstract, Wilson had more freedom to build political coalitions at home than he did abroad. His status and reputation as president, his persuasive skills, and the deference accorded to any chief executive over questions of foreign policy counted for more domestically than they did internationally. Ironically, however, it was in the domestic realm where his League idea ultimately failed to win political support. This failure was not due to some sort of all-encompassing "isolationism" as such, either in Congress or in the country. It was due to the fact that Wilson simply asked for too much in the way of new overseas commitments, and thereby ran up against the still powerful American tradition of limited liability in strategic affairs. The majority of Republicans were in fact willing to enter into a concrete alliance with France and Great Britain; they were willing to sign on to a modest sort of League. But Wilson insisted on more: a broad U.S. commitment to a global collective security system through Article 10 of the League Covenant. This clash of ideas, both genuine and profound, prevented any real agreement or coalition building between the president and his opponents. Rather than compromising on essentials, each side tried to force the other into defeat: Republicans through parliamentary maneuvering, and Wilson through the mobilization of public opinion. Senate Republicans turned out to have a better grasp of political realities than Wilson did. The president's underestimation of his opponents and his miscalculation of public sentiment ultimately sealed the defeat of his vision in the Senate. No winning coalition was or could be built around the idea of a strong commitment to the new League of Nations.

The domestic political hurdles facing Wilson's League were straightforward, and focused on the Senate. The U.S. Constitution of course specifies that the ratification of any international treaty require the approval of two-thirds of the Senate. In 1919, this meant the approval of sixty-four senators. As we saw earlier, senators were divided between three very different alternatives. The first group, consisting of Wilson's Democratic supporters, favored a firm and unequivocal commitment to the League of Nations as it had been negotiated at Versailles. Wilson could count upon the support of the vast majority of Democratic senators, especially in the South; but since the Democrats had been reduced to forty-seven Senate seats in the elections of 1918, this still left him a long way from the necessary two-thirds. The second group of senators, led by Senate Foreign Relations Committee Chairman Henry Cabot Lodge, favored a nonbinding commitment to the new League together with a French alliance. Specifically, Lodge and his supporters offered a number of "reservations" to the Treaty of Versailles, clarifying above all else that the United States would assume no obligation to go to war under Article 10 of the League Covenant without separate and prior approval from Congress.[72] This group of "reservationists" included the majority of Senate Republicans: at least thirty senators, depending upon the exact circumstances. Finally, the third group of senators, informally led by nationalist and progressive western Republicans William Borah and Hiram Johnson, favored a return to a policy of strategic disengagement from Europe. This group of "irreconcilables" numbered anywhere from five to twenty senators, again depending upon the circumstances of each vote.[73]

The lines between these groupings were somewhat fluid. Some Republicans, for example, were torn between the positions of Lodge and Borah, or Lodge and Wilson. But the underlying logic of the situation was clear: not one of these alternatives had anything like sixty-four senators to support it. In order to win a two-thirds majority in the Senate, Wilson needed the votes of almost twenty Republican reservationists; in effect, he needed Lodge. But neither Wilson nor Lodge was willing to compromise on essentials at any point over the course of the treaty fight, and as a result the two-thirds majority failed to materialize.

But *why* were Wilson and Lodge both so unwilling to compromise? In the case of Wilson, the most common explanations are psychological and medical. The psychological explanation, first championed by Alexander and Juliette George, is that Wilson had an unusually inflexible personality, and a deep-seated need to dominate his opponents. Seeing the Republicans' position on the League as a challenge to his autonomy, the president rationalized his intransigence and convinced himself that he had a moral obligation to be unbending.[74] The medical explanation, championed by Edwin Weinstein, is that a series of strokes, culminating in October 1919, undermined Wilson's mental agility. Wilson may have intended to compromise, after some hard bargaining, but his October stroke left him a different man—rigid, inflexible, and unimaginative.[75]

These two explanations provide very different pictures of Wilson before 1919: flexible and practical, according to Weinstein; inflexible and compulsive, according to the Georges. On these grounds, Weinstein is more convincing, since Wilson did in fact show considerable agility and pragmatism in many political battles before 1919. But the trouble with both theories is that neither of them take seriously Wilson's own explanation for his inflexibility. That explanation was that the Republicans wanted to destroy his vision of a League of Nations by gutting the crucial Article 10 commitment to a collective security system. On this, Wilson was exactly right, and in their more candid moments Republicans admitted as much. They did not want the United States to sign on to any such system. Wilson could have accepted Lodge's reservations on Article 10, but that would have meant a very different sort of League: modest, conservative, harmless. It would have meant, in Wilson's view, a "rejection of the Covenant."[76] It also would have meant a very different grand strategy for the United States: one much more limited and regional in scope. Of course, in the search for middle ground, Wilson's admitted obstinacy did not help matters; neither did his increasingly poor health. But the most important reason for his unwillingness to compromise was ideational: he simply did not share the Republicans' belief in a strategy of limited liability.

Similar questions have surrounded the motives of Republican reservationists in the Senate. Why were they so reluctant to compromise with Wilson? Partisan politics provides an important part of the answer, for three reasons. First, Republicans were deeply concerned by Wilson's domestic political program.[77] Wilson had amassed greater power to the federal government, specifically to its executive branch.[78] He had increased the government's role in the economy significantly. Conservative Republicans resented this growth of governmental power, and they associated the League of Nations with more of the same. Once the war against Germany had been won, they reacted with pent-up fury against the president and all that he stood for. As Lodge put it, "underlying the whole question of the treaty is the determination to put an end to executive encroachments and to re-establish the legislative branch of the government and its proper constitutional power."[79] Second, Republicans were simply tired of losing elections to Wilson, and they wanted to deal him a political defeat, regardless of the issue. The thought of Wilson entering the 1920 presidential elections with another great legislative victory under his belt was too awful to contemplate. Albert Beveridge, for example, believed that Republican candidates in 1920 would suffer if Wilson could claim that he had brought about "the greatest constructive world reform in history."[80]

Third, Republicans were divided between internationalist and noninterventionist factions: the former, based on the East Coast, and the latter, based in the Midwest. A series of strong reservations to Wilson's League was the only position that could keep the Republican Party unified. All three of these domestic political considerations helped bring Republicans together in resistance to Wilson's strategic idea.

Nevertheless, while partisan considerations were significant, they were not the only cause of opposition. A crucial source of resistance came from the fact that the great majority of Republican senators actually felt Wilson's version of the League to be profoundly misguided. As Elihu Root put it, speaking for most Republican reservationists:

> If it is necessary for the security of Western Europe that we should agree to go to the support say of France if attacked, let us agree to do that particular thing plainly, so that every man and woman in the country will understand that. But let us not wrap up such a purpose in a vague universal obligation, under the impression that it really does not mean anything [is] likely to happen.[81]

Even apart from these kinds of practical objections, Wilson's League—and especially Article 10 of its Covenant—appeared to violate traditional American assumptions of limited liability in strategic affairs. This was a common concern of Republican senators, felt with special intensity by irreconcilable nationalists like William Borah. As early as February 21, 1919, on the Senate floor Borah described the "draft covenant" of the League as "the most radical departure from our policies hitherto obtaining that has ever been proposed at any time since our Government was established." The fundamental issue for nationalists like Borah was that under the League, the United States would be robbed of its national sovereignty along with its traditional freedom of action in international affairs. As Borah said in the same speech:

> I may be willing to help my neighbor, though he be improvident or unfortunate, but I do not necessarily want him for a business partner. I may be willing to give liberally of my means, of my council and advice, even of my strength or blood, to protect his family from attack or injustice, but I do not want him placed in such a position where he may decide for me when and how I shall act or to what extent I shall make sacrifice.[82]

While such sentiments were strongest among the irreconcilable senatorial faction, they were not limited to this group. Indeed, Lodge paid homage to the continuing power of limited-liability assumptions by referring to them again and again on the Senate floor. For example, on August 12, 1919, Lodge declared that it was "important to keep the United States out of European affairs"—a sentiment he expressed repeatedly in public.[83]

Lodge did not actually believe that the United States needed to stay clear of European alliances altogether; as we have already seen, his first preference was for a peacetime alliance with France and Great Britain. But in public, he referred to the American tradition of limited liability in order to build support against Wilson. So did GOP leaders in general, because they understood the cultural and political power of that tradition. On March 7, 1919, Republican National Committee Chairman Will Hays expressed the mainstream Republican position regarding the League: "While we seek earnestly and prayerfully for methods lessening future wars, and will go far indeed in an honest effort to that end, and will accomplish very much, we will accept no indefinite internationalism as a substitute for fervent American nationalism."[84]

Senate reservationists like Lodge were willing to entertain a modest and constrained departure from the tradition of nonentanglement, but they genuinely viewed membership within Wilson's very ambitious League of Nations as a gross violation of America's limited liability in strategic affairs, and they referred to symbols of nonentanglement regularly in order to win support in their fight against the president. Wilson's central contribution to the League Covenant—the commitment to uphold the independence and integrity of member states—was viewed by virtually all Republicans as excessive, unclear, and potentially very costly. It ran directly against the tradition of limited liability in strategic matters, a tradition that Senate reservationists as well as irreconcilables took very seriously. Any sweeping U.S. commitment to a global collective security system was simply incompatible with most Republicans' conception of the national interest. For this reason, as well as for partisan political ones, Lodge and his supporters refused to concede to the president.

Since Wilson needed sixty-four senators to secure treaty approval, and since compromise seemed out of the question to both sides, the president was left with few political choices. His hope was that public pressure would eventually force the necessary number of senators to sign the treaty as it stood.[85] This strategy was not quite as naive or futile as it has sometimes been made out to be. There were in fact several Republican senators—so-called mild reservationists, as many as ten in all—who wavered between Wilson's and Lodge's versions of the League.[86] Wilson had succeeded in drumming up public support for difficult measures before by going on speaking tours and employing the presidential bully pulpit against congressional resistance. It was on the basis of this precedent that Wilson undertook his famous speaking tour through the West in September 1919.[87] He made his case with great eloquence, and his speeches were largely well received, but the tour did not fundamentally alter the political dynamic on the issue of the League. The President and his advisors had overestimated support for their position in the country, as well as in the

Senate. Wilson's tour brought about no breakthrough in terms of public opinion, and Republican senators refused to change their views.[88]

Rather than winning new backing for his version of the League, Wilson actually *lost* support over the course of 1919 on a variety of fronts. The most visible defections came from a number of previously supportive interest groups, publicists, and intellectuals on the Left. The apostasy of Walter Lippmann and Herbert Croly, editors of the *New Republic*, was representative of this trend. In 1917 both men had been enthusiastic champions of Wilson's idea for a League of Nations.[89] By the summer of 1919, however, once it was clear that liberal ideals had been seriously compromised by the Treaty of Versailles, the *New Republic* turned against Wilson's League.

This sense of disappointment on the part of liberal opinion spread into the Senate, as well. Progressive Republicans like Borah and Johnson, in particular, railed against the supposed sell-out of liberal ideals at Versailles. Senator Johnson spoke for many Americans when he described that diplomatic settlement—along with potential U.S. membership in a League of Nations—as "the halting and betrayal of New World liberalism, the triumph of cynical Old World diplomacy, the humiliation and end of American idealism."[90] Such senators sincerely believed that they, and not Wilson, spoke for the best progressive tradition in American diplomacy: pacific, anti-imperialist, and militarily noninterventionist.[91] And while only a few senators were fully committed to this purist liberal position, they and their arguments had an impact far beyond their numbers. Specifically, liberal disillusionment with Versailles had the effect of giving many other leading Republicans and Democrats doubts about Wilson's League. It also provided intellectual ammunition for all of Wilson's critics. And conservative Republican leaders were eager to keep the party unified; the progressive faction within the GOP thereby had an influence out of proportion to its size.[92] During the League debate, observers were therefore treated to the spectacle of watching hardened foreign policy realists like Henry Cabot Lodge criticize Wilson for being insufficiently true to America's progressive ideals. In private, of course, Lodge believed that Wilson was dangerously utopian. He would not have employed such arguments unless he felt they would have had an impact. The fact that he criticized Wilson from the left, in effect, was testimony to the power of liberal and idealistic assumptions within the American political arena. It also raises the question of how Lodge could have ever made the case effectively for a simple Franco-American alliance. If liberal and progressive opinion even within the GOP felt the League of Nations to be an unacceptable concession to Old World realpolitik, how could Lodge have ever built support for a straightforward and unadorned peacetime alliance with France?[93]

Progressives within every political party were disillusioned not only by Wilson's obvious concessions to the imperial interests of France, Britain, and Japan but also by his failure in 1919 to deliver reform-minded legislation on the domestic front.[94] Add to this Wilson's approval of military intervention against the Soviet regime, and the blind eye that he turned to a crackdown on radicals and socialists at home, and the alienation of the Left became complete.[95]

As Wilson lost support for the League on the left, so he also lost support on the right. Conservative realists and nationalists, of course, had long been skeptical of Wilson's League. But with the war against Germany won, support for progressivism and the Democratic Party ebbed significantly. A conservative backlash set in against six years of political experimentation and upheaval, and the Republican Party regained much of its pre-1912 popularity in northern and western states. The association of the League with domestic reform, and with the Democratic Party, was therefore something of a political liability as the country readjusted to peace.

Given Wilson's weakened political standing in 1919, and his need for two-thirds of the Senate to pass the Treaty of Versailles, the task for Republican leaders was largely negative: to stake out a credible position on the issue, rally support for it, and maintain a coalition of at least thirty-three senators opposed to Wilson. Their task was complicated by the fact that Republicans themselves were deeply divided over their preferred outcome. The larger faction, led by Lodge, wanted the League to pass with reservations so as to render it harmless. This faction also wanted the treaty with France to pass through the Senate. The smaller group of irreconcilables, led by Borah and Johnson, did not want any League or any alliance with France whatsoever. This raised the possibility of tactical cooperation between Wilson and one of the two Republican factions: a possibility very much feared by leading figures in the GOP. But the most likely alliance, both logically and on party grounds, was for Republicans to cooperate in defeating Wilson, and here the leadership of Henry Cabot Lodge was crucial.

Lodge succeeded brilliantly in building and maintaining a broad coalition of Republicans in opposition to the president. The position that he took was in favor of the League, but with major reservations, particularly with respect to Article 10. In effect, he called for an American commitment to the League without any strict obligation to collective security. Having laid out his reservations in public as early as February, he encouraged interest groups with similar concerns about the League to come forward and testify before the Senate.[96] This process of testimony and debate served to publicize and popularize doubts regarding the League. Lodge was not overly scrupulous in using any available arguments to beat Wilson. The conservative senator drew, for example, on liberal disillusion-ment with the Treaty of Versailles to bolster his case. He also drew upon the arguments of isolationists like Borah and Johnson, even though he did not share their commitment to a strategy of absolute disengagement. Most importantly, Lodge, like the most fervent irreconcilables, made re-peated references to Washington's Farewell Address, and to the historic tradition of U.S. nonentanglement, in order to defeat Wilson, even though he did not actually favor a return to that tradition. "I would keep America as she has been," he announced, "master of her own fate."[97] The rhetori-cal linkage of nonentanglement with American national identity, though very effective politically, was not entirely genuine, and Republican inter-nationalists would later pay a price for having made that link.

The clear difference between Wilson's position and that of Lodge had two effects. First, it allowed anyone with a latent grievance against Wil-son's League to rally to a credible alternative. Support for the idea of a League had initially been very broad, but somewhat shallow. There were bound to be questions and criticisms once the issue actually came to a vote. The reservations offered by Lodge permitted critics to voice their objections to the League without appearing to be purely destructive. Ad-ministration officials with doubts regarding the Treaty of Versailles—in-cluding, notably, Secretary of State Lansing, and former State Department employee William Bullitt—were encouraged to testify before the Senate.[98] Latent grassroots opposition to Wilson's vision for American grand strat-egy materialized from unexpected sources. Not only Irish- and German-American, but Polish- and Italian-American and Jewish interest groups came forward against the treaty.[99] Midsized businesses and local labor organizations formed anti-League lobbies.[100] An exceptionally broad range of criticisms from every direction on the political spectrum were brought against Wilson and his strategic designs.

Second, the clash between Wilson and Lodge forced wavering interna-tionalists to choose one side or the other. "Mild reservationists" were obliged to come out either for or against a firm commitment to collective security. In the end, most came out in favor of Lodge. By early July, even former President Taft, a longtime advocate of a League of Nations, came out in favor of reservations.[101] The LEP was weakened and divided in the process. But this was actually a rather healthy development, in that the conflict between Wilson and Lodge forced senators to make an honest and inescapable choice between two incompatible versions of the League.

In the final Senate vote, in mid-November 1919, Wilson's version of the League failed to win even a simple majority. Every Republican but one held firm against the treaty, and five Democrats actually crossed the floor to vote against the president. But the amended version of the treaty proposed by Lodge also failed, as irreconcilable Republicans joined loyalist Democrats in opposing it. Almost eighty senators had voted for some form of League commitment, but neither Wilson nor Lodge could muster anywhere near sixty-four votes for their preferred version of it.[102]

The next four months saw Wilson's political strength on the issue of the League deteriorate even further. The president was under increasing pressure to accept the reservations favored by Lodge. Former members of the American negotiating team at Versailles begged Wilson to compromise. A growing number of Democratic senators grew restless at the obvious possibility of the League's complete rejection.[103] A variety of interest groups—farm, labor, religious, and educational—called on Wilson to negotiate with the Senate. The French sent word that any League would be better than no League at all.[104] But Wilson answered these solicitors in the same way that he always had, with a refusal to yield, and for the same reason: his League and the Republicans' were two entirely different things. He now rested his hopes on the 1920 presidential election, in the apparent expectation that a Democratic victory would revive popular and congressional support for his foreign policy program.[105] A final vote on the amended version of the treaty, held on March 19, 1920, led to further defections from Democratic senators, but still failed to produce the necessary two-thirds majority for Lodge and his supporters. A large bloc of mostly southern senators remained loyal to the president, and this bloc, together with the votes of Republican irreconcilables, prevented any modified American commitment to the new League of Nations.[106]

Wilson never built the necessary winning coalition in support of his version of the League. But this failure was not due to some minor tactical error or personality flaw on Wilson's part. It was due to the fact that such a winning coalition simply did not exist. Certainly, there was broad support in the country, and in the Senate, for some sort of limited League, but Wilson's League and his opponents' were two very different things. Wilson favored a clear obligation to act militarily, if necessary, against any international aggression. Lodge favored, in essence, an obligation to act only against a German invasion of France. There was probably a majority in the Senate, and in the country, willing to undertake certain limited and new strategic obligations overseas, but there was no such majority in favor of a general commitment to the principle or practice of collective security. The tradition of limited liability was still too strong for that.[107]

Strategic Outcomes, 1920–1921: The Triumph of Disengagement

Once the Senate had definitively ruled out Wilson's League, two grand strategic alternatives still remained: a Western alliance within a modest

League commitment, or disengagement from Europe. Most accounts of the treaty fight end with the final vote against ratification, and treat the triumph of disengagement as a foregone conclusion. But as we have seen, disengagement was by no means a majority position in 1919. Given the fact that foreign policy realists and internationalists like Lodge, Root, and Hays dominated the Republican party at that time, the question is: why did they fail to secure their preferred strategy in 1920–1921?

The first reason, of course, is that Wilson dealt their foreign policy program a blow by instructing Democrats to vote against the Lodge reservations. Wilson had also made a French alliance conditional on ratification of the Versailles treaty. It was therefore obvious by the spring of 1920 that any new departure in American grand strategy, such as that favored by Lodge, would have to await the inauguration of a new president. In itself, however, Wilson's veto power was not sufficient to block all hopes for a peacetime alliance with France and Britain, since Republicans might have nominated and elected an internationalist presidential candidate in 1920.

The crucial developments of 1920, then, were: (1) the waning of both public and congressional support for any new international commitments, (2) the steady ascendancy of the noninterventionist position within the Republican party, and (3) the nomination and election of a Republican presidential candidate supportive of a policy of disengagement.

Political backing for the idea of strategic disengagement had never died out completely. Irreconcilables like Borah and Johnson had carried a torch for it through the war. Internationalists of both parties recognized the persistent power of the traditional strategic paradigm, and they paid tribute to it by arguing that their preferred policies were really most consistent with American traditions of nonentanglement. Not only Republicans, but Wilson himself regularly referred to the evils of "entangling alliances"—a position that forced him into the false argument that the League, far from being entangling, was entirely compatible with disengagement from Europe. The unintended consequence of this expedient rhetoric was that it made both Wilson and Lodge sound like less convincing versions of Borah. But if Borah was right and nonentanglement was really the best policy, then why not go for the real thing? Wilson was loathe to challenge the concept of nonentanglement, or to explain why it was no longer useful; Lodge and his colleagues were even less forthcoming in making the case for an alliance with France and Britain. Such efforts would have run directly against American cultural assumptions.

The lack of public effort by leading politicians on behalf of the treaty with France was compounded by a general decline in support for new international commitments of any kind. By 1920, the window of opportunity for a great departure in foreign policy was closing, and Americans were growing tired of the issue. As Lodge admitted to Lord Bryce, Britain's former ambassador to the United States, "the protracted debate on the League both inside and outside the Senate has wrought a great change in public opinion and the feeling is growing constantly stronger against the United States involving itself in quarrels of Europe at all."[108] The conservative backlash against Wilson, and the unpopularity of his administration by this time, only added to the general unwillingness to take up the League idea again. For all of these reasons, support for any form of internationalism ebbed over the course of 1920, while support for disengagement grew.

The growing support for disengagement gained political expression in the Republicans' nomination of presidential candidate Warren Harding at their national convention in the summer of 1920. Harding has often been ranked by historians as one of the worst presidents in American history. Admittedly the man was no intellectual giant. But he was actually quite effective in unifying the Republican Party leading up to the 1920 presidential election. At heart, Harding favored a policy of disengagement, and his stand on this issue could have divided the GOP.[109] But Harding straddled the League issue quite skillfully, and leading advocates of American strategic engagement like Lodge, Root, and Hughes came out in support of Harding after his nomination. They supported him for several reasons: because of his conservatism on domestic issues; to keep progressive-nationalists within the Republican fold; and because they believed that he might be open to a more internationalist strategy once in office.[110] They also supported him because, whatever his views on foreign policy, they could not be worse—in the eyes of party leaders—than those of Wilson and his protégé, Democratic presidential candidate James Cox, who had taken a firm position on behalf of Wilson's League.[111] As Lodge said to Root in May 1920, "I am much more interested in getting the whole party to fight together against Wilson and the League than I am in myself or anything else."[112] In this way, intraparty division was trumped by interparty competition, and Harding was given the freedom to take the Republicans in the direction of disengagement.[113]

It was at this crucial moment that Theodore Roosevelt, having died in January 1919, was most missed by Republican realists and internationalists. Roosevelt was extremely popular and would have probably been the favorite to capture the nomination in 1920. He would have advocated a combination of policy stands almost diametrically opposed to that of Harding: progressive and reform-minded at home, expansive and assertive abroad. If his actions and words over previous years were any indication, he would have advocated an alliance with France and Britain, and an American commitment to some sort of League, both as a presidential candidate and as president. Indeed, he did precisely that in the months just before his death. His passing removed the one champion of a Western alliance who might have achieved power in 1920.[114] As it was, Republican internationalists were left with Harding, for fear of something worse.

Having united Republicans behind him, Harding went on to win the November election in a landslide. His victory was mostly due to factors other than foreign policy.[115] Nevertheless, the decisive victory over Cox was widely interpreted as a mandate against the League, and that is also how Harding chose to interpret it.

Only after the new president's inauguration in January of 1921 was it obvious that the strategy of disengagement had triumphed. Lodge continued to hope for some "new treaty or agreement with our Allies," but no such initiative was forthcoming from the White House.[116] Instead, the energy of talented, erstwhile internationalists, such as Charles Evans Hughes, was directed for the most part into economic diplomacy, into the pursuit of opportunities for American trade and investment abroad, and into disarmament efforts. Among leading Republicans, the fear of opening up a bitter intraparty debate trumped any interest in reconsidering the League issue.[117] New strategic commitments abroad were off the government's agenda. To put them back on the agenda would, by 1921, have required heroic efforts politically, and in any case, Harding did not believe that such commitments were merited. As he said candidly in October 1920, referring to America's obligations under the League: "I do not want to clarify these obligations. I want to turn my back on them."[118]

Instead of expending any effort on new strategic commitments to Europe, Harding and his cabinet oversaw a return to the traditional American strategy of nonentanglement. As revisionist historians have made clear, this strategy was not isolationist in any strict sense. The new Republican administration was actually quite aggressive in promoting opportunities for American trade and investment overseas, in consolidating the predominance of U.S. influence within Latin America, and in encouraging a nascent liberal order of democracy, open markets, and limited armaments in Europe and East Asia. These foreign policy goals were pursued through the mechanism of the "associational" or "cooperative" state, through close but informal cooperation between government and the private sector.[119] Direct investment by American corporations proceeded at an unprecedented pace. In Western Europe, the Harding administration encouraged conditions of economic recovery, free trade, stable and convertible currencies, and multilateral disarmament, notably through the renegotiation of German war reparations.[120] In East Asia, it encouraged mutual arms reduction, an end to the Anglo-Japanese alliance, and an Open Door in China through the Washington treaties of 1921–1922.[121] In those same treaties, Harding's foreign policy team also achieved the goal that had eluded Wilson three years before: recognized parity in naval power with Britain. All of these initiatives point to a coherent, active, and "progressive" grand strategy in the early 1920s: that is, the pursuit of American interests abroad, and of a liberal international order, primarily through economic means, and at limited expense.

This strategy of diplomatic and military nonentanglement has been commended by revisionist historians for having sought liberal and ambitious ends at so little cost, both in human and material terms. The question ignored by revisionists is whether this strategy actually secured its own ambitious ends. However grandiose the stated goals of Harding's foreign policy team, the fact is that the unwillingness to back up those goals with significant material sacrifices—whether economic or military—left the United States with little leverage over most international disputes in Europe and Asia. The determination to avoid higher taxes or expenditures, and to let the private sector take the lead, left government officials with very few sticks or carrots on international economic questions, despite the country's great wealth. American financiers, for example, could not be directed to invest in areas of dubious profitability since their losses were not about to be subsidized. In terms of the military, the lack of leverage was even more obvious. The General Staff of the War Department had called in 1919 for a peacetime standing army of 500,000; General Pershing had indicated that 300,000 was the minimum number necessary to defend American lives, territories, and interests overseas. Congress itself initially agreed to a standing army of 280,000, but by 1921 that force was limited to 175,000. Within Harding's first two years as president, the army's numbers had fallen to 135,000. As Allan Millett and Peter Maslowski put it, "the United States had disarmed itself more effectively than the Versailles treaty disarmed Germany."[122] With an army this size, and of a strictly constabulary nature, the United States could not expect to have much influence over international questions that might involve the use of military force. The U.S. Navy, while comparatively much stronger, was also cut significantly. The imperatives of arms control were permitted to outweigh those of actually preparing for the possibility of war in the Pacific. As a result, the possibility of forcibly backing up putative interests overseas—the independence and integrity of China, for example—was explicitly foreclosed.[123] Of course, America was not isolated from the rest of the world. But the unwillingness to support supposed U.S. interests outside the Western Hemisphere with material sacrifices—and, specifically, the unwillingness to make any strategic commitments to peace and stability in Europe—left a weakened political and military structure to sustain the nascent liberal order of the 1920s.

Nevertheless, the strategy of nonentanglement was politically very appealing, and it soon regained overwhelming congressional and popular support within the United States. Pacifists and progressives appreciated

the repudiation of new military commitments. Nationalists and conservatives appreciated the minimal costs of the new strategy. Even the most
fervent Republican internationalists from Wall Street's financial firms supported Harding's foreign policy—in part, because they were given a direct
role in making it. Ethnic lobbies, business, and labor all agreed that repeated military adventures in Europe or Asia were best avoided. On left
and right, the revitalized concept of nonentanglement became the focus
of strong political support. The window of opportunity closed for any
real commitment to peace and stability in Europe or Asia. The idea of
nonentanglement was locked in, institutionalized in government circles,
and solidified in the public mindset, as a guiding principle for U.S. grand
strategy. Obviously the triumph of this idea in 1919–1921 was to have
fateful consequences for both the United States and the world since it
continued to dominate American thinking on strategic matters even as
Hitler marched into Paris twenty years later. Only with the attack on Pearl
Harbor was the mentality of nonentanglement really broken.

The possibility still existed in 1920–1921 that Republican internationalists might engineer the Senate's approval of an alliance with France,
together with a qualified commitment to the League of Nations. But as
long as he was President, Wilson blocked this possibility, and public support for any such foreign commitments continued to wane. The crucial
victory for proponents of disengagement came with the nomination and
election of a presidential candidate in 1920. Internationalists were outma-
neuvered, first, within the Republican Party, second, in the November
election, and finally, in the new course set by President Harding after his
inauguration. Harding favored U.S. strategic disengagement from Europe, ruled out any real alternative from within the Republican Party, and
assembled a winning coalition in support of his policy. The revived concept of nonentanglement was institutionalized as the reigning paradigm
in American grand strategy, and a period of maximum uncertainty over
U.S. foreign policy ended.

In effect, cultural factors had made it surprisingly difficult for any political leader within the United States to prevent a return to strategic disengagement. Classical liberal assumptions made it difficult for realists such
as Lodge to make the case for a simple, balance-of-power alliance with
France. And since neither Wilson nor Harding believed in this approach,
they were unlikely to make the case for it themselves. In this sense, liberal
assumptions had causal effects at the domestic political level, as well as
at the decision-making level. At the same time, assumptions of limited
liability, as enshrined in the doctrine of nonentanglement, made it difficult
for leaders such as Wilson or Lodge to argue for a new set of strategic
commitments abroad. Admittedly, the situation in 1918–1921 was, in
domestic political terms, highly unstable, and might have ended differ-

ently if Wilson had adopted a more modest approach. In the absence of flexible and responsive leadership, however, the cultural preference for limited liability won out.[124]

Conclusion

In the period immediately after World War One, there were three basic strategic alternatives open to the United States: membership in a world-wide League of Nations, disengagement from Europe, or a simple military alliance with France and Great Britain. From a realist perspective, any of the three options were at least viable, and in fact, an alliance with France and Britain would have been preferable. Certainly, international conditions at the time cannot explain the actual outcome of disengagement. Given America's immense relative power by 1918, a structural realist would have expected the United States to reject such an approach. Relative to other eras, however, such as 1945–1951, the international pressures against disengagement were not overwhelming. Consequently, there was considerable room for cultural factors—as mediated by political ones—to influence the final outcome.

In the end, domestic patterns of agenda setting and coalition building on the part of President Wilson, conditioned by cultural assumptions, shaped and directed the process of strategic choice. For cultural reasons, decision-makers like Wilson and Lodge were unable and/or unwilling to build support for any *limited* and *realistic* strategic commitment to Europe. A simple balance-of-power alliance with Western European countries was ruled out by Wilson and many other Americans, because it seemed to violate liberal foreign policy goals. Similarly, membership in a strong League of Nations was ruled out by the Senate, because it seemed to violate the American tradition of limited liability in strategic affairs. The culturally influenced result was a return to the default option of disengagement, in spite of the fact that the United States was materially ready to assume a larger role in world affairs. International conditions set the boundaries of what was feasible, pointed to certain alternatives, and very much shaped the process of international coalition building. But international conditions did not actually determine the final selection of strategic disengagement on the part of American decision-makers after 1918.

Chapter Four

CONCEIVING CONTAINMENT:

IDEAS AND ALTERNATIVES IN

AMERICAN GRAND STRATEGY, 1945–1951

IN THE YEARS IMMEDIATELY AFTER World War Two, the United States broke with its own foreign policy traditions and made a series of military, economic, and political commitments on the Eurasian continent that were unprecedented in peacetime. These commitments were made under the rubric of a new strategic idea, that of containment. The adoption of containment is generally viewed today as a foregone conclusion; most political scientists and historians find it difficult to imagine that America could have taken any other course. But in fact, the United States had multiple foreign policy options after 1945 apart from containment. It could have returned to a more traditional and inexpensive stance of strategic nonentanglement, buttressed by a powerful navy, atomic air power, and the geographical buffer offered by two great oceans. It could have engaged in "rollback" against the Soviet Union and its allies. Or, it could have come to an explicit agreement with the USSR regarding mutual spheres of influence in Europe and Asia—an option I examine in greater detail in this chapter. All three of these options had serious and credible advocates at the time within the United States. So why were all three alternatives rejected in favor of containment?[1]

Structural interpretations suggest that the United States was bound to play a much greater role in the international system after 1945, not only because of America's newfound material supremacy but also because of a clear threat from the Soviet Union. At first glance this seems to be an entirely plausible explanation for the expansion of U.S. strategic commitments under President Truman. Changes in international conditions do go a long way in explaining America's rise to world power during the mid-to-late 1940s. Certainly, the USSR after 1945 posed a serious threat to the balance of power in Europe as well as in Asia. On closer examination, however, the structural realist explanation looks incomplete. Even assuming that a more expansive international role on the part of the United States was inevitable, why did U.S. officials adopt containment and not some other strategy? After all, containment was strikingly global and ideological in nature. As we shall see, under containment, U.S. officials did not seek a balance of power with the Soviet Union; they sought American predominance. They also took for granted the existence of a transnational conflict between liberal democracy and Marxist Leninism. They refused to engage in negotiations with the Kremlin, or to recognize the legitimacy of Stalin's de facto empire in Eastern Europe. They sought to check communist expansion worldwide; to promote a liberal international order outside of the Soviet bloc; to pressure the USSR out of Eastern Europe; and, ultimately, to encourage the collapse of communism within the Soviet Union. These features of containment, which distinguished it from a pure balance-of-power or sphere-of-influence approach, worked admirably in the long run, but they are inexplicable from a structural realist perspective; they cannot be explained simply by referring to international pressures.

The insight revealed by a neoclassical realist approach is this: in the wake of dramatic international changes, U.S. strategic behavior after 1945 was determined not only by structural conditions but also by contingent processes of agenda setting and coalition building on the part of leading state officials, involving cultural as well as international pressures. If international pressures had been the only significant source of American behavior, U.S. officials could have settled just as easily on a policy of mutual spheres of influence within Europe and Asia. A pure sphere-of-influence approach, however, lacked powerful and credible advocates, and it lacked such advocates, in large part, because it simply did not resonate with Americans culturally. U.S. officials would accept an "open," liberal sphere, but not a "closed" Soviet sphere in Eastern Europe. Cultural factors—specifically, U.S. liberal norms and ideas—acted as a crucial filter on strategic options, rendering a strict sphere-of-influence approach literally unthinkable. Whatever the virtues of containment, then, the United States was not forced to follow such a strategy by international pressures. The adoption of containment cannot be explained simply by referring to such pressures. Containment became U.S. policy because it was the first feasible strategic idea to win the support of leading executive officials, including the president, and it won their support because it suited American liberal assumptions.

ALTERNATIVE STRATEGIC IDEAS, 1945–1951

The strategic ideas available to American officials after 1945 were in part the result of the shock of wartime experience. Up until 1941, U.S. grand strategy was dominated by the idea of nonentanglement in relation to Europe and Asia. The Japanese attack on Pearl Harbor, and the subse-

quent American involvement in World War Two, acted as a strong external shock, discrediting the old idea of strict nonentanglement. A window
of opportunity opened up for more expansive conceptions of America's
role in the world. Many Americans began to think aggressively about the
need to sustain a permanent equilibrium in Europe and Asia. U.S. officials, along with the American public, also proved willing to think of
U.S. war aims in terms of the promotion of a broadly liberal international
order. Beyond this, however, there was considerable uncertainty as to
what sort of strategic, diplomatic, and economic commitments the
United States would undertake in the postwar era. Franklin Roosevelt
envisioned the United States as the leading power in Latin America and
the Pacific, on good terms with both Britain and the Soviet Union, and
detached from European affairs—but he also refused to renounce America's worldwide interest in the promotion of certain liberal goals, such as
open markets and self-determination. Since these goals came into direct
conflict with the declared interests of the Soviet Union in Eastern Europe,
and since the Soviet Union was the only other power with anything like
the military capabilities of the United States, by 1945 the great question
for American policymakers was how to handle the USSR. Stalin was not
about to accept subordinate status in a liberal international order led by
the United States, nor was he prepared to sacrifice what he viewed as
basic security interests to Western liberal sensitivities. In practice that left
four broad alternatives for American grand strategy. The United States
could (1) return to an insular strategy of nonentanglement, (2) roll back
the Soviet sphere through military means, (3) come to an agreement with
the USSR on unrestricted spheres of influence in Europe and Asia, or (4)
adopt a strategy of "containment." I will briefly discuss the first two
alternatives, and then go into some detail regarding the last two, in order
to distinguish between them.

Neoisolationism

The first alternative to containment after World War Two was to return
to a posture of disengagement from European or Asian wars and alliances.
The essence of such a neoisolationist strategy was to keep strict limits
on U.S. military spending, and to avoid strategic commitments overseas,
especially in Europe and Asia. The neoisolationist option was put forward
most seriously during the Korean War by leading conservatives such as
Senator Robert Taft and former president Herbert Hoover. Hoover argued for a strategy, "Fortress America," by which the United States would
maintain a series of island strong points in the Atlantic and Pacific, relying
upon its navy and air force for security, instead of being dragged in to
new strategic commitments on the Eurasian continent.[2] Taft made similar

arguments in his 1951 book, *A Foreign Policy for Americans,* in which he warned of the dangers of strategic overextension.[3] Neoisolationism held considerable appeal for western and midwestern conservatives within the Republican Party, who feared that a strategy of containment would ultimately undermine traditions of limited government at home.[4] But the neoisolationist alternative also had some support on the left wing of the Democratic Party, among progressives such as Secretary of Commerce Henry Wallace, who feared that containment would undermine domestic reform and lead to war with the Soviet Union.[5] It was precisely these fears that led Wallace to break with Truman and run for president in 1948. Conservatives like Taft, and progressives like Wallace, disagreed on the relative value of foreign aid, the United Nations, and good relations with the USSR. But, interestingly, they both criticized containment on the classical liberal grounds that it would undermine America's way of life, and turn the United States into an "armed camp," while entangling the United States in supposedly Old World patterns of militarism, imperialism, and balance-of-power alliances.[6] Strategic disengagement may not have been a viable option for the United States after World War Two, but it still held a certain appeal to many Americans, if only because of these classical liberal concerns.[7]

Rollback

The second alternative to containment after 1945 was to "roll back" the Soviet sphere in Eastern Europe by force. Such a strategy would have gone beyond containment by intervening militarily on behalf of anti-Communist uprisings in Eastern Europe, or possibly even by attacking the Soviet Union itself. Like the Fortress America strategy, the alternative of rollback was put forward by some very influential figures, mostly toward the end of the period 1946–1951. Some of the very same people that advocated a neoisolationist approach, such as Senator Taft, also made the case for a strategy of rollback after the outbreak of the Korean War.[8] Logically, however, a strategy of rollback was incompatible with neoisolationism, because rollback would have involved even greater costs and greater risks than containment.

There were really two versions of rollback. The first version, offered by anti-Communists like James Burnham, suggested that the Soviet Union be attacked and defeated in its satellite states before it grew too powerful.[9] According to this line of reasoning, containment was unsatisfactory because it never took the offensive against Moscow. In the long run, containment only seemed to invite a series of retreats by the United States and its allies. Anti-Communists like Burnham therefore called for the "liberation" of Eastern Europe from Soviet influence through direct American support of anti-Communist uprisings—a strategy that received the explicit approval of the Republican Party at its 1952 convention.[10] The second version of rollback was to launch a preventive air strike on the USSR itself, thereby destroying Moscow's emerging nuclear weapons capabilities. Again, this option was very seriously considered by U.S. officials, such as Secretary of the Air Force Stuart Symington and Secretary of the Navy Francis Matthews.[11] Of course, a preventive strike against Moscow was never launched, but it is worth noting that in 1950–1951, the Truman administration did make a concrete, if limited, effort at rollback by attempting to reunite Korea under a non-Communist government—an effort that General Douglas MacArthur would have expanded to the Chinese mainland had he been permitted to do so.[12] So while rollback was never implemented as the overall strategy of the United States, it was very much in the minds of U.S. officials as an alternative to containment.

Spheres of Influence

The third alternative to containment after World War Two—and the alternative, apart from containment, with the most support inside official circles—was to come to a clear agreement with Stalin on mutual spheres of influence for the victorious powers in Europe and Asia. Such an agreement would have entailed the explicit recognition of the Soviet Union's unquestioned predominance within Eastern Europe in exchange for the recognition of American and British predominance in Western Europe, the Middle East, and Japan. Presumably it would have also involved the partition of Germany into Eastern and Western zones, since neither the United States nor the USSR could accept the possibility of a unified and hostile Germany.[13] At the same time, a sphere-of-influence arrangement would have necessitated a limited but active U.S. military and diplomatic presence in Western Europe, the Middle East, and Northeast Asia; without such a presence, Soviet power would have been unchecked, Stalin would have pressed his advantage, and the arrangement would have inevitably broken down. In purely geographic terms, a sphere-of-influence deal would have led to an international outcome much like the one that actually transpired: Germany, divided; the Soviet bloc, dominant in Eastern Europe and parts of mainland Asia; the United States and its allies, dominant in Western Europe, the Middle East, and the Asian littoral. Undoubtedly, the United States and the USSR would still have been rivals. The crucial difference would have been that by agreeing in explicit terms to a geographic division of influence, the two superpowers might have avoided some of the most costly and risky features of the early Cold War period: a complete breakdown of diplomatic relations, spiraling arms production, violent proxy conflicts, and hair-raising nuclear crises.

It has sometimes been suggested that Moscow and Washington did eventually work out a kind of informal sphere-of-influence arrangement over the course of their Cold War competition.[14] By practice, trial and error, rather than explicit agreement, the two superpowers learned to abstain from direct interference within each other's spheres. But this observation requires several important qualifications. First, no such understanding ever existed outside of Europe. On the contrary, most Cold War crises after 1949 grew from the failure to agree upon any clear lines of influence within Asia, Africa, and Latin America. Second, even in Europe, it took decades for any such understanding to fully develop; the lengthy process of reaching it was costly and significant. It is therefore worth asking whether such an understanding could have been accomplished earlier, at less risk and expense. Third, it was not until the 1970s that the United States—under Richard Nixon and Henry Kissinger—moved toward something like a pure realist or sphere-of-influence approach with the strategy of détente.[15] This modification of containment opened up serious negotiations with Moscow and played down the aspiration for internal change within the Soviet bloc. But even Nixon and Kissinger could not completely escape the domestic influence of classical liberal assumptions, and consequently, American grand strategy continued to pursue certain Wilsonian goals under their leadership. The period of détente soon ended in renewed confrontation, primarily because the two superpowers never reached a mutually acceptable understanding of détente's meaning.[16] Finally, there never was any comprehensive sphere-of-influence arrangement or condominium between Moscow and Washington at any time during the Cold War, in part because neither side recognized the legitimacy or inviolability of the other's domestic political system. Incompatible strategic cultures—liberal versus Marxist-Leninist—rendered void any halting attempts at a lasting, explicit, and mutual partition of international influence between the two superpowers.

An effective sphere-of-influence arrangement—as opposed to a sphere of influence strategy—is of course an international outcome, rather than a unilateral decision on the part of one country; all interested parties have to agree on its essentials for it to work.[17] The nature of Soviet strategic culture under Stalin certainly complicated any efforts at a postwar sphere-of-influence arrangement; we will examine this point in greater detail later on. But the nature of American strategic culture had a similar complicating effect.

As late as 1945, American officials supported a certain kind of sphere-of-influence arrangement with the USSR. A few such officials, like Joseph Davies and Harry Hopkins, were New Deal holdovers, eager to maintain good relations with Moscow. But some of the most hard-nosed foreign policy experts and officials in the United States also initially supported such an arrangement—men like George Kennan, Charles Bohlen, and Walter Lippmann, who had no illusions about the purity of Soviet intentions. Kennan spoke of dividing "Europe frankly into spheres of influence—keep ourselves out of the Russian sphere and the Russians out of ours."[18] Bohlen stressed that "we should not in any sense attempt to deny the Soviet Union the legitimate prerogatives of a great power in regard to smaller countries resulting from geographic proximity."[19] Lippmann argued for "a modus vivendi by which the Russians and ourselves, neither fearing they are predestined enemies nor believing they are members of the same society, are able to live and let live by practical adjustments around the edge where their power and influence meet."[20] Indeed, before 1946 the acceptance of a Soviet sphere of influence within Eastern Europe was virtually unquestioned among leading U.S. foreign policymakers.[21] Franklin Roosevelt himself had expected and allowed for the territorial expansion of Soviet influence after the war, and the Yalta conference seemed to enshrine this influence, albeit in vague and informal terms.[22] Nor were there strong indications after Truman's succession to the White House that the new president planned to abandon hopes for Soviet-American cooperation.[23] As late as October 1945, Secretary of State James Byrnes publicly advocated a "regional arrangement" to augment "the efforts of the Soviet Union to draw into closer and more friendly association with her Central and Eastern European neighbors."[24]

A key condition from the American perspective, however, was that any such Soviet sphere remained "open," rather than oppressive or "exclusive." The USSR was expected to rule with a light hand, to permit its allies internal autonomy, to be respectful of free elections and plebiscites within its zone of influence, and to allow foreign trade and investment there. On these points, again, there was broad agreement among American officials. U.S. foreign policymakers never seriously advocated granting the Soviet Union a "closed" or unlimited sphere of influence over Eastern Europe. And this insistence on open or limited spheres would prove to be a major stumbling block in negotiations with Moscow.[25]

Containment

The strategy of "containment" involved drawing lines of resistance around the Soviet bloc, and denying the USSR further gains, through the provision by the United States of economic, political, and military aid to non-Communist countries. This entailed a dramatic expansion in the normal or peacetime level of America's defense expenditures and commitments. In the late 1940s, for example, military spending was maintained at about $13 billion per year, or 5 percent of GNP, a much higher proportion than the levels of military spending maintained in the 1920s and

1930s.[26] Billions more were spent every year on economic and military aid to American allies. Formal and informal alliances were built with dozens of countries in Europe and Asia; many of these alliances involved explicit security guarantees from the United States.

The implementation of containment was such a massive process that it took years to complete. From 1945 to 1951, as Stalin and his allies probed and challenged non-Communist governments in Europe and Asia, the United States responded by steadily increasing its diplomatic, economic, and military commitments overseas. In this sense, the period under examination here involved multiple strategic adjustments. But this process had more to do with the unfolding of international events than with changes in the basic strategy or mentality of U.S. policymakers. Most of the central and defining assumptions of containment were established in the minds of American officials by the end of 1946: the sense that continued negotiations were futile; the profound anti-Communism; the sense of global interests and global ambitions; the desire to promote a liberal international order; and, finally, the willingness to draw lines against Soviet expansion and deny the USSR further gains. The United States would not have acted as it did between 1946 and 1951 in the absence of those assumptions.[27]

Containment had several distinct characteristics that distinguished it from alternative strategies, such as, for instance, a sphere-of-influence approach. First, containment was influenced by *liberal* assumptions. That is to say, it was animated not simply by a determination to balance Soviet power, but by the desire to foster the strength of an international order characterized by free trade, national self-determination, and liberal democracy. This meant that outside of the Soviet bloc, among non-Communist countries, U.S. policymakers sought to encourage free trade and economic interdependence, democratic reform, and gradual decolonization. Occupied countries such as Germany and Japan were liberalized, politically and economically. Europe's colonial powers were pressed to coopt nationalist movements in the developing world by devolving formal control over imperial holdings. Of course, these efforts were often modest and halting. The long-term goal of liberalization was often sacrificed to the immediate goal of combating Communist expansion. But the interesting thing is that such long-term liberal goals were pursued at all. U.S. policymakers evidently believed that economic interdependence, democratization, and national self-determination outside the Soviet bloc would undercut the appeal of communism, strengthen the unity of a loose American-led coalition, and serve U.S. interests. They further believed that such a liberal world order would be conducive to the ultimate preservation of America's distinct form of government at home.[28]

Containment was influenced by liberal assumptions in another sense: in the expectation that the Cold War could only end with what George

Kennan called "either the breakup or the gradual mellowing of Soviet power."[29] This assumption was liberal, and not realist, because it placed primary importance upon the domestic political and cultural makeup of the Soviet system rather than the international distribution of power. The Clifford-Elsey Report of September 1946 put it this way: "Even though Soviet leaders profess to believe that the conflict between Capitalism and Communism is irreconcilable and must eventually be resolved by the triumph of the latter, *it is our hope that they will change their minds* and work out with us a fair and equitable settlement when they realize that we are too strong to be beaten and too determined to be frightened."[30] Cynics might have been forgiven for viewing this hope as naive. Yet such protestations were common, even in the private correspondence of leading American officials. The strategists of containment were convinced that the USSR could eventually be converted away from communism, and that the very example of a free society would have a transforming effect on the Soviet bloc. Again, this was no realist assumption.[31]

If containment was liberal in its program and aspirations, it was also *anti-Communist*. That is, the goal of containment, from the start, was not simply to stem the advance of Soviet power, but to combat the spread of communism.[32] As Kennan put it in his "long telegram" of Febraury 1946, the "inner central core of Communist parties . . . are in reality working together as an underground operating directorate of world communism, a concealed Comintern tightly coordinated and directed by Moscow."[33] This meant that, for all practical purposes, Communist successes anywhere constituted a gain for the Kremlin and a loss for the United States. Consequently, the strategy of containment had to be applied not only against the USSR, but against Communist parties everywhere.

Under containment, U.S. officials took Marxist-Leninist ideas seriously. The basic American assumption regarding Moscow's intentions was that Soviet policymakers were bent on the destruction of capitalism and the promotion of world revolution, and would inevitably try to expand until forcibly stopped. As Kennan put it in the same telegram: "We have here a political force committed fanatically to the belief that with [the] U.S. there can be no permanent modus vivendi, that it is desirable and necessary that the internal harmony of our society be disrupted, our traditional way of life be destroyed, the international authority of our state be broken, if Soviet power is to be secure."[34]

The central implication of this assumption was that the expansionist drives of the USSR were irreconcilable. This did not mean that war was inevitable. But it did mean that diplomatic concessions or negotiations with Moscow were pointless. As Clark Clifford put it in September 1946, reflecting the common views of American officials, "compromise and concession are considered, by the Soviets, to be evidence of weakness and they are encouraged by our 'retreats' to make new and greater demands."[35]

The above belief helped encourage one of the most distinctive features of containment: an unwillingness to engage in serious diplomacy. No strict foreign policy realist would have sanctioned this refusal to engage in meaningful negotiations with another state.[36] Neither would such a realist have taken very seriously the declarations of Marxist Leninism issuing forth from the Kremlin. Instead, a purely realist strategic conception would have assumed that the USSR was motivated by geopolitical interests. Certainly, the balancing of Soviet power would have still been necessary under such a strategy, but the door would have been open for hard-nosed and substantive negotiations over matters of mutual interest. In this sense, containment was not a realist strategy.[37]

Another major and consistent feature of containment was its *global* nature. At no time were U.S. officials willing to simply designate defensible "strong points" like West Germany, Britain, and Japan, while leaving less vital territories to the USSR. For one thing, U.S. policymakers believed that the economic revival of Western Europe and Japan depended upon access to food, raw materials, and markets located in the developing world.[38] Furthermore, the liberal and anti-Communist elements of containment undermined sharp distinctions between regions of vital importance versus regions of lesser interest. If communism as such was a threat, then it had to be contained everywhere; if a liberal international order was to be established, then it had to be promoted worldwide. Great emphasis was therefore placed on the vigorous containment of communism even in countries of little intrinsic interest to the United States. Kennan himself agreed that containment had to be applied to a large number of countries beyond Europe and Japan for reasons of security, credibility, and economic access.[39] As a result of such concerns, American officials self-consciously drew a vast perimeter or line of defense around the entire circumference of the Soviet bloc, from 1946 onward.

As part of this line of defense, anti-Communist containment was applied early on not only to vital regions in Europe, the Middle East, and Japan but to the East Asian mainland, as well. For example, Southeast Asia was integrated into the strategy of containment several years before the Korean War. French Indochina, in particular, was viewed as a test case for the development of a popular, non-Communist regime in the colonial world—the elusive "third force."[40] U.S. officials earnestly pressured the French to reform their colonial system and devolve power over Indochina. But Communist nationalists such as Ho Chi Minh were an unsatisfactory alternative to French rule, since they seemed, for all practical purposes, to be Soviet allies. Consequently, the Truman administration felt that it had no choice but to offer its support to France against the Vietminh, through economic and military aid, from as early as 1946.[41] Whatever his discomfort with the situation, Kennan agreed that it was the task of the United States "to ensure, however long it takes, the triumph of Indochinese nationalism over Red imperialism."[42]

From a very early date, containment was also applied against Mao Zedong's Chinese Communist Party (CCP). In the abstract, American officials would have preferred to support some sort of third force in China, free from the corruption and incompetence of Chiang Kai-shek's Nationalist forces. But no such force existed, and since Mao in the late 1940s was not about to merge his party into an anti-Soviet coalition, the only practical options available to the United States were either to aid the Nationalist Kuomintang (KMT) or allow the CCP to come to power. Given that choice, American officials consistently chose to support the KMT with economic and military aid—over $3 billion worth between 1945 and 1949.[43] U.S. officials also remained consistently supportive of an independent, non-Communist regime in South Korea throughout the mid-to-late 1940s. They continued to believe, in the words of a 1947 interagency committee, that if South Korea were lost to the Soviet bloc, "the resulting political repercussions would seriously damage U.S. prestige in the Far East and throughout the world, and would discourage those small nations now relying on the U.S. to support them in resisting internal or external Communist pressure."[44]

Under the strategy of containment, the declared interests of the United States extended not only into Western Europe, the Middle East, Japan, Korea, China, and Southeast Asia but also into the Soviet bloc itself. With a straightforward sphere-of-influence agreement, presumably the United States would have given up hope of seeing Eastern Europe freed from Soviet control. With containment, however, this long-term goal was never abandoned. Through the use of propaganda, covert operations, and imaginative diplomacy with nationalist regimes such as Tito's Yugoslavia, American officials planned to undermine the coherence of the Soviet bloc. Moreover, by implementing a broad-based and aggressive strategy of worldwide containment, the United States sought to intensify the political, economic, and military pressures on the USSR and bring about its ultimate retreat from Eastern Europe.[45] George Kennan was especially insistent on this point, arguing that "our first aim with respect to Russia in time of peace is to encourage and promote by means short of war the gradual retraction of undue Russian power and influence from the present satellite area."[46]

In sum, containment was a strategy of breathtaking scope. U.S. officials sought to contain Soviet power, but they also sought to do more: to promote a liberal international order characterized by free markets, democratic governments, and national self-determination in order to check

Communist expansion worldwide, to force the retraction of Soviet power, and, ultimately, to bring about a change of attitude within the Kremlin itself. To these ends, the United States entered into an unprecedented set of diplomatic and military peacetime commitments, not only in core regions such as Japan and Western Europe but around the world. A simple balance-of-power strategy would not have required such extensive aims and commitments. This was not a strategy of balance, but of preponderance.[47] The one gaping hole in this strategy, at least up until 1950, was the yawning gap between America's stated international aims and its military capabilities. Washington was, in effect, offering to help defend dozens of countries in Europe and Asia from the threat of Soviet pressure or attack. Yet in the late 1940s, it simply did not have the conventional military capability to do so reliably.[48] As a result, the United States went through an initial period under Truman during which the goals of containment were seriously out of proportion to the means at hand. With the outbreak of the Korean War, the means were finally increased to match the goals. But the goals were extremely ambitious from the very beginning.

REALISM AND INTERNATIONAL PRESSURES, 1945–1946

Having outlined both the nature of containment, and the various alternatives to containment in 1945–1946, the question remains: why were these other alternatives ultimately rejected? Why did U.S. officials not adopt a strategy of neoisolationism, rollback, or competitive cooperation with Moscow through a sphere-of-influence arrangement? And what role did international pressures, as opposed to cultural factors, play in this process of strategic adjustment?

Both structural realists and neoclassical realists would agree that international pressures are the single most important constraint upon strategic choice, as well as the ultimate trigger for strategic adjustment. In this particular case, international pressures offer a convincing explanation for both the rejection of neoisolationism and the rejection of rollback.

First, with regard to neoisolationism, a realist explanation would point out that the rise of U.S. power to unprecedented heights, together with the appearance of a clear threat from the USSR, made the adoption of a more expansive grand strategy on the part of the United States inevitable. The mid-1940s witnessed a revolution in the international distribution of power.[49] Germany and Japan were temporarily destroyed as great powers; Britain and France were significantly weakened. The United States, on the other hand, emerged from the war with immense and growing material capabilities. In 1945, for example, about 50 percent of all the manufactured goods in the world were produced in the United States.[50] Nor was

U.S. power confined to the purely economic. Again, by 1945, the United States spent more on its armed forces than any other country, making it the leading air and naval power in the world, and it had a monopoly on atomic weapons.[51] In fact, by the end of World War Two, the USSR stood as the only other major power with the ability and the desire to threaten America's vital interests. And whatever its economic weaknesses, the Soviet Union did possess great military power on land, along with a willingness to expand Soviet influence where possible. It was entirely plausible in 1945 that Soviet influence would spread, directly or indirectly, not only to regions of secondary interest, but to vital industrial centers such as Germany and Japan. There was simply no guarantee at the time that these two powerful nations—or others, such as France and Italy—would remain friendly to the United States. Communist electoral victories, as well as nationalist or neutralist foreign policy stands by major regional powers were distinct possibilities. It seems unlikely that any equilibrium could have been established around the edges of the Soviet bloc without the counterweight of U.S. economic aid, political support and military guarantees to various European and Asian states. A neoisolationist strategy would therefore have entailed immense risks for the United States. Given the new international conditions of 1945–1946—that is, given the rise in U.S. power, the existence of a serious threat from the USSR, and the weakness of Stalin's neighbors—a neoisolationist strategy on the part of the United States was neither very feasible nor very likely. Structural realism can explain the rejection of that strategy simply by pointing to material conditions in the international system at the time.

Structural realists can also explain the United States' rejection of rollback by referring to material constraints at the international level. The fundamental problem with rollback was that the United States did not have the capability to eject Soviet troops from Eastern Europe. As General Omar Bradley rightly put it, if the United States were to initiate a war against the USSR, "we might be in danger of losing."[52] A conventional assault on Soviet forces east of the Elbe was deemed utterly implausible; any attack would have had to rely upon a strategic bombing campaign against the USSR itself. But in the period immediately after World War Two, the United States possessed very few atomic bombs, and delivery systems were considered inadequate.[53] Even if industrial, military, and urban targets within the Soviet Union had been destroyed, there was hardly any guarantee that the USSR would actually surrender or withdraw from Eastern Europe. Indeed, it seemed more likely that Moscow would respond by using its conventional military forces to overrun Western Europe, the Middle East, and Northeast Asia. The United States would then be faced with international conditions infinitely worse than before the attack.[54] Militarily, the USSR was simply too strong to be vulnerable to a strategy of rollback. Nor was such a strategy popular with the United States' European allies.[55] An attack on the USSR would have been immensely costly, pointless, and disproportionate. From a structural perspective, rollback was not a viable strategy, and it is hardly surprising that it was rejected.

International pressures can explain the rejection of both rollback and neoisolationism satisfactorily. We can explain the adoption by the United States of a more global and expansive grand strategy simply by pointing to changes in international conditions. But international pressures cannot explain why U.S. foreign policymakers adopted a strategy of containment rather than a sphere-of-influence approach. From a realist perspective, a sphere-of-influence agreement should have been a viable strategic alternative in 1945–1946.

Clearly, the nature of Soviet strategic culture, and the nature of Stalin's leadership, complicated all efforts at a sphere-of-influence arrangement.[56] There was never any possibility that Stalin would accept the U.S. recipe for an open sphere of influence in Eastern Europe. Obviously, the Soviet dictator did not share in any Western liberal consensus regarding democracy, self-determination, and open markets, nor did he pretend to. Stalin wanted to promote the socialist system within the Soviet sphere of influence, and tie occupied countries closer to Moscow, for strategic, economic, and ideological reasons.[57] This meant that client states in Eastern Europe were subject to an unusually invasive form of imperial control—"Sovietized" in an effort to clone the Stalinist system. As Stalin put it, "this war is not as in the past . . . whoever occupies a territory also imposes his own social system."[58] Moscow's client states were to be integrated into an autarchic Soviet bloc and cut off from the West, in preparation for future conflict. Stalin's own personality—specifically, his inordinate paranoia and brutality—also tended to work against light-handed diplomatic arrangements. Wherever possible, Stalin wanted obedient, subservient clients, not independent allies.[59] Consequently, the "popular front" governments under Soviet occupation turned out to be a sham. Communists controlled the key ministries, backed by the Red Army, and when democratic methods failed, they used every fraudulent and coercive method to seize absolute power. For all of these reasons, there was no possibility of an open sphere of influence in Eastern Europe after 1945. The only sort of sphere of influence possible, and the only sort that Stalin would accept, was one based upon coercion and direct control.[60]

A diplomatic arrangement between Washington and Moscow involving closed spheres of influence, however, was a possible alternative in 1945. From what we know of Soviet diplomacy at the time, there is reason to believe that Stalin might have welcomed a sphere-of-influence arrangement, provided that such spheres were exclusive and unrestricted.[61] Indeed, Stalin did negotiate such an arrangement with Winston Churchill, in the infamous "percentages agreement" of October 1944, whereby Britain was left with predominant influence in Greece, while the USSR was left with predominant influence in Bulgaria and Romania.[62] By Churchill's own admission, Stalin lived up to his end of the bargain, refusing to aid the Greek Communists in their insurgency against the royalist government in Athens.[63] In 1945–1946, Stalin also acted to restrain Communist Party activity in France and Italy for much the same reason: in order to maintain reasonably good relations with the West.[64]

Stalin was often flexible and pragmatic with regard to foreign policy. His very cynicism, together with his desire for control over Communists outside of the USSR, actually made him a willing partner in straightforward geopolitical bargains with non-Communist countries. Certainly, Stalin probed for weaknesses in neighboring countries, but when these probes were resisted, as in Turkey and Iran in 1945–1946, he usually backed down. Soviet leaders took it for granted that strategic and ideological competition would continue between the United States and the USSR, but they saw no reason why such competition should rule out diplomatic expediencies designed to serve the interests of both sides.[65] As one Soviet diplomat said in 1945, in reference to a speech by U.S. Secretary of State James Byrnes, "Why doesn't he stop talking about principles, and get down to business and start trading?"[66] A sphere-of-influence deal in 1945 was therefore a possibility from Moscow's point of view, as long as the United States made no demands on the internal nature of the Soviet sphere. So why was a closed sphere-of-influence arrangement rejected by the United States in favor of containment? International pressures alone do not provide the answer.

DOMESTIC AGENDA SETTING, 1945–1946

It is at this point that U.S. strategic culture can and must be brought in to explain the final choice between containment and spheres of influence. The evidence suggests that cultural factors—in the form of liberal beliefs and assumptions—acted as a crucial filter on the American consideration of strategic alternatives in 1945–1946, rendering a pure sphere-of-influence approach unacceptable. The classical liberal vision is of course that of an international system characterized by peaceful trade, open markets, international law, national self-determination, and democratic government. Interestingly, such liberal ideals were virtually the only war aims expressed by Franklin Roosevelt beyond the unconditional surrender of the Axis powers. They were certainly at the heart of wartime declarations like the Atlantic Charter and the Declaration on Liberated Europe. The implication of such declarations was that the war's true purpose was not simply to defeat a coalition of hostile powers, but to usher in a new kind of international system. As Roosevelt told Congress shortly after meeting Churchill and Stalin in 1945: "[the Yalta conference] ought to spell the end of the system of unilateral action, the exclusive alliances, the spheres of influence, the balances of power, and all the other expedients that have been tried for centuries—and have always failed."[67] Such millennial rhetoric was unsurprising in a public forum, since the president needed to build popular support for the war effort. Roosevelt knew that no set of war aims could possibly win popular approval in the United States unless they were framed in broad, liberal, and idealistic terms. But the striking thing about Roosevelt's wartime diplomacy is that it was deeply informed by liberal ideas, even in private.[68] As Harry Hopkins told Robert Sherwood in 1941: "[Roosevelt] sometimes tries to appear tough and cynical and flippant, but that's an act he likes to put on, especially at press conferences. . . . You can see the real Roosevelt when he comes out with something like the Four Freedoms. And don't get the idea that those are any catch phrases. He believes them! He believes they can be practically attained."[69] To the immense distress of both British and Soviet officials, Roosevelt and his advisors actually pressed for the realization of liberal goals, such as free trade and national self-determination, in both the British Empire and the liberated territories of Europe.[70]

Obviously the promotion of a liberal international order by the United States was not strictly disinterested. American foreign policymakers expected that the growth of such an order would serve U.S. interests. But the interesting point is that American officials, from Roosevelt down, followed liberal (and not simply balance-of-power) assumptions regarding the nature of the national interest. By promoting an international system characterized by free trade, democratic governments, and national self-determination, U.S. officials hoped to discourage military and political rivalries between the major powers, bind other countries economically to the United States, and create a more peaceful and prosperous world order.[71] It is precisely for this reason that U.S. foreign policymakers were so persistent in calling on the USSR to demonstrate some minimal respect for democratic norms in liberated territories. Roosevelt understood that the Soviet Union would exercise special influence over Eastern Europe in the postwar era. Nevertheless, he wanted Stalin to observe basic democratic procedures in countries such as Poland, and to cooperate with the United States in the creation of a new security regime based upon open exchange, self-determination, and nonaggression.[72] These liberal demands were not simply meant as window dressing; they were at the core of America's wartime diplomacy.[73] And they were quite incompatible with Stalin's own demands for a secure buffer zone in Eastern Europe.

Once it became clear that the USSR would not accept an open sphere of influence in Eastern Europe, the United States began to shift toward a strategy of containment. The possibility of a more straightforward and traditional sphere-of-influence approach, in which each side exercised exclusive rights within its own sphere, was never seriously considered by American officials. As we have already seen, this was not for lack of feasibility at the international level; Stalin was willing to negotiate. On the contrary, a pure sphere-of-influence approach was ruled out within the United States for domestic, cultural reasons.

First, there was simply no domestic political support for any such bargain with Moscow. The slightest hint of a secret deal with Stalin drew fierce criticism from across the political spectrum.[74] Roosevelt and Truman both knew that Congress, as well as the press, would lash out against an explicit abandonment of East European self-determination. They knew that liberal justifications would be needed in order to secure popular and congressional support for any new U.S. commitments abroad. For either President to have embraced a sphere-of-influence strategy in 1945 would have undermined not only his own popularity, but the popularity of the internationalist cause.[75] A sphere-of-influence strategy simply did not resonate with liberal cultural assumptions within the United States, and, for this reason, such an approach was judged by leading American officials to be politically infeasible.[76]

Second, even if a straight sphere-of-influence deal had been politically feasible at home, U.S. foreign policymakers themselves were opposed to the idea. Again, this opposition was not for humanitarian reasons. Rather, it was based upon an interpretation of U.S. interests informed by liberal assumptions. To have accepted a pure sphere-of-influence deal with Stalin would have been to abandon the wartime goal of a liberal international regime, free from rival, autarchic, military blocs.[77] This was not a concession that American officials were prepared to make, either during or immediately after the war. As Deputy Under-Secretary of State Orme Sergeant put it: "It would no doubt be easy to strike a bargain with the Soviet government if we were prepared to recognize their exclusive interest in certain countries. On such terms we might be able to save Czechoslovakia, Yugoslavia, Austria and Turkey at the cost of sacrificing Poland, Romania and Bulgaria. But it is inconceivable that we should adopt this course."[78]

Harry Truman, for his part, shared the liberal cultural assumptions of his leading foreign policy advisors, and was not inclined to question their rejection of a sphere-of-influence approach.[79] Certainly, like many other U.S. officials during 1945, Truman wavered on the question of how to handle relations with Moscow; he was reluctant to see Soviet-American cooperation end.[80] But like Franklin Roosevelt, Truman never really wavered on the basic demand that Stalin allow reasonably free and fair elections in Poland, as well as elsewhere in Eastern Europe.[81] Once it became clear, by the beginning of 1946, that no such elections would be held, Truman was ready to adopt a more hard-nosed approach—one consistent with liberal assumptions.[82]

For present purposes, the immediate origins of containment need only be briefly summarized. Already in 1944–1945, leading State Department officials with Soviet experience were arguing for a less naive approach toward Stalin.[83] Certain cabinet officials, such as Admiral Leahy, Truman's chief of staff, and James Forrestal, the Secretary of the Navy, also called early on for a toughening of U.S. policy toward the Soviet Union.[84] By February 1946, Soviet behavior seemed to confirm that the hard-liners were right. The USSR seemed to be acting in an aggressive and heavy-handed manner, not only in Eastern Europe but also in Turkey and Iran. George Kennan's "long telegram," sent on February 22, did not in itself alter American grand strategy, but it did articulate the assumptions that were coming to dominate U.S. government thinking in relation to the Soviet Union.[85] With both Congress and public opinion calling on him to get tough with the USSR, and genuinely alarmed by the threat of Soviet expansion, President Truman decided early in 1946 to embrace a new, hard-line approach.[86] Advocates of Soviet-American cooperation, such as Henry Wallace, were soon won over or marginalized from power.[87] By the fall of 1946, there was virtual consensus in U.S. government circles behind the strategy of containment.[88] The precise implications of that strategy were still unclear, but all of the key assumptions were already there: that is, that the USSR was expansionist and implacable; that negotiations with Moscow were pointless; that the United States should provide diplomatic, economic, and military aid to non-Communist countries worldwide in order to check the spread of communism; that the Soviet sphere in Eastern Europe could not be recognized as legitimate; and that the United States should aim, in the long run, for the eventual retreat of Soviet influence.[89]

The crucial point about containment, however, is that it was not the only internationally viable grand strategy open to U.S. foreign policymakers in 1945–1946. Rather, it was the only internationally viable grand strategy that also resonated with American cultural—which is to say, liberal—assumptions. The strategy of containment resonated with the American public, with Congress, and with leading U.S. officials in a way that no strictly realist, sphere-of-influence approach ever could have. The very features of containment criticized by realists—the fact that it had a distinctly ideological, crusading, and uncompromising bent to it—were precisely what made it popular at home. With containment, Americans were asked to take up an active, global role in championing democracy, halting the spread of totalitarianism, and preserving America's own system of limited government.[90] This was a role that was culturally meaningful to Americans in terms of their sense of their nation's history and identity. Nor were such cultural references only for public consumption. As pragmatic as they were, U.S. foreign policymakers really did think and speak, in private, in terms that were colored by classical liberal assumptions; that is to say, the assumptions behind containment were culturally bound, at the highest levels, and those assumptions were genuine.[91] By emphasizing the classical liberal goals behind containment, U.S. officials were able to link this new strategy to a sense of American national identity, build domestic support for expensive, new foreign policy initiatives, and prevent a return to isolationism.[92] Beginning in 1946, the strategy of containment gained broad popular and congressional support, in spite of serious concerns about this unprecedented new role for the United States overseas. There is no reason to believe that such support would have been forthcoming, if U.S. officials had adopted a sphere-of-influence arrangement with the Soviet Union.[93]

International Pressures, 1946–1951

The adoption of the idea of containment did not mean that the new strategy was secure from all challenges. In fact, U.S. officials faced a serious and practically insoluble dilemma in trying to implement containment without completely sacrificing the U.S. preference for limited liability. First, we look at the growing international pressures on U.S. decisionmakers between 1946 and 1951, then the domestic political challenge of building and maintaining support for the strategy of containment.

In the years immediately after 1946, international pressures continued to stimulate new American commitments overseas. Despite later accusations of American imperialism, U.S. allies in Europe and Asia willingly supported these new commitments. Indeed, American economic aid, political support, and military guarantees were positively encouraged by foreign governments, to an extent that actually made U.S. officials uneasy.[94] Initially, under the basic assumptions of containment, U.S. officials intended to limit America's economic, political, and military commitments on the Eurasian mainland.[95] The hope in Washington was that the United States could contain the expansion of communism, and promote the security and stability of a liberal international order, without sacrificing limited liability in strategic affairs. Between 1946 and 1951, however, non-Communist governments in Europe and Asia came under new pressures. It became increasingly obvious that the goals of containment could not be met without a more direct U.S. presence overseas. American officials were forced to abandon their hope that the strategy of containment could be maintained at low cost to the United States; they agreed instead to enter into an unprecedented set of formal, direct strategic commitments toward numerous allies in the Middle East, Europe, and East Asia. Through this set of commitments, the feasibility of containment was maintained, but it was maintained only through major concessions on the part of the United States, in that Americans were forced to play a more direct and expensive military role overseas than they would have liked. International pressures thus ran contrary to the U.S. preference for limited liability.

In Western Europe, between 1947 and 1951, steadily increasing pressures for U.S. diplomatic engagement, economic aid, and military support forced American policymakers to abandon their initial hope that the goals of containment could be met without direct and extensive U.S. financial, political, and strategic commitments on the European continent. These pressures from Europe triggered a complex and staggered process of transatlantic bargaining, whereby the United States attempted to extract certain concessions in exchange for its aid and support. In the end, however, it was the United States—and not its European allies—that made most of the crucial concessions. The feasibility of containment was maintained, but only through a series of escalated and unexpected political, economic, and military commitments on the part of the United States.

The first stage of transatlantic bargaining began in 1946–1947, with pressures for new U.S. economic assistance. Economic conditions in Western Europe immediately after World War Two were even worse than expected. Britain's finances were stretched to the breaking point, endangering its ability to maintain a strong anti-Soviet presence in Germany and the Middle East.[96] And on the European continent in 1945–1947, communism and neutralism held considerable political and ideological appeal.[97] The fear in Washington was that deteriorating economic conditions would play into the hands of Marxist-Leninist parties, leaving Western European governments drawn toward autarchy, neutralism, and communism.[98] Such developments could only benefit the USSR, and undermine containment. Consequently, in spite of intense domestic pressures toward fiscal conservatism, U.S. officials initiated a sweeping program of economic aid for Western Europe—the European Recovery Program, or Marshall Plan. In exchange for this aid, the United States asked for several important concessions from European governments: first, that they liberalize their economies, reducing barriers to trade and investment; second, that they move toward a much more cooperative, integrated approach to economic and political problems; third, that they accept the economic and political rehabilitation of Germany; and fourth, which was implicit, that they align with the United States in the Cold War against the Soviet Union.[99]

The European response to these demands was mixed, to say the least. On the one hand, expectations of Marshall aid did play a key role in the "Western choice" of continental European governments in 1947–1948. The resulting anti-Soviet alignment of ruling coalitions throughout Western Europe was a great victory for the United States. But initial U.S. hopes for a fully integrated and economically liberal European union—with a rehabilitated Western Germany at its core—were badly disappointed. There would be some liberalization of trade and money in Western Europe in 1947–1948, and some limited movement toward economic cooperation, but not nearly as much as U.S. officials had desired.[100] Worst of all, France continued to resist one of the United States' key demands: the economic and political rehabilitation of Western Germany.[101]

The Franco-American impasse over Germany led directly to a second stage of transatlantic bargaining—this time, centering around the question of a U.S. military commitment to Europe. French officials simply would not accept the rehabilitation of Germany without the promise of formal security guarantees from Washington.[102] Indeed, by the spring of 1948, most Western European governments sought military alliance with the United States. One reason for such requests was direct alarm over Soviet behavior—particularly after the Czech coup of February 1948. But for the most part, European fears were more indirect. Britain, France, Belgium, and the Netherlands faced opposition and rebellion from within their colonial empires; France and Italy faced Communist-inspired labor unrest. All of these countries sought economic, political, and military relief from multiple challenges at home and abroad. U.S. economic aid was no longer enough to provide that relief. Only a direct alliance with the United States seemed to offer Western Europeans the prospect of security against Russia *and* Germany, without forcing them to direct their limited resources away from imperial and domestic reconstruction.[103]

Initially, U.S. officials were very reluctant to offer formal security guarantees in Western Europe. The American hope was that increased military aid and staff coordination would be enough to satisfy friendly European governments.[104] But over the course of 1948 it became obvious that nothing less than a military alliance would suffice. Only such an alliance would give European governments the confidence to resist Soviet pressures while focusing on domestic economic reconstruction.[105] And only such an alliance would give France the confidence to accept Germany's rehabilitation. As Dean Acheson put it in February 1949, "It was doubtful that, without some such pact, the French would ever be reconciled to the inevitable diminution of direct allied control over Germany and the progressive reduction of Allied troops."[106] Accordingly, after prolonged negotiations, in April 1949 the U.S. government signed the North Atlantic Treaty—in effect, guaranteeing that the United States would come to the defense of Britain, France, Italy, Portugal, Norway, Denmark, the Low Countries, Canada, and Iceland in case of armed attack on any of those countries.

The French government did in fact respond to the United States' North Atlantic Treaty Organization (NATO) guarantees by accepting a considerable revival of German sovereignty and power—notably, with the creation of the Federal Republic of Germany in September 1949. Beyond that, NATO gave French officials the confidence to take a bold, new approach toward European integration, beginning with the proposal for a European Coal and Steel Community (ECSC) in May 1950.[107] But with the outbreak of the Korean War the following month, even America's NATO commitment was insufficient to reassure Europeans of their security. The notion that the United States would bomb the USSR after allowing the Red Army to march to the Atlantic (the standard U.S. war plan at the time) was naturally uncomfortable for the inhabitants of Western Europe. As General Omar Bradley noted as early as April 1949, "It must be perfectly apparent to the people of the United States that we cannot count on our friends in Western Europe if our strategy in the event of war dictates that we shall first abandon them to the enemy with a promise of later liberation."[108] Nor did such a war seem too distant a possibility. There was genuine alarm in European capitals over the North Korean attack, and fear that a Soviet invasion of Western Europe might follow.[109] Europeans wanted a significant, direct U.S. military presence in Europe; they wanted to see U.S. divisions on the ground.[110] This led to the third and final stage of transatlantic bargaining.

U.S. officials recognized the need for an augmented conventional military force capable of defending Western Europe from attack, and they were willing to increase the American contribution to it, but they expected the Europeans themselves to provide the bulk of such a force. Specifically, they expected their NATO allies to accept the fact that Europe could not be defended without a major contribution from the Germans.[111] France, however, balked at the prospect of a new Wehrmacht, and European rearmament was slow to get off the ground. In the short term, assuming Soviet superiority in conventional forces, there seemed to be no way of actually defending Western Europe without a major U.S. military presence on the ground. Accordingly, in 1951 American officials again entered into a new strategic commitment that they had long hoped to avoid by adopting a forward military presence in Europe and deploying four heavily armed divisions to West Germany.

By 1951 the essential outlines of the postwar transatlantic bargain between the United States and Western Europe were already in place. The governments of most Western European nations had chosen to align with the United States against the USSR. Stable, centrist, democratic forces had taken office in most West European capitals, and Marxist-Leninist parties had been marginalized from power. Germany had been restored to levels unanticipated in 1945, and locked into the North Atlantic community, through the creation of a separate, rehabilitated West German republic. And the process of European economic integration had begun. These historic achievements—which were undoubtedly in America's own national interest—were secured only through a new set of strategic commitments on the part of the United States. Yet these commitments were offered with the greatest reluctance. American officials had never intended for the United States to play such a direct role in the defense of Western Europe, and even after 1951 they still refused to view that role as permanent. Expectations of limited liability persisted in spite of international pressures to the contrary.

In Japan, as in Western Europe, international pressures led to unexpected alliance commitments on the part of the United States. The adoption of the strategy of containment led U.S. foreign policy officials to view Japan as a potentially crucial ally, in need of protection and support, rather than a onetime enemy in need of punishment and reform. By 1947 U.S. officials had already begun to "reverse course" on Japan, emphasizing political stability and economic reconstruction rather than the democratization of Japanese society and the decartelization of Japanese industry.[112] This change in emphasis on the part of the United States was not unwelcome to leading Japanese authorities. But the victory of the Communist Party in mainland China, and the outbreak of the Korean War, led U.S. officials to propose a new set of political and military arrangements for Japan. From 1949–1950 onward, U.S. policymakers were willing to offer a substantial restoration of national sovereignty to Japan, along with a generous peace treaty stipulating the virtual end of postwar economic controls. U.S. officials, however, expected a number of key concessions in exchange. First, they wanted the right to maintain a permanent garrison and a set of military bases on Japanese territory.[113] Second, they wanted Japan to cooperate in the diplomatic and economic isolation of Communist China by abstaining from political ties or commercial relations with Beijing.[114] And third, they insisted that Japan rearm against the Soviet Union.[115]

Japanese authorities welcomed an end to the strictures of occupation, but they did not quite share the American vision regarding Japan's new role in East Asia. Officials in Tokyo hoped to focus national efforts on economic growth and commercial expansion, rather than on anti-Communist containment. So while Japan sought close political ties with the United States—indeed, sought guarantees of military protection—it resented any restrictions on trade with mainland China, and resisted U.S. pressures toward national rearmament. Ironically, early postwar efforts to root out militaristic values from Japanese society had succeeded so well that by 1950–1951, the U.S. attempt to "remilitarize" its onetime enemy ran into fierce opposition within Japan.[116] In 1951–1952, under the terms of the San Francisco peace treaty, a compromise was struck. The period of occupation was ended, and Japanese sovereignty restored. A de facto military alliance was formed between Tokyo and Washington. The United States retained basing rights and military garrisons on Japanese territory. Japan agreed to accept the U.S. foreign policy line with regard to Communist China.[117] But the Japanese successfully resisted any serious rearmament efforts, agreeing only to maintain a "police reserve force" of some 50, 000 men.[118] As in Western Europe, the United States was left with the primary military obligation to uphold containment.[119]

The U.S. decision to embark upon a strategy of containment led to an outcome in Japan remarkably similar to that in Germany. A defeated enemy was rehabilitated in the hopes of staving off local Communist expansion. The Far Left was marginalized from centers of political power. Local authorities actually welcomed a continuing U.S. military presence, and the United States entered into an unexpected set of strategic commitments toward its onetime enemy. In the case of Japan, however, the convergence of interests with the United States was even greater than in the case of Germany. For one thing, Americans had long intended to be the predominant military and political power in the Pacific region; they did not have to be dragged reluctantly into a strategic commitment toward Japan. The Japanese, unlike the Germans, were not asked to rebuild their armed forces to any great extent, or to accept the indefinite partition of their country. Nor was there any Asia-Pacific equivalent of France to act as a powerful, independent, and complicating factor in U.S.-Japanese relations. In sum, few compromises were needed on the part of the United States in order to maintain the viability of containment with relation to Japan. For the most part, the new alliance between Tokyo and Washington served the interests of both sides very well.

In the Middle East, as in Western Europe, the United States entered into unexpected military and economic commitments after 1946 in order to preserve the friendly diplomatic alignment of regional governments. Initially, under the strategy of containment, U.S. commitments in the Middle East were meant to be limited. American officials hoped that Britain would check Soviet expansion in the region, allowing the United States to remain somewhat disengaged. From 1946 to 1951, however, it became increasingly clear that Britain would no longer be able to play its traditional role, balancing Russia in the "northern tier." As British influence waned, local governments—as well as Great Britain itself—turned to the United States for aid and support. This process had already begun by 1946, with U.S. economic, political, and military support for Turkey and

Iran. By February 1947 British officials were forced to notify Washington that they would be unable to maintain a military presence in Greece, supporting the local government against Communist insurgents. In the following year, Iran pressed for U.S. economic and military aid.[120] Turkey demanded a formal alliance commitment from the United States, while the Saudis asked for security guarantees as well as military aid.[121] In each of these cases, the stimulus for a new U.S. commitment came from abroad, not from the United States. Indeed, regional governments sought U.S. aid not only to better resist Soviet or Communist political pressures, but in order to combat regional and domestic non-Communist adversaries. Still, American officials responded willingly to requests for assistance, because under the assumptions of containment, the continued strength of allied, non-Communist regimes was in itself of vital interest to the United States: if one friendly government fell to hostile forces, for whatever reason, the reverberations might be global. As Truman put it:

> If we were to turn our back on the world, areas such as Greece, weakened and divided as a result of the war, would fall into the Soviet orbit without much effort on the part of the Russians. The success of Russia in such areas and our avowed lack of interest would lead to the growth of domestic Communist parties in such European countries as France and Italy, where they were already significant threats. Inaction . . . could only result in handing the Russians vast areas of the globe now denied to them.[122]

Britain, Greece, Turkey, Iran, and Saudi Arabia had asked for increased support from Washington; U.S. officials responded by upgrading economic and military aid to local governments. In March 1947 Truman announced a $400 million package of economic aid for Greece and Turkey.[123] Military aid to Iran was increased. Economic aid and informal military guarantees were extended to Saudi Arabia.[124] And in 1952 the United States agreed to extend formal alliance commitments to Greece and Turkey by including them within NATO. U.S. officials were left with a set of military and economic commitments in the Middle East, both formal and informal, that were much more extensive than they had anticipated. But as of 1951–1952, local regimes in Athens, Istanbul, Tehran, and Riyadh remained essentially friendly and non-Communist; the core goals of containment had been met.

In their efforts to contain the spread of Soviet influence between 1946 and 1951, the most frustrating region for American officials was undoubtedly East Asia. As in Western Europe, the Middle East, and Japan, the United States was drawn into a more direct set of military commitments in East Asia by 1951. In mainland Asia, however, the strategy of containment met with very high costs and some devastating setbacks.

Initially, American officials planned to minimize U.S. political and military commitments on the East Asian mainland, while denying the region to Soviet influence. Before 1950, U.S. policymakers were determined to check the spread of communism in East Asia, but they hoped to do so through limited amounts of economic and military aid to non-Communist forces in China, South Korea, and Indochina.[125] U.S. officials also hoped to pressure local allies in each of these three countries—including the French in Indochina—into enacting liberal political reforms. In this way, it was reasoned, the force of postcolonial Asian nationalism would be diverted into democratic and pro-Western channels, rather than into Communist hands.[126]

This detached version of containment proved unsustainable in the face of repeated setbacks and increased pressure for American involvement. On China's mainland, the complete collapse of the Nationalist army in mid-1949 constituted an unavoidable but shocking defeat for the strategy of containment. From their redoubt on the island of Formosa, Chiang Kai-shek's Nationalist forces subsequently called for American aid and support. In Indochina, the French continued to suffer military setbacks against Ho Chi Minh's revolutionary forces. Paris asked for increased support from Washington. And in South Korea, in June 1950, a full-scale invasion by Kim Il-Sung's northern regime threatened to leave the entire peninsula under Communist rule.

Non-Communist regimes in South Korea, French Indochina, and Formosa were coming under severe pressure by 1950; the American response was to enter into new military commitments toward each of these countries. In Indochina, U.S. officials recognized a semiautonomous French protectorate under Bao Dai and gave increased military aid to the new regime—$300 million per year by 1951.[127] The French were no longer pressed quite so hard by Washington to devolve power over their Southeast Asian colony.[128] In Formosa, as a result of the Korean War, the United States moved to consolidate the strength of Chiang's remaining Nationalist forces by shifting from simple economic and military aid to an effective security guarantee. Vessels from the Seventh Fleet were deployed in the Taiwan straits on June 27, 1950, indicating that the People's Republic of China would not be permitted to invade Formosa.[129] And in Korea, the United States made its most dramatic new strategic commitment by coming to the defense of Syngman Rhee's regime in a major military effort costing billions of dollars per year and involving hundreds of thousands of American troops.

As officials at the time recognized, the Korean peninsula was of no vital inherent interest to the United States, either strategically or economically. But under the strategy of containment, the security, prosperity, and stability of the entire non-Communist world was viewed as interdependent; any

Communist gain, no matter how intrinsically insignificant, might raise questions concerning the strength and credibility of America's worldwide alliance system.[130] This was all the more true in a case of blatant military aggression by a Communist state against a non-Communist government—really, the first such case that the United States had had to face. Consequently, Truman and his advisors did not hesitate to come to South Korea's defense. As the president put it, expressing the general consensus, "If we let Korea down, the Soviets will keep right on going and swallow up one piece of Asia after another. We had to make a stand some time, or else let all of Asia go by the board. If we were to let Asia go, the Near East would collapse and no telling what would happen to Europe."[131]

By the end of 1951, then, the United States had entered into an unprecedented set of direct military commitments in East Asia. U.S. military aid was pouring into French Indochina. Washington had made an implicit defense commitment toward Chiang's nationalist regime on Formosa/Taiwan. And American forces were fighting in Korea at great cost to preserve the independence of Syngman Rhee's southern regime. Communist forces had triumphed in mainland China—a great disappointment for the strategists of containment. Ho Chi Minh's forces were gradually making gains in Indochina. But while U.S. policymakers could not yet know it, the feasibility of containment had already been confirmed at selected points, in South Korea and Formosa, where viable, non-Communist regimes would flourish under the U.S. security umbrella. The viability of these regimes, and the feasibility of containment in the region, was secured only through certain critical concessions on the part of the United States. U.S. officials had to enter into clear military commitments toward Seoul and Taipei, and temporarily accept the authoritarian nature of both regimes. These commitments and concessions were more costly and definitive than U.S. officials had originally intended. But as in Europe, the Middle East, and Japan, such concessions were necessary given the ambitious end goals of containment.

DOMESTIC COALITION BUILDING, 1946–1951

Prior to the Korean War, concerns over limited liability encouraged the Truman administration to keep a relatively low ceiling on defense expenditures. The conventional reading of U.S. foreign policy during these years is that the strategy of containment became increasingly "militarized" after 1949.[132] But given that U.S. officials were determined to contain communism throughout Europe and Asia, and given that they had made an explicit commitment to defend Western Europe from any Soviet attack, U.S. defense spending up until 1950 was, if anything, inadequate to the task at hand. The initial preference for strategic detachment actually undermined the credibility of America's diplomatic commitments. Yet prior to the outbreak of the Korean War, domestic constraints on rearmament prevented Truman from bringing military means into line with diplomatic ends, while during that war, the costs of the struggle triggered a sweeping set of attacks on the whole concept of containment. In a word, Americans wanted to have the benefits of containment without paying the price.

The fundamental strategic dilemma for the United States centered on the perceived superiority of the Soviet Union's conventional military capabilities in Europe and the Middle East.[133] In the event of war, American military planners expected that the USSR would probably be able to overrun most of continental Europe and the Middle East within a few months.[134] Nuclear weapons were an appealing means of overcoming this imbalance in conventional forces, and the American war plan was to strike back at the USSR with strategic bombers based in Britain and Egypt. But this strategy faced a number of problems. It was not clear that the possibility of nuclear retaliation would deter Communist forces from piecemeal acts of aggression; certainly it had not done so in Eastern Europe or China after 1945. Western Europeans were hardly comforted by the thought that their American ally would be unable to actually help defend them from Soviet attack. And there were also serious questions as to whether a U.S. nuclear strike would necessarily compel the surrender or collapse of the Soviet regime.[135] Failing such a surrender, the USSR would be left weakened by bombing, but still in effective control of Western Europe and the Middle East. This was bound to be true, even under conditions of an American nuclear monopoly; once the USSR tested its own atomic bomb in 1949, the U.S. strategic dilemma only worsened. New questions arose as to the credibility of the U.S. nuclear deterrent. Would Washington actually risk a nuclear strike on the USSR once Moscow had the ability to respond in kind? The solution was obvious: for both military reasons, and political ones, the United States and its allies needed to increase their ability to actually *defend* Europe and the Middle East from Soviet attack through conventional military forces, rather than simply relying on nuclear retaliation.[136]

This was the international diplomatic and strategic reality in the late 1940s: America's broad international commitments were lacking in credibility so long as the United States refused to strengthen its conventional armed forces. Within the United States, however, between 1946 and 1950 the domestic political reality was that any large-scale increase in military spending was out of the question. In part, this was a reflection of Truman's own policy preferences. Up until the Korean War, Truman's inclination was to maintain a balanced budget, suppress inflation, and, if possible, build on Roosevelt's New Deal programs.[137] Increased defense spending was simply not on Truman's list of priorities. This constraining pressure on military expenditures was multiplied by domestic political considerations. The Republican Party made spectacular gains in the congressional elections of 1946, retaking control of both houses. Conservatives were especially well represented among the freshmen of 1947. Their common demand was for not only a balanced budget, but significant cuts in both taxes and government spending.[138] These demands were supported by an unprecedented political mobilization of business interests, and by a broad trend in popular opinion after World War Two in favor of fiscal retrenchment.[139] So while Truman and the Republicans disagreed on domestic priorities, when it came to defense expenditures all domestic political principles and considerations pointed in one direction: downward.

In domestic political terms, of course, the strategic incoherence of containment before 1950 was part of its attraction. The very fact that military spending was held at such low levels in the late 1940s—relative to U.S. goals and commitments—was one of the things that lent containment its domestic political appeal. The long-term military and financial implications of this strategy—a strategy already in place by 1947—were permitted to develop slowly, in response to external shocks such as the Czech coup of 1948, the Berlin crisis of 1948–1949, and, finally, the attack on South Korea in 1950. This gradual increase in costs and commitments allowed both Congress and the American public to digest the awesome implications of this ambitious new strategy piece by piece. Had Truman announced in 1947 that defense spending would be increased to a level consistent with U.S. foreign policy goals, it is inconceivable that Congress would have approved. In any case, there was little disagreement over the need to keep costs down.

The impact of these domestic political constraints, however, was to encourage a widening gap between America's strategic commitments overseas and its ability to meet those commitments.[140] This gap only widened over the course of the late 1940s. U.S. conventional military forces were not expanded significantly. Military expenditures were kept at a ceiling of approximately $13 billion per year.[141] Indeed, after approving a modest military supplement of $3.2 billion in 1948, Truman actually cut defense spending the following year.[142] In spite of the USSR's successful test of an atomic bomb in August 1949, in spite of the proclamation of the People's Republic of China a few weeks later, and in spite of a growing feeling among leading state officials that defense spending was dangerously low, Truman remained committed to strict limits on military expenditures.[143] In effect, the administration gambled—in light of U.S. superiority in nuclear weapons—that the USSR and its allies would not actually test America's willingness or ability to check armed aggression against non-Communist countries. On the Korean peninsula, at least, this gamble turned out to be misplaced.

With the outbreak of the Korean War in June 1950, political constraints on U.S. defense spending were finally lifted.[144] The North Korean attack revealed that conventional military forces had not been rendered obsolete by nuclear weapons; it also highlighted NATO's military weakness relative to the USSR.[145] The administration was stunned into action. In Truman's eyes, Fair Deal programs and balanced budgets now took a back seat to national security concerns.[146] Congress temporarily accepted the administration's new fiscal priorities, as did public opinion.[147] The result was a dramatic increase in U.S. military spending: supplemental expenditures of $10.5 billion in July 1950, $5.6 billion in August, and another $16.8 billion in December.[148] Only half of this combined supplemental expenditure was spent on forces directly assigned to Korea; the other half was spent on an overall increase in U.S. military readiness. Total manpower in every service was more than doubled, and four American divisions were sent to Western Europe. Military spending remained at a very high level throughout 1951—more than three times what it had been before the Korean War. In other words, the administration not only sent U.S. forces to Korea, but took advantage of the shock provided by Korea to enhance America's overall strength in conventional military forces. This set of initiatives is often derided by historians and political scientists as an unnecessary "militarization" of containment. But in fact, it was the first time since 1946 that U.S. officials had made a concerted effort to close the growing gap between America's strategic commitments, on the one hand, and its military capabilities, on the other. Given the broad geographic scope of containment, and the strength of enemy forces, an increase in U.S. conventional military capabilities was both necessary and inevitable. Had such an increase been implemented before 1950, and had U.S. officials clearly indicated their strategic commitment to Seoul, it seems unlikely that Stalin would have permitted North Korea to launch its attack. So the increase in U.S. military spending made sense, strategically and internationally. The only question was whether it would be politically sustainable at home.

During Truman's first term in office, congressional Republicans had been mostly supportive of containment.[149] From 1949 on, however, Republican attacks on the administration's foreign policy increased dramatically.[150] The reasons for these attacks were both partisan and genuine. Republicans resented their unexpected defeat in the election of 1948. They resented their seeming inability to make any political headway on domestic policy questions.[151] The repeated disasters and frustrations of U.S. policy in East Asia from 1949 onward offered the GOP a new set of issues with which to attack the president, as did rumors of domestic

Communist subversion.[152] But Republican attacks on Truman were not entirely political in nature: the party's conservative old guard, in particular, really was infuriated by news of domestic espionage scandals, by the administration's half-hearted support of Chiang Kai-shek, and by the seemingly endless expenses and entanglements of containment.[153] For conservatives such as Robert Taft, the one concern that outweighed all others—particularly in the wake of Truman's Fair Deal proposals—was limiting the role of government inside the United States.[154]

Because they associated containment—via Truman—with new social welfare legislation at home, and because containment involved a massive expansion of the national security state, old guard Republicans were eager to find a low-cost alternative strategy.[155] During 1950–1951, with the Korean War in the background, they came as close as they ever would to offering such an alternative to the public. In a series of publications, addresses, and debates, conservatives spelled out their recommendations for American grand strategy. In effect, Taft and his supporters tried to fuse a strategy of disentanglement with a strategy of rollback. On the one hand, they called for greater reliance on atomic airpower, a reduction in defense spending, the speedy resolution of the Korean conflict, and the avoidance of any new troop commitments in Europe.[156] At the same time, they supported General MacArthur's demands for an expanded war against China, including the blockading of the Chinese coast and the bombing of Manchuria.[157] Popular frustration with the Korean War allowed Republican critics to make considerable headway against the president. In the wake of continued American casualties in Korea, Truman's overall handling of foreign policy met with widespread disapproval.[158] But when it came time to vote on the president's central foreign policy proposals—such as whether to send four more divisions to Europe—even critics like Senator Taft voted in favor.[159] The arguments, and the international pressures in favor of such actions, were simply too strong. Consequently, the administration continued to pursue a policy of limited war in Korea, and global anti-Communist containment worldwide, in spite of Republican attacks. Concerns over limited liability continued, especially among conservatives, but the strategy of containment held.

CONCLUSION

U.S. foreign policy makers had four basic strategic options open to them after 1945: first, a return to strategic disengagement; second, the alternative of rolling back the Soviet Union by military means; third, an explicit sphere-of-influence arrangement with the USSR; and fourth, the containment of Soviet influence worldwide. International conditions at the time ruled out neoisolationism, as well as rollback, but such conditions by themselves cannot explain why U.S. officials ultimately selected containment. From a realist perspective, a sphere-of-influence strategy was feasible and even preferable to containment. Containment was selected not because it was the only strategy that matched international conditions but because it was the only strategy that matched international conditions as well as domestic cultural concerns. American classical liberal assumptions regarding international affairs worked against a pure sphere-of-influence strategy and in favor of containment.

The tradition of limited liability continued to exert pressure on U.S. officials, even after 1945, leading them to select a version of containment that was extremely ambitious but relatively inexpensive—a combination that could not last, and indeed broke down after the outbreak of the Korean War. The Truman administration finally closed the gap between capabilities and commitments by increasing defense spending after 1950. Yet the cost of these expenditures, and the costs of the war in Korea, triggered sharp attacks by conservative Republicans against the whole concept of containment. In the end, containment was not abandoned. But, as always in U.S. grand strategy, a tug of war continued between the stimulus of international pressures, a preference for limited liability, and the desire to remake the international order in America's own image.

Chapter Five

HEGEMONY ON THE CHEAP:

IDEAS AND ALTERNATIVES IN

AMERICAN GRAND STRATEGY, 1992–2000

IMMEDIATELY AFTER THE collapse of the Soviet Union, many foreign policy observers expected to see a dramatic reassessment of America's Cold War commitments overseas. Some experts called for a sweeping retrenchment of America's worldwide strategic commitments. Others called for a reorientation of U.S. foreign policy goals, away from the longstanding aim of promoting a liberal international order, and toward the somewhat more modest task of upholding a balance between the various major powers of Europe and Asia. But whether such experts advocated or feared major changes in America's strategic and diplomatic posture, most of them agreed that such a change was inevitable.

As it turned out, the 1990s witnessed few dramatic changes in America's basic strategic commitments overseas. While the Clinton administration did encourage a modest reduction in military spending from Cold War levels, one of the most striking features of America's national security policy under Clinton was its essential continuity with Cold War assumptions. Some 200,000 troops remained deployed by the United States in Western Europe and Northeast Asia, the United States spent much more on its armed forces than any possible combination of hostile powers, and an historically unprecedented and worldwide array of alliance commitments persisted. If anything, the pace of U.S. military intervention overseas actually increased under Clinton. And all of these strategic commitments were justified, just as they were during the Cold War, by two central claims: first, that the United States is and ought to be the preeminent world power, with significant interests and obligations in every corner of the globe; and second, that the United States has a special responsibility to promote and uphold a liberal international order characterized by free markets and democratic government.

Why the striking continuity with Cold War assumptions? Why not a strategy of retrenchment, or a strategy of balance of power, given the revolutionary geopolitical changes and opportunities following the events of 1989–1991? These are questions that will be addressed in this brief examination of American grand strategy during the Clinton years. The answer to these questions will be found to lie not simply in international pressures but in the lasting power of certain cultural legacies, and in the absence of a number of crucial, contingent conditions that might have permitted a more dramatic reassessment of U.S. strategic commitments and assumptions. Certainly, from a structural realist perspective, a return to isolationism was unlikely given the sheer relative power of the United States. But international conditions cannot explain the particular strategy followed during the 1990s.

As always, given the liberal assumptions of American strategic culture, grand strategies based upon pure realpolitik or balance-of-power assumptions found little favor with U.S. policymakers. And in the absence of any real sense of policy failure, U.S. foreign policy officials were strongly inclined to preserve the internationalist assumptions and commitments of the Cold War era. Hence, because of the legacy of liberal internationalism—and in the seeming absence of any compelling case for change—the Clinton administration embarked upon a national security policy of "engagement and enlargement," which in its essence preserved the basic outline of America's Cold War strategic assumptions and commitments overseas. At the same time, however, Clinton and his advisors tried to pursue this very ambitious foreign policy agenda at minimal cost to the United States. A pervasive concern over limited liability continued to inform American foreign policymaking, especially on questions of military intervention. The result was a paradoxical combination of liberal internationalist goals, pursued worldwide, by strictly limited and often inadequate means.

Alternative Post—Cold War Strategic Ideas

After the collapse of the Soviet Union, the United States could have followed one of a number of grand strategies. While in theory there are probably as many alternative strategic ideas as there are strategists, for our purposes we can simplify the available options into four broad schools of thought.[1] First, there are those who clearly reject the notion of the United States as a world power, with its troops and alliances scattered around the globe, and who favor a withdrawal from strategic commitments incurred as a result of the Cold War. Second, there are those who question the liberal assumptions behind U.S. grand strategy, and who advocate a balance-of-power strategy—an internationalist strategy—but one shorn of globalist and liberalizing ambitions. Third, there are those who favor a strategy of primacy for the United States, one that aggressively promotes both an "Americanized" international order and the worldwide preeminence of the United States. Finally, there are those who advocate a strategy of liberal internationalism, one that promotes a liberal world order through the use of multilateral institutions.

Strategic Disengagement

Advocates of strategic disengagement favor a complete withdrawal from political and military commitments made during the Cold War, and a return to America's interwar policy of "strategic independence" or "hemispheric defense." The essence of this alternative is that the United States abandon its posture of forward deployment in Europe and Asia, that it withdraw from its Cold War alliances and bring its troops home. While this neoisolationist alternative is rarely articulated in mainstream political circles today, it does have a certain appeal to both the left wing of the Democratic Party and the right wing of the Republican Party—that is, to left-liberal progressives as well as conservative nationalists.[2] Indeed, the two leading third-party candidates of the 2000 presidential election—Ralph Nader and Pat Buchanan—could both be said to advocate strategic disengagement.[3] The most thoughtful advocates of strategic disengagement, however, have not come from the political arena, but from a small group of foreign policy commentators like Eric Nordlinger, Christopher Layne, Ted Galen Carpenter, Daryl Press, and Eugene Gholz.[4]

Advocates of strategic disengagement argue that the collapse of the Soviet Union has removed any lingering necessity for the United States to maintain a vast assortment of military commitments overseas. Since these commitments were justified by referring to the Soviet threat, they are no longer relevant or necessary. As Eugene Gholz puts it, "Now that the Cold War is over, George McGovern is right."[5] The United States itself is in a position of unparalleled strength and security. No threat comparable to Hitler's Germany or Stalin's Russia looms on the horizon. Economic interdependence and democratization have encouraged a deep and growing peace in most of Europe and much of Asia. International peace and prosperity no longer depend, if they ever did, on a U.S. military presence overseas.[6] This overseas presence, moreover, is a heavy burden on the United States, a distraction from domestic concerns. It prevents allies such as Germany and Japan from carrying a fair share of their own defense. It is also a positive danger, in the sense that Americans constantly risk being entangled in local conflicts of little concrete interest.[7] In a word, according to neoisolationists, no pressing need exists to justify the maintenance of America's Cold War military commitments. On the contrary, these commitments have become a real danger to America's domestic welfare.

The direct implications of these arguments is that the United States should withdraw from its European and Asian alliances, bring the vast majority of U.S. forces home from their stations overseas, abstain from military adventures abroad, and reduce military spending.[8] Neoisolationists agree that defense spending should be cut dramatically—by approximately 50 percent from Cold War levels.[9] The only military force that neoisolationists favor is one capable of protecting core U.S. interests in the Western Hemisphere, along with a minimal capacity for military intervention abroad. Consequently, under a strategy of disengagement, the United States would not require much more than a million soldiers, sailors, airmen, and marines.[10] This standing force would be heavily weighted toward naval and air power, and supported by a small nuclear arsenal. Even these reduced forces would leave the United States invulnerable to attack. And with more resources to direct inward, and less risk of military entanglement, the United States would actually be stronger, and more secure, as well as truer to its own democratic traditions.[11]

These arguments receive little support in elite circles, and are considered beyond the fringe of mainstream political discourse.[12] But they do have a certain resonance with many Americans. One recent study of public opinion found that 41 percent of the American public believes that the United States should "mind its own business" when it comes to world affairs.[13] Mass public opinion tends to be less interventionist than are elite opinion leaders; this is especially true of voters who are less wealthy or less educated.[14] So while there is hardly a grassroots demand for strategic disengagement at present, the latent support for such a strategy is always there, particularly among nationalists and progressives.

Balance of Power

The second major strategic alternative for the United States since the end of the Cold War has been to abandon what Walter McDougall calls "global meliorism," and to simply support a geopolitical balance between the major powers.[15] Henry Kissinger has been the leading advocate of this alternative, but a number of foreign policy commentators with realist inclinations have voiced a similar approach—commentators like James Schlesinger, Alan Tonelson, James Kurth, and Sam Huntington.[16] These balance-of-power advocates seek to preserve U.S. alliance commitments to Europe and Asia. They also favor the continued deployment of U.S. troops to these critical regions. Like their liberal internationalist counterparts, they view these strategic commitments as an insurance policy that dampens security competition and undergirds stability overseas. Unlike liberal internationalists, however, they define American interests, and the threats to those interests, in strictly realist terms.

Balance-of-power realists do not view the promotion of a liberal world order, characterized by the reproduction of market democracies overseas, as a central U.S. national security interest. They do not expect the incidence of international conflict to disappear as a result of institutions, democratization, and interdependence. Rather, they anticipate continued competition between the major powers of the world. Nor do they view U.S. interests as identical with those of other powers.[17] For this reason, the desire to remake the world in America's own image is viewed by balance-of-power realists as a distraction at best, and as self-defeating at worst. Ideological goals such as democratization, human rights, and collective security are downplayed in favor of concrete economic, strategic, and political interests.

Rather than attempting to reshape the international system in a profoundly liberal direction, realists such as Kissinger stress the need to preserve a functioning equilibrium between the great powers of Europe and Asia. Each power is viewed as having its own autonomy, its own legitimate interests, and its own sphere of influence. So while the United States remains, in the realist vision, first among equals, it does not attempt to exercise any sort of worldwide hegemony over the other major powers, or impose its own political system upon them.[18] Rather, it simply acts to maintain a balance among these other powers while preserving decent relations with each one of them.[19]

In practical terms, this means that the United States would abstain from making the domestic political complexion of other countries a subject of foreign policy.[20] Humanitarian interventions such as those in Bosnia and Kosovo would be avoided. Russia would no longer be lectured on the need for market reform. China would no longer be hectored on its human rights abuses. The democratization of those two countries would no longer be central to Sino-American and Russo-American relations. Nor would the United States define its international enemies as "rogue states," in need of democratic revolution or conversion. Rather, Washington would protect its vital interests overseas while recognizing the inevitability of both conflict and diplomacy with countries whose self-defined interests run counter to America's own.

By abstaining from interference in peripheral civil wars, and by playing down its pretensions as a moral guide for other nations, realists expect that the United States would be able to avoid costly commitments and controversies in areas of little concrete interest. The United States would thus avoid strategic overextension. At the same time, however, realists advocate a vigorous defense of U.S. interests in those areas and on those subjects that *are* deemed vital.[21] So in terms of their core strategic commitments to peace and security in Western Europe, Northeast Asia, and the Persian Gulf, balance-of-power realists would be just as engaged as any internationalist.

To sum up: a balance-of-power strategy would redefine U.S. national security interests so as to avoid interference in the domestic affairs of other countries. Democratization and human rights would no longer be a criterion for economic aid, diplomatic relations, and/or military intervention. As a result, U.S. grand strategy would be more selective in choosing those cases where military force was actually required. But the United States would not retreat into a Fortress America strategy. The balance of power in Europe and Asia would be carefully managed and monitored, and the central strategic commitments, alliances, and forward deployments of the Cold War era would be energetically upheld.

Primacy

The third alternative open to the United States since the end of the Cold War has been to pursue a strategy of primacy, which would entail acting aggressively to maintain America's political and military predominance in the world while preempting any conceivable challenges to a U.S.-led international order. The goal of this strategy, however, is not only U.S. dominance, but an "Americanized" international order, characterized by an expanding zone of market-oriented democracies—what Robert Kagan and William Kristol call a "benevolent global hegemony."[22] Primacy is therefore an internationalist strategy with a very strong dose of realism. While de facto support for a strategy of primacy comes from a wide variety of sources, the most pointed and explicit calls for such an approach have come from a group of neoconservative foreign policy commentators, including writers, journalists, and former government officials like Kagan, Kristol, Charles Krauthammer, Richard Perle, Joshua Muravchik, Zalmay Khalilzad, Elliot Abrams, and Paul Wolfowitz.[23]

Primacists argue that in spite of the collapse of the USSR, the international system remains a very dangerous place, characterized by multiple threats to American security and international stability. The most worrying of these threats include: (1) terrorism; (2) the proliferation of weapons of mass destruction; (3) revisionist "rogue states"; and (4) the development of any hostile great power or "peer competitor," such as China, which might seek to challenge American interests overseas.[24] More subtle, but equally serious, is the danger that the entire international order might begin to erode or fall apart through a lack of strong leadership on the part of the United States.[25] Primacists fear that in some ways the world is actually more unstable since the fall of the Soviet Union than it was during the Cold War. In the words of Clinton's director of central intelligence, James Woolsey, the United States has "slain a large dragon" only to discover "a jungle filled with a bewildering variety of poisonous snakes."[26] At the same time, advocates of primacy believe that the United States has the ability to meet all of these threats, and to sustain a U.S.-led international order, because of America's unparalleled political, military, economic, and ideological power.[27] For primacists, the problem is not so much a dearth of national resources as a lack of political will in mobilizing those resources to meet both the challenges and the opportunities of what Charles Krauthammer calls "the unipolar moment."[28]

A number of specific policy recommendations follow from these premises. First, primacists call for the containment of China, while pushing for the liberalization of that country's political and economic system. They also suggest supporting Taiwan, and refocusing America's East Asian policy on its traditional alliances with South Korea and Japan, while maintaining a strong military presence in the region.[29] Second, primacists call for containing Russia, or at least preventing the creation of a Russian sphere of influence in the former Soviet Union, while maintaining businesslike relations with Moscow.[30] Third, primacists advocate the expansion of NATO and the maintenance of America's forward presence in Europe. They are highly skeptical of any movement toward European unification—such as an independent defense identity—that might undermine America's role as a European power.[31] Fourth, primacists call (and have long called) for aggressive policies of counterproliferation toward "rogue states" like Iran, Iraq, and North Korea—including, if necessary, the use of preventive military strikes against nascent weapons-of-mass-destruction (WMD) capabilities in those countries. The advocates of primacy believe that neither containment nor engagement constitute desirable strategies in relation to rogue states; in language reminiscent of Taft-era conservatives, they call for policies of "regime change."[32]

Primacists suggest that the United States should be more, not less, willing to intervene militarily in cases of aggression or humanitarian disaster in semiperipheral regions, such as the Balkans. They make this argument both because they believe that such cases are intrinsically important, for humanitarian or idealistic reasons, and because such situations test the credibility of America's general claims to world leadership.[33] And in order to support this broad conception of American national interests, strategists of primacy call for major increases in defense spending across the board, including the construction of a national missile defense system. Estimates during the mid-1990s were that a strategy of primacy would require anywhere from $60 to $100 billion more in defense expenditures each year.[34] Finally, primacists do not expect international regimes or organizations to be of much help in promoting international order, or in sustaining America's worldwide interests. For this reason they tend to resist treaties, covenants, or institutions that limit American autonomy on matters of national security.[35]

Primacists are hawkish and hard-line, with a keen appreciation for the role of power, force, conflict, and national self-interest in international relations; they share this appreciation with balance-of-power realists. But they are distinct from such realists in two important ways. First, they are more aggressive in terms of the policies and strategies they advocate.[36] Like leading members of the Truman administration, they seek not a "balance" of power, but a preponderance of power on the part of the United States and its close allies. Continued U.S. predominance over other potential great powers is their goal.[37] Second, primacists are more idealistic than balance-of-power realists. They genuinely believe that America's democratic and free market values can be promoted successfully worldwide. And they believe that this is not only in the interests of the United States—although it certainly is that—but also in the interests of the international community as a whole.[38] In this sense, they are as much Wilsonian internationalists as they are realists.

Liberal Internationalism

The final alternative open to the United States since 1992 has been to pursue a strategy of liberal internationalism. Liberal internationalist authors in the post–Cold War era have included former officials as well as scholars, among them Graham Allison, David Callahan, John Ikenberry, Joseph Nye, and John Ruggie.[39] Like primacists, liberal internationalists favor the promotion of an "Americanized" world order, characterized by the spread of democratic governments and open markets. Unlike primacists, however, liberal internationalists believe that a strong set of multilateral institutions—rather than America's military predominance—is really the key to creating and sustaining a more friendly and democratic world order. Contemporary liberal internationalism is therefore heavily influenced by progressive as well as internationalist traditions in American strategic culture.

Liberal internationalists believe that the nature of world politics has changed fundamentally in recent decades. A new set of global issues has become more important and more pressing than the traditional balance-of-power preoccupation of previous eras. This new set of issues includes: the threat of widespread environmental degradation, population growth and migration, international economic development, world poverty, ethnic conflict, human rights violations, democratization, globalization, terrorism, and the proliferation of WMD.[40] On balance, these are issues over which common interests between nations exist. And for the most part, they cannot be addressed in any useful way by the exercise or the threat of force. Nor can they be addressed by individual nation-states, alone, however powerful.[41]

According to liberals, the best way to address these new issues is to promote international cooperation and coordination through a world-wide network of multilateral institutions. Such multilateral institutions and practices will promote world order. They will make American power less alarming to others.[42] They will secure U.S. engagement in the world.[43] And they will promote America's own self-interest—its influence, security, and prosperity—in a manner that is far-sighted and enlightened rather than confrontational or threatening. Liberals therefore suggest that the United States act multilaterally whenever possible, and in so doing observe a certain self-restraint in the exercise of power.[44]

In the post–Cold War era, liberals have often favored military intervention in civil conflicts or peripheral regions for purely humanitarian reasons, although again, they tend to prefer that such actions be taken multilaterally.[45] In 1992, for example, liberal internationalists were at the forefront in calling for U.S. intervention in both Bosnia and Somalia: in the former case, to stop "ethnic cleansing," and in the latter, to address widespread starvation.[46] Liberals have also been enthusiastic regarding the prospects for UN and/or U.S. peacekeeping missions. But apart from this affection for humanitarian intervention, liberal internationalists tend to downplay the importance of military power as a central tool of American grand strategy. Instead, they emphasize the importance of nonmilitary policy instruments, and the rising significance of "soft power," as exercised through diplomacy, foreign aid, international organizations, economic dynamism, and cultural appeal.[47] Most liberal internationalists believe that American grand strategy during the Cold War was overly militarized, at great cost to the United States. In the early 1990s, many of them went on record calling for deep cuts in defense spending.[48] Certainly, mainstream liberal internationalists do not believe that the United States can simply disarm and walk away from its strategic commitments abroad. But they place great emphasis on nonmilitary instruments of U.S. power, and they are optimistic that the significance of military power in world politics is in long-term decline.

Arms control is a key element in the liberal internationalist approach to grand strategy.[49] Liberals advocate the preservation and strengthening of international nonproliferation regimes.[50] They call for increased transparency in the production, sale, and deployment of weapons. They favor "confidence and security-building measures," (CSBMs), along with new, stringent verification procedures surrounding arms control agreements in order to reduce the chances of misperception between national armed forces. Together, these commitments and restraints are said to amount to a new paradigm, one of "cooperative security," whereby each nation's safety is assured in a manner that does not threaten that of others.[51] Europe is often mentioned as a regional model for the benefits and possibilities of such an approach. As Ashton Carter and William Perry put it, nicely summarizing the liberal internationalist view, cooperative security through arms control entails "a commitment to regulate the size, technical composition, investment patterns, and operational practices of all military forces by mutual consent for mutual benefit."[52] Again, multilateral institutions are seen as a way of dampening down security competition, to the benefit of both the United States and the international community as a whole.

Liberal internationalists favor the promotion of democracy and human rights worldwide, and they suggest that the United States do so with greater consistency than has often been the case.[53] Pressure should be applied to allies as well as adversaries, great powers as well as small ones. In the case of both Russia and China, liberals do not view human rights violations as purely internal matters. They view them as necessary and legitimate issues for the United States to raise in its pursuit of a more progressive world order. Liberals therefore put democratic reform at the top of their foreign policy agenda in relation to Russia and China, as well as other authoritarian or semidemocratic countries. In the long run, liberals do not believe that there can be peace or stability in a world characterized by autocratic or dictatorial regimes. Conversely, in a world dominated by democracies, liberals expect cooperation and nonviolence to be the norm.[54] For the most part, liberals favor peaceful methods of democracy promotion, by relying on tools like economic sanctions, diplomatic pressure, foreign aid, and international organizations. But just as many liberals are willing to consider military intervention abroad for humanitarian reasons, so, too, are the more hawkish among them willing to consider intervention for reasons of democracy promotion.

To an even greater extent than with other schools of thought, liberal internationalists are divided amongst themselves. The question that causes greatest division relates to the use of force in American grand strategy. Some liberal internationalists are quite sanguine about military intervention in pursuit of their agenda. They recognize the persistent importance of military power in world affairs, and call for the continuation of America's forward strategic presence abroad.[55] Because they favor a liberalized, or "Americanized," international order, supported by U.S. military power, such liberals have a great deal in common with primacists. This group has been in the ascendancy within the Democratic Party since the end of the Cold War, at least at the elite level. Other liberal internationalists, in the progressive tradition of Hiram Johnson and Henry Wallace, are convinced that the United States should truly demilitarize its presence overseas, cut defense spending still further, and avoid the use of force in all but the most extreme cases.[56] For all practical purposes, such liberals have much in common with isolationists. The current differences between liberals, of course, date back to the division between hawks and doves as a result of the war in Vietnam.[57] Liberals are still divided amongst themselves over how hawkish they should be on questions of national security. But they all agree on the need for multilateralism; they all agree that soft power is becoming more important; and they all agree that the nature of international relations has changed dramatically enough in recent years to outmode any sort of traditional balance-of-power, isolationist, or unilateralist approach to the world.[58] This is what sets them apart from the other three schools of thought.

REALISM AND INTERNATIONAL CONDITIONS

To what extent do international conditions account for the particular strategy actually chosen by the Clinton administration? How would structural realists explain post–Cold War American grand strategy? In realist terms, the end of the Cold War was a revolutionary change—the sort of change usually associated with the aftermath of a major war. The central feature of that change was the collapse of a previously bipolar international system. But in such circumstances it is not entirely obvious what sort of foreign policy behavior realists would expect from the world's only remaining superpower. In the early 1990s, realists did not offer clear predictions regarding the probable course of post–Cold War U.S. foreign policy. Instead, they offered predictions regarding systemic outcomes. Authors like Kenneth Waltz and John Mearsheimer, in particular, predicted that the international system would evolve in a multipolar direction, and that previously quiescent powers, such as Germany and Japan, would begin to assert themselves on political and strategic, as well as economic, matters.[59] The implicit prescription was that the United States accept the inevitable trend toward multipolarity and scale back somewhat on its global role.[60] In recent years, Mearsheimer has come out with a much more explicit prediction that the United States will soon disengage strategically from Europe and Northeast Asia.[61] But Mearsheimer's prediction is based in large part upon a questionable premise: that the "stopping power of water" prevents the United States from being able to aspire to any sort of hegemonic role outside the Western Hemisphere.[62] His prediction is all the more curious, since he argues elsewhere in the same book that all major powers try consistently to maximize their relative power in the world at the expense of potential rivals.[63] This hardly seems to lead to the conclusion that the United States will soon disengage strategically from Europe and Northeast Asia.

Kenneth Waltz, for his part, has long insisted that structural realism cannot explain or predict foreign policy behavior.[64] Yet he seems willing to make implicit predictions regarding the future foreign policies of Germany and Japan when he suggests that they will soon assert their strategic independence from the United States.[65] Certainly, Waltz is right to say that international pressures are simply that—pressures—rather than determinate causes. As he points out, states are free to ignore such pressures.[66] This is all the more true of a country as powerful as the United States is today: free to ignore systemic imperatives, free to act in a capricious, and even a "foolish," manner.[67] But Waltz is actually quite vague as to what sort of grand strategy a realist would expect from the world's only superpower. He states that isolationism is "impossible" for the United States in the current international system. He also obviously believes that the United States would be well served by abandoning its globalist pretensions, and by acting with greater "forbearance" internationally. But then he adds that he "would not bet on it."[68] What we are left with, from Waltz, is the sense that the United States *ought* to avoid isolationist, primacist, or liberal internationalist grand strategies, without any *predictive* sense of whether it will actually do so. This unwillingness to offer any sort of clear foreign policy predictions only lends credence to the argument, common among realism's critics, that international pressures are highly indeterminate, and that, consequently, realism explains nothing at all. Realists can do better than this. A more useful and convincing approach—a neoclassical realist approach—would be to begin by admitting that international conditions allow states varying degrees of latitude, but that, nevertheless, we can and should form clear hypotheses regarding the magnitude and direction of international pressures on individual states.

The basic problem with the arguments of both Waltz and Mearsheimer, in terms of their actual understanding of world politics today, is that neither allows for a state that truly dominates the international system, nor for the possibility of "unipolarity" or "hegemony" as anything other than: (1) an unattainable state of global empire (for Mearsheimer), or (2) a very fleeting and unstable condition (for Waltz).[69] But this does not necessarily mean that realism itself is invalid. There is in fact a long tradition of realist thought that recognizes that hegemonic international systems have been at least as common, historically speaking, as balance-of-power systems.[70] Relative to other countries, the United States is so dominant today that balance-of-power theory may have actually become a hindrance to understanding the current world order.[71] Just to note a few indicators: In terms of defense expenditures, the United States spends more than all of its potential adversaries, as well as all of its major allies, combined.[72] In particular, America's lead in precision weaponry over any potential rival is unquestioned. And a vast system of worldwide bases and alliances serves to magnify American military power. In terms of economic capabilities, the imbalance of power is less stark, but the United

States still possesses a gross national product at least twice that of Japan or China, its closest rivals.[73] Politically, the United States possesses unmatched influence as the only power with interests and reach in every part of the globe. The international institutions that shape political and economic affairs in the world today were created largely by the United States, to serve U.S. interests, as they continue to do. And the United States exercises influence abroad not only through these institutions, but through its universalistic ideals and popular culture, and through the undoubted recognition by other countries that the United States is, for better or worse, the world's preponderant power.[74] Many Americans like to play down the predominance of the United States in the current international system, but America's allies and adversaries both know that the United States is truly a hegemon.

If we take the current distribution of power in the international system as our starting point, and recognize that U.S. capabilities are truly unmatched, then we reach a somewhat different set of predictions from those offered by realists such as Waltz and Mearsheimer. For one thing, we would not necessarily expect to see other states balancing against the United States all that vigorously, since such balancing may simply be beyond their capabilities; the United States may be so powerful that the costs of balancing against it tend to outweigh the benefits.[75] More to the point, the prediction in terms of U.S. foreign policy behavior would clearly be to expect no disengagement from America's international role. In the words of Michael Mastanduno: "According to realist logic, any great power should prefer to be a unipolar power, regardless of whether or not it possesses expansionist ambitions. For the state at the top, unipolarity is preferable to being a great power facing either the concentrated hostility and threat of a bipolar world, or the uncertainty and risk of miscalculation inherent in a multipolar world."[76]

Realists believe that the definition of "security" tends to flow from the amount of power that a given state possesses. A country as powerful as the United States can afford to define its interests, and its security, in very broad terms. It can afford to intervene militarily against distant, potential dangers. It can afford to have a low tolerance for external threats.[77] There are of course a number of ways in which hegemonic powers can respond to threats and challenges. They can retreat in the face of danger, or appease potential challengers. But as Robert Gilpin points out, hegemonic powers seldom act in this way unless they have to. Their preference, for the most part, is to weaken potential rivals, preempt potential threats, and expand their sphere of influence even further, in order to "eliminate the source of the problem."[78] Again, this is not a question of whether dominant states *should* act in this way. It is, rather, a question of what a structural realist would expect or *predict*. Surely no realist would actually expect any nation to voluntarily relinquish its status as the world's preeminent political and military power. On the contrary, from a realist perspective, it seems reasonable to predict that the United States would try to prolong the unipolar moment for as long as possible.[79] In this sense, realists should not have expected the United States to disengage from Europe and Asia in the wake of the Soviet Union's collapse.

Still, realists face a puzzle, and a problem, in explaining post–Cold War U.S. grand strategy. Given that the United States was not about to retreat into a new Fortress America, that still left three broad strategic alternatives. The United States could have pursued a strategy of primacy, a strategy of liberal internationalism, or a more modest balance-of-power strategy. In other words, the United States could have acted in precisely the way that realists themselves actually favor—that is, by abandoning any attempt to promote a liberal world order. Yet such a course was generally rejected by U.S. policymakers. There is simply no basis within conventional structural realist theory—which looks to international systemic pressures first and foremost—to explain the rejection of a balance-of-power strategy on the part of the United States. International pressures cannot explain that policy choice. Realists might have expected the rejection of neoisolationism after the end of the Cold War; they cannot explain the adoption of any distinctly liberal grand strategy on the part of the United States without leaving realist explanatory categories behind.

Liberalism, Limited Liability, and American Grand Strategy Under Clinton

The end of the Cold War presented U.S. foreign policymakers with a dramatically changed international environment. The opportunity had finally arisen for truly sweeping changes in America's strategic posture overseas. Analogies were drawn to similar moments after the World Wars. But this third potential turning point in U.S. grand strategy had one great difference from 1918–1921 and 1945–1951. In this case, unlike the prior two, there was no sense of disaster, no sense that previous policies had failed to keep America prosperous and secure. Since the Cold War had ended—successfully—without the occurrence of a general war, Americans did not really feel the need to reassess the policies that had preceded the events of 1989–1991. On the contrary, these events were generally taken to confirm the wisdom of the long-term policy of containment, and of the liberal internationalist and globalist assumptions that surrounded it. Since Americans experienced no adverse effects from the end of the Cold War, it failed to act as a shock to policymakers. Consequently, in spite of radical changes in the international system, the premises of both liberal internationalism and primacy, as viable strategies, were never really called into question. On the contrary, the premises of these two strategies were reinforced. At the same time, however, American strategic behavior continued to be influenced, to an inordinate extent, by the desire to maintain limited liability in strategic affairs. The tension between these two longstanding features of U.S. strategic culture—liberalism, on the one hand, and limited liability, on the other—continued to create contradictions and shape U.S. grand strategy under the Clinton administration.

Liberal Internationalism under Clinton

The persistent power of liberal internationalist ideas was revealed in the abortive debate over U.S. foreign policy in the early 1990s, and in the words and actions of the first real post–Cold War presidency. Initially, it seemed as though America's global strategic commitments might be radically reduced. In 1991–1992, for example, there was considerable pressure on the Bush administration to decrease spending on defense. A number of leading commissions called for significant cuts in military expenditures, and these calls were reflected in both public opinion polls and in pressure from Congress.[80] The sense among many elite opinion leaders was that the United States had become "overextended" internationally, and that new geopolitical circumstances offered a chance to redirect attention toward domestic concerns.[81] The Democratic nominee for president in 1992, Bill Clinton, made exactly this case for a shift toward domestic priorities. Yet at the very same time, Clinton and his supporters embraced the argument that the United States ought to be, if anything, *more* willing to intervene overseas on questions of democracy and human rights.[82]

During the 1992 presidential campaign, for example, Clinton criticized the Bush administration for its reluctance to punish Serbian aggression in Bosnia. "President Bush's policy towards the former Yugoslavia," claimed Clinton, "mirrors his indifference to the massacre at Tiananmen Square. . . . Once again, the administration is turning its back on violations of basic human rights and our own democratic values."[83] Candidate Clinton made similar statements with regard to other cases of humanitarian concern, arguing that Bush was violating American "values" by turning back Haitian refugees, and by failing to act in the face of widespread starvation in Somalia.[84] Clinton's statements reflected the new optimism of the immediate post–Cold War era, especially on the Left. The feeling among leading Democrats was that the Soviet Union's demise presented the opportunity for the United States to promote liberal goals internationally with more energy and consistency than had been possible during the Cold War.[85] Most such Democrats did not question the fundamental premises of liberal internationalism, inherited and passed down from one administration to the next since the 1940s. Certainly, Clinton did not question these premises. Far from rejecting liberal internationalist assumptions, he and his supporters hoped to renew them, albeit at somewhat less cost to Americans in military spending.

It is often suggested that the Clinton administration had no foreign policy design at all, and that, in any case, political and international conditions made any such design extremely unlikely after the fall of the USSR. It is certainly true that Clinton showed an unusual lack of interest in foreign policy issues, particularly national security issues, early in his administration.[86] The division of powers in the American political system, together with the byzantine structure of the national security bureaucracy, always complicates U.S. strategic planning, and the absence of any strong sense of external threat during the Clinton years made it unusually difficult to formulate and execute a coherent grand strategy.[87] Nevertheless, the foreign policymakers of any major power are always forced by necessity to make strategic decisions, even in times of relative peace and quiet, and these decisions are informed by underlying assumptions that delimit the range of acceptable policy alternatives. This was no less true under Clinton than under any previous U.S. president.

Clinton's national security team initially included Warren Christopher at the State Department; Anthony Lake, as national security advisor; Madeleine Albright, as ambassador to the United Nations; Les Aspin at the Pentagon; and Al Gore as vice-president. Important figures such as Strobe Talbott, Joseph Nye, Richard Holbrooke, and William Perry were also brought into the administration. Many of these officials had served under President Jimmy Carter in the late 1970s. Like Carter, a significant number of them—including the president himself—were torn between their instinctive aversion to the use of force, their desire to promote a more liberal international order, and their concern not to seem weak on national security issues.[88]

Important differences existed within the administration. Warren Christopher, for example, was significantly less hawkish than Madeleine Albright on questions of intervention.[89] But Clinton and his leading advisors did share a relatively coherent set of foreign policy assumptions. As gathered from their public statements, these assumptions were as follows:

First, the administration believed that the post–Cold War world would be dominated by nontraditional threats to both national and global security. As Tony Lake put it, "old threats like ethnic and religious violence have taken on new and dangerous dimensions. And no one is immune to a host of equal opportunity destroyers: the spread of weapons of mass destruction, terrorism, organized crime, drug trafficking, and environmental degradation. . . . Together, they have the potential to cause terrible chaos around the world and in our own society."[90] Traditional balance-of-power concerns would no longer be particularly important in the new international order.

Second, Clinton and his advisors argued that the best way to address these new threats would be to act through multilateral institutions. A multilateral approach was believed necessary given the distinctive nature of the new security challenges. It was also expected to encourage burden sharing between the United States and its allies.[91] One central consequence—at least initially—was that U.S. military interventions overseas would occur under the rubric of institutions like the United Nations. But the administration's preference for institution building was also evident in its broad commitment to new multilateral economic arrangements such as NAFTA (the North American Free Trade Agreement), APEC (Asia-Pacific Economic Cooperation), and the WTO (World Trade Organization).[92]

The third assumption was that the United States would have to be more willing than ever before to intervene politically and even militarily in cases of civil war or civil disorder for what were largely humanitarian reasons: to end mass starvation, to stop "ethnic cleansing," and so on. To that end, nontraditional missions of peacekeeping, peacemaking, humanitarian intervention, and nation building were embraced as both legitimate and necessary. As Under Secretary of Defense, Frank Wisner, said in 1993, peacekeeping was to lie "at the core" of the Defense Department's activities in the post–Cold War world.[93] The preoccupation with internal, humanitarian conditions in peripheral countries was both novel and striking. And again, humanitarian interventions were to occur, if at all possible, through international institutions: an approach that Madeleine Albright described as "assertive multilateralism."[94]

Fourth, the Clinton administration stressed the heightened importance of globalization, foreign economic policy, and economic "competitiveness" in the new international order. One might even say that the Clinton team believed that "geoeconomics" had replaced "geopolitics" as the driving force behind international relations. Clinton seems to have been convinced early on that an expansive, internationalist foreign policy could help reverse U.S. economic decline by opening up new opportunities for trade and investment.[95] In this sense, as Clinton himself suggested repeatedly, domestic economic concerns tended to trump and supplant security concerns in the administration's hierarchy of priorities.[96]

Fifth, the United States was to actively promote an international order characterized by free trade, open markets, democratic governments, non-aggression, and respect for human rights. It was assumed that such a democratic and interdependent world order would encourage an upward spiral of international peace and prosperity, allowing the United States to de-emphasize military capabilities as the primary source of American power. It was also assumed that an increasingly liberal world order would be in America's best interest in that the United States would be safer, more prosperous, and more powerful as a result.[97] As the White House put it in *A National Security Strategy for a New Century*, released in May 1997:

> In designing our strategy, we recognize that the spread of democracy supports American values and enhances both our security and prosperity. Democratic governments are more likely to cooperate with each other against common threats and to encourage free and open trade and economic development—and less likely to wage war or abuse the rights of their people. Hence, the trend towards democracy and free markets throughout the world advances American interests.[98]

A crucial implication of this assumption was that undemocratic regimes were, by their very nature, a standing threat to America's interests, as well as a threat to international order. As Clinton's first national security advisor, Anthony Lake, put it in 1993: "our own security is shaped by the character of foreign regimes."[99] This was a classically liberal assumption—indeed, a classically American assumption—and it was central to the thinking of the Clinton administration.

These five assumptions can all be categorized as entirely consistent with a strategy of liberal internationalism. But there was also another set of assumptions articulated by the Clinton foreign policy team—assumptions that sound much more consistent with a strategy of primacy, or at least a hawkish version of liberal internationalism.

First, the United States was viewed by Clinton and his advisors as the "dominant power" in the world, the "indispensable nation," with a unique obligation to uphold international order through "global leadership."[100] While Clinton officials did not use the phrase "hegemonic stability," this was clearly the sort of stabilizing role that the United States was expected to play.

Second, the United States was to maintain a diplomatic-strategic posture of forward defense in Europe and Asia. This meant that the core alliances and troop deployments of the Cold War—era were preserved intact. It was assumed that these alliances and deployments would promote stability, deter aggression, stifle local conflicts, bolster regional balances of power, reassure allies, and facilitate military action when necessary.[101]

Third, the United States was to remain the "world's only military superpower."[102] It was to maintain military forces of global scope and reach, by far the most expensive and powerful armed forces of any in the world. Again, the goal was not a balance in terms of military capabilities, but clear military superiority over any potential adversary.

Two further and final assumptions were consistent with liberal internationalism, as well as with a strategy of primacy. The first of these was that threats are interdependent, and peace indivisible. In other words, while an armed conflict in some small, distant locale might have seemed peripheral, such conflict could have spread to places of great intrinsic value, threatening the peace and stability of countries that were of truly vital interest to the United States. In essence, this was an updated version of the Cold War "domino theory," somewhat discredited by America's experience in Vietnam but never fully abandoned.

Finally, U.S. national security policy under Clinton was informed by crucial lessons drawn from the history of the twentieth century. The primary lesson was that U.S. isolationism in the 1930s permitted the spread of fascism, the Depression, and World War Two, while American internationalism since the 1940s has preserved peace, stability, prosperity, and freedom. As Clinton's first Secretary of State, Warren Christopher, put it in 1995: "the imperative of American leadership . . . is the central lesson of this century."[103] In this sense, the case for "global leadership," forward defense, a powerful armed forces, the promotion of a liberal international order, and the indivisibility of peace and stability was bolstered by the argument that these things have historically been linked to success, while their absence has been linked with failure.

On balance, looking at the stated goals and assumptions of the Clinton foreign policy team, it seems fair to say that they were those of liberal internationalism, with a strong dose of primacy.[104] Clearly, Clinton and his advisors rejected a strategy of isolationism. And by placing such emphasis on the internal character of states, on multilateralism, on nontraditional security issues, on humanitarian intervention, and the promotion of a liberal world order, they also rejected balance-of-power realism. The combination of primacy and liberal internationalism is harder to disentangle. Clinton rejected a "dovish" liberal internationalism, which would have essentially abandoned America's forward strategic presence in the world. At the same time, the assumptions behind U.S. grand strategy under Clinton were "liberal" enough to distinguish it from the kind of approach that a true primacist would have favored.

The internationalist assumptions of the Clinton foreign policy team had been explicitly articulated over the course of the 1992 election campaign, so that observers could be in little doubt as to the basic intentions of the new administration. Indeed, Clinton made it clear during that campaign that he, as president, would maintain America's position of world leadership, preserve its basic strategic commitments overseas, and bring renewed effort to the promotion of liberal goals worldwide. As he put it in his remarks to the Foreign Policy Association on April 1, 1992: "I believe it is time for America to lead a global alliance for democracy as united and steadfast as the global alliance that defeated communism."[105] At the same time, he promised during the course of that campaign to place new emphasis on domestic concerns, nonmilitary dimensions of power, foreign economic policy, multilateral institutions, and humanitarian goals.

Clinton's advocacy of a relatively hawkish liberal internationalism seems to have been motivated both by genuine conviction and the anticipation of political reward. Certainly, it was his judgment that no Democrat could win back the White House without projecting a reliable image on national security policy. In practice, this meant abandoning any sort of 1970s left-liberal argument that the United States could safely withdraw from its worldwide alliance commitments.[106] As David Halberstam writes,

> The Clinton people studied the Bush record and saw . . . that he was most vulnerable on Bosnia, part of the old Yugoslavia, where the world was watching the beginning of what would become a human catastrophe. They would hit Bush hard on Bosnia and on China, where there were also human rights violations. That would be tailor-made, they believed, to put Bush on the defensive and show that they were tougher than the Democrats who had run in recent years. Their words on Bosnia would also show that Democrats need not be wimps.[107]

The very fact that Clinton felt compelled to campaign as a firm "internationalist" revealed the persistent power of anti-isolationist foreign policy assumptions, not only among elite opinion-makers but also among public opinion in general. Moreover, in attacking Bush's policies toward China, Haiti, Bosnia, and Somalia as insufficiently true to American ideals, and in arguing for the expansion of democracy internationally, Clinton demonstrated the continuing impact of liberal ideas on U.S. foreign policy debates. It seems unlikely that as skillful and flexible a politician as Clinton would have taken these positions had he not known that they could pay political dividends. Still, there is no reason to doubt that Clinton himself was actually a convinced internationalist, particularly on economic issues of trade and globalization. The legacy of liberal internationalism and American primacy clearly shaped his thinking on national security policy, just as it shaped the thinking of his constituents, and this led him to occasionally take some surprising political risks.

Clinton's embrace of the post–World War Two internationalist legacy had the incidental effect of stifling any fundamental debate over U.S. foreign policy in the immediate post–Cold war era. Since the nominees of both major parties in 1992 were staunch internationalists, the major disagreements between them were tactical, with Clinton positioned as more of a liberal and Bush as more of a realist. This was a fair reflection of elite opinion, which was characterized after 1991 by broad, bipartisan agreement on the need for U.S. "global leadership." The only major political figure to question this consensus, and to offer a radically different alternative, was the conservative nationalist Pat Buchanan. Challenging Bush for the Republican nomination in 1992, Buchanan advocated a return to isolationism.[108] But the extreme conservatism of his domestic political views, and the difficulty of challenging an incumbent president from within the same party—together with the limited appeal of the neoisolationist position—undermined Buchanan's candidacy and ensured his defeat. No major elected official in either party was about to seriously question America's purported mission of promoting democratization, open markets, and human rights overseas. Consequently, the 1992 election campaign only served to cement the internationalist foreign policy consensus among the leadership of both major parties. And in the absence of serious division over national security policy among elite opinion, the public was unlikely to rebel.[109]

Once in office, and in spite of his relative disinterest in foreign policy, Clinton played an important role in building and maintaining domestic support for a strategy of "engagement and enlargement." This sometimes entailed taking genuine political gambles, particularly on questions of military intervention, where popular opinion proved to be quite skeptical.[110] Nevertheless, throughout the 1990s a clear majority of the American public continued to support the idea that the United States take an active part in world affairs, and this widespread opinion constituted a potential base of support for an active foreign policy.[111] This was doubly true of elite opinion, where isolationist voices were almost entirely absent from public policy discourse. The result was that Clinton could generally expect a certain amount of public support from congressional Republicans like Newt Gingrich and Robert Dole on national security policy, since conservative elites shared many of the administration's core assumptions about America's role in the world.[112] And on the left, the fact that Clinton's national security policy included the promotion of democracy and human rights among its central goals was precisely what made it palatable to a large section of liberal opinion.[113]

What were the implications overseas of the Clinton administration's liberal internationalist foreign policy assumptions? It can and has been argued that U.S. grand strategy during the 1990s was not consistently liberal—that the rhetoric was more idealistic than the actual policies.[114] This argument is absolutely correct. A myriad of narrow, self-interested, and mundane motives, including domestic political concerns, interest group pressures, bureaucratic politics, and particular economic interests shaped and constrained the conduct of U.S. grand strategy throughout the Clinton years. The United States had a tendency to pick and choose its implementation of liberal ideas, in a very self-serving way. Historically, this would hardly be unique to Clinton. Foreign policy is always the result of a mixture of motives; nations do not act out of altruism. But then again, mainstream liberal internationalism was never intended to hurt U.S. interests; it was meant to serve them. So the dichotomy between interests and ideals is something of a red herring. And in Clinton's defense, many of the inconsistencies in his promotion of liberal goals were due to understandable, pragmatic concerns about how to best implement those goals. The impact of internationalist (as opposed to strictly liberal) assumptions during the 1990s is less controversial, though some have questioned how committed Clinton really was to a robust version of internationalism. As we shall see, a common pattern during the 1990s was for the United States to stake out a liberal internationalist position rhetorically while initially refusing to bear the costs of that position: a consequence not simply of Clinton's idiosyncrasies, but of a broader U.S. strategic tradition of limited liability. Nevertheless, the contradiction between U.S. words and U.S. actions would not have arisen in the first place—in cases as diverse as China, Bosnia, Somalia, and Haiti—had a liberal internationalist position not been taken. U.S. strategic behavior during the Clinton years was in fact visibly and powerfully influenced by both liberal and internationalist assumptions. The impact of these assumptions was evident worldwide.

In core, democratic regions such as Western Europe and Japan, under Clinton the United States maintained a large military presence—about 200,000 troops altogether—in the assumption that this continued presence would reassure America's allies, prevent regional security competition, and preserve the stability, security, and interdependence of an extensive, U.S.-led zone of advanced industrial democracies. The goal of "strategic reassurance" was viewed as especially important with regard to Germany and Japan. Allies were encouraged to take up more of the burden of their own defense, so long as these efforts did not supplant U.S.-led alliances. The administration also continued to encourage trade and investment between the United States and its core allies in the belief that this would not only benefit the U.S. economy but also tie the advanced democracies ever closer together.

In Russia, and in the newly independent members of the Commonwealth of Independent States, the United States tried to help manage the difficult transition from communism by pressing for democratic, market reforms. Such reforms were actually made central to U.S.-Russian relations—for example, as a condition of economic aid—in the expectation that Russia's internal makeup would ultimately be the chief determinant of Russia's foreign policy. The United States under Clinton also sought to engage Russia, and to turn it into a "strategic partner," by arranging for international loans, bringing Russia into the G-7, continuing negotiations over nuclear arms reductions, and agreeing that Moscow share a certain level of involvement in Balkan peacekeeping operations. The overarching

U.S. goal in all of this was to see Russia become a stable, modern democracy, unthreatening to the United States.

In Eastern Europe, again, the leading priority of the Clinton administration was the integration and consolidation of an expanding zone of market democracies. Two initiatives, in particular, served to underscore this commitment. First, the United States decided to take the lead in extending NATO membership to Poland, Hungary, and the Czech Republic. The primary motivation behind this expansion seems to have been the belief that it would help lock in democratic market reforms and peaceful international relations throughout Central and Eastern Europe.[115] Second, the United States intervened militarily against Yugoslavia in both Bosnia and Kosovo, ultimately to stop "ethnic cleansing," but also to prevent further conflict while demonstrating the credibility of America's role as a leading "European power." U.S. peacekeepers were subsequently deployed in each of these two Balkan cases to help encourage political reconciliation and democratization on the ground.

In China, the Clinton administration changed strategies significantly over time. The administration was conflicted over the question of how to best promote liberal goals in that gigantic country—conflicted, even, over whether to view China as a potential partner in transition from communism, or as a "rogue state," dangerous and aggressive. Clinton initially pressed for progress on human rights, suggesting that Sino-American trade relations would be held hostage to such progress. But this punitive approach was soon shelved. The administration instead began to encourage trade and investment in China, regardless of human rights violations, while continuing to maintain a military deterrent in the region. The strategy became one of "engaging" the Chinese, through economic exchange and diplomacy, on the assumption that liberalization through foreign trade and diplomatic pressure would eventually lead to a friendlier regime in Beijing.

A recurrent pattern of humanitarian intervention was one of the most striking results of Clinton's liberal internationalist assumptions. Obviously, this pattern was selective, half-hearted, and frequently characterized by a mixture of motives. In the most extreme case of human rights violations during the 1990s—Rwanda—the United States and the rest of the international community did nothing at all. Nevertheless, the Clinton administration repeatedly engaged in significant military interventions overseas at least partially in order to promote liberal and humanitarian goals. The cases of Bosnia and Kosovo have already been mentioned. In Haiti and Somalia, the United States took on the remarkable task of trying to create or re-create stable, democratic polities out of extremely unfavorable conditions.[116] In Haiti, the United States intervened to restore a democratically elected leader to power. In Somalia, the Clinton administration essentially gave itself the mission of rebuilding a failed state, after realizing that humanitarian aid would be ineffective in the face of continuing anarchy.

In all of these cases, the assumptions behind U.S. policy were strikingly liberal. In all of these cases, too, the assumptions were strikingly global and expansive. It was simply taken for granted that no corner of the earth, no matter how devoid of intrinsic interest to Americans, could fail to constitute at least a potential case for U.S. involvement and intervention, whether military or political. Indeed, in many cases, as in the Balkans, the need to demonstrate "leadership" actually became the chief argument for military intervention.[117] The combined effect of liberal and globalist assumptions on U.S. national security policy was to lead to some extraordinary new strategic and diplomatic commitments. Here, for example, is the ambitious list of goals that the Peace Implementation Council set for Bosnia in the wake of the Dayton Accord:

1. regional stabilization (arms control)
2. security (law and order)
3. human rights
4. democratization
5. elections (municipal in 1997 and general in 1998)
6. freedom of movement
7. repatriation of refugees and displaced persons
8. arrest of war criminals
9. reconstruction
10. a market economy
11. reconciliation
12. education, and
13. mine removal.[118]

All of this in a country of no obvious economic, strategic, or political importance to the United States.

Limited Liability under Clinton

In spite of the ambitious, liberal internationalist agenda set out by Clinton foreign policy officials, one of the most striking features of U.S. strategic behavior during the mid-1990s was an intense reluctance to back up this internationalist agenda by force. The typical pattern was that the administration would rhetorically stake out an assertive and idealistic foreign policy position—for example, against ethnic cleansing in Bosnia—but then refuse to act on that rhetoric in any meaningful way. These refusals and delays were no doubt heavily influenced by domestic political pressures, but they also matched the preferences of the administration, where the priority was clearly to avoid the costs and risks of serious military action. Yet in each case where Clinton had staked out an aggressive rhetorical position, he would ultimately be forced to act, if only to protect the credibility both of the United States and of his presidency. The result was a series of half-hearted interventions, which only served to reinforce the impression that Americans were unwilling to sustain any significant costs on behalf of their role in the world.

In Somalia, the Clinton team began with the laudable intention of maintaining the flow of food supplies to Somali civilians, under a mission first approved by outgoing President George H. W. Bush. But the administration soon realized that such supplies could not reach these civilians in the face of continued civil disorder and warlordism. Clinton and his advisors then took the fateful step of expanding the U.S./UN mission significantly. In March 1993, at Washington's suggestion, the United Nations approved a resolution calling for the reconstruction of Somalia as a "failed state."[119] Madeleine Albright described this new mission as "an unprecedented enterprise aimed at nothing less than the restoration of an entire country."[120] Yet the United States was actually neither willing nor able to impose law and order in Somalia. It quickly became apparent that the conditions for nation building and democracy-promotion in that country were quite unfavorable. A manhunt for one particularly offensive warlord, Mohamed Aideed, led to a fierce firefight in the streets of Mogadishu, culminating in the death of eighteen American soldiers on October 3, 1993. Clinton's reaction, in spite of some tough rhetoric at the time, was in fact to withdraw the American mission in Somalia a few months later.[121]

In Haiti, Clinton called for the restoration to power of Jean-Bertrand Aristide, elected as president in 1990 but then forced out of office by a military junta. Again, the stated American aim was admirably democratic and humanitarian, and included concern not only for the sanctity of the elections but for the plight of Haitian refugees trying to escape to the United States. But the Clinton administration proved unwilling, for over a year and a half, to make anything but the most half-hearted threats on behalf of its demands. The resulting series of humiliations eventually convinced Clinton of the need for stronger action. Only when the United States indicated that it was prepared to invade Haiti in September 1993 did the junta leadership finally step down.[122]

The case of Bosnia was probably the single most disturbing example of the disconnection between rhetoric and behavior in U.S. national security policy under Clinton. From the very beginning, the administration had called for an end to ethnic cleansing, especially on the part of Serb forces against Moslem civilians. At the same time, the United States did very little to stop these atrocities.[123] Not only did Clinton rule out the use of American ground troops in the Balkans; for over two years, he took no meaningful military action whatsoever. Only in June 1995, when the crisis over Bosnia became so severe as to seemingly threaten both Clinton's political standing and America's credibility as a European power, did the United States finally embrace a strategy of "lift and strike" against the Serbs.[124] Yet the methods that were used in that campaign were illustrative of America's continued preference for limited liability in strategic affairs. The United States relied upon airpower, as well as mercenaries, to aid Moslem and Croatian forces against their opponents.[125] No regular U.S. ground troops were involved. Once the war was over, however, U.S. ground troops would be required to serve as peacekeepers for much longer than Clinton cared to admit.

Four years later, in Kosovo, the Clinton team acted more rapidly to stop Serbian atrocities against ethnic Albanians. A lesson had apparently been drawn from the Bosnian experience—to act sooner rather than later. Another lesson drawn was that airpower could achieve desirable political results without the need for U.S. ground troops. Consequently, soon after the war over Kosovo began, in March 1999 Clinton indicated that he "had no intent" to commit U.S. ground forces.[126] The United States would rely upon airstrikes, together with the Kosovo Liberation Army (KLA), to quickly defeat the Serbs. The actual results defied the initially optimistic expectations. The Yugoslav government held out for over two months, refusing to concede. There is still considerable debate over what finally convinced Yugoslavia's leader, Slobodan Milošević, to sue for peace in June 1999. But it is reasonable to suggest that one of the crucial factors was the threat that the United States and its NATO allies might actually introduce ground forces into the war.[127] Both the administration and the Pentagon had been extremely reluctant to even consider such a contingency.[128] Yet by May 1999 Clinton was willing—indeed, forced—to say in public that militarily "all options are on the table."[129] It was soon after this point that Milošević agreed to relinquish Serb control over Kosovo.[130]

In keeping with the preference for limited liability, there were numerous other cases of minimal or low-risk military action under Clinton. In August 1998, in response to terrorist attacks by Al Qaeda against American diplomatic missions in Africa, the Clinton administration authorized cruise missile strikes against terrorist bases in Afghanistan, as well as against a supposed chemical weapons production site in the Sudan. Four months later, in response to continued Iraqi defiance of UN weapons inspectors, the administration launched a new campaign of precision airstrikes against Iraq—one of many over the course of Clinton's tenure. In some cases of potential humanitarian intervention, such as Sierra Leone and East Timor, the United States was able to rely on regional allies to bear the burden of military action. And in other cases, of course, neither the administration nor its allies did anything at all, most notably in

Rwanda, where approximately one million Tutsi people were massacred in the space of a few weeks.

The point here is not to decry the handling of every one of these cases, but rather to point out a pattern of extremely low-cost, low-risk military interventions during the immediate post–Cold War era. Some authors described it as a "new American way of war."[131] The new way of war would involve airstrikes, cruise missiles, precision guided weapons, arms sales, economic, and even covert military aid, but it would not involve risking the lives of U.S. troops on the ground. Instead, the United States would rely upon proxy forces, such as the Bosnians, the Croats, or the KLA, to do much of the heavy lifting while contributing to the war effort at minimal risk with long-range precision airstrikes—a combination of "gunboats and gurkhas," as Andrew Bacevich has pointed out, much like the one favored by Great Britain during its imperial heyday.[132]

Why the remarkably high sensitivity to the costs and risks of serious military action during these immediate post–Cold War years? Why the reluctance to act forcefully? One answer is that the geopolitical stakes were in fact unusually low in all of these cases.[133] The Clinton administration could define U.S. national security policy in terms of humanitarian missions to peripheral regions, but it could not convincingly argue that serious national interests were endangered, and as a result, it was constrained from taking costly military action in these regions. There is considerable truth to this assertion. But from a realist perspective, the answer in that case would have been to avoid putting America's reputation on the line in the first place—to avoid defining U.S. interests in such an expansive manner as to then call the nation's credibility into question. The fact is that the Clinton administration *said* that in cases like Bosnia that the United States had a vital interest in the pursuit of liberal or humanitarian goals. Then it refused to protect this stated interest with the requisite seriousness until U.S. credibility had already been undermined. This may have been partially the result of a president characterized by unusual inattention to matters of national security. But it was also a pattern of behavior very much in the liberal internationalist tradition: sweeping commitments, too often supported by inadequate means.

Benign international conditions or low geopolitical stakes cannot entirely explain why the Clinton administration was so sensitive to the risk of U.S. military casualties. In order to explain that sensitivity, we must look to domestic cultural constraints, as expressed through public opinion, Congress, the bureaucracy, and the president himself.

Mass public opinion in the United States is of course sensitive to the possibility of U.S. military casualties, and tends to be unenthusiastic about the prospect of military action overseas.[134] This has been especially true since Vietnam. In the abstract, even when asked if they would favor U.S.

military intervention to defend any of America's European or Asian allies from attack, a majority of the public says no.[135] And when military action goes badly, and casualties mount, the evidence suggests that the public will eventually withdraw its support.[136] Presidents are aware of this phenomenon and are naturally attuned to it.[137] Having said that, the public's aversion to casualties, like its aversion to military intervention, is often overstated.[138] Public opinion polls in recent years by organizations such as Duke University's Triangle Institute for Security Studies have established this quite convincingly. The common belief—even among politically savvy government officials—that the American public is *hyper*sensitive to casualties is in fact a misperception.[139] Whenever the president actually initiates military action, there is usually a sharp jump in popular support.[140] The public will to a certain extent defer to the president, and to elite opinion, in cases of intervention, especially if elite opinion seems united.[141] If a given military operation seems likely to succeed; if it seems to have a coherent goal; and if it appears to address some vital national interest, then the public will be more supportive.[142]

This last point goes to the heart of the matter. Under the Clinton administration, as we have seen, force was often used in a half-hearted fashion, in the service of what were essentially liberal or humanitarian ends. In such circumstances, popular support for military action was naturally rather low. As Bruce Jentleson has shown, the American public does not look particularly favorably on the use of force to spread democracy, promote nation building, or engineer internal political change in other countries.[143] Nor does it look favorably on using force in a confused and timid fashion. Yet this was precisely the pattern of humanitarian intervention under the Clinton administration: ostensibly disinterested, but often incoherent. As a result, the very nature of the mission, in cases like Somalia, ensured that public opinion would be averse to the prospect of U.S. casualties.

During the Clinton years, Congress also frequently proved to be intolerant of the risks and costs associated with military intervention. In the 1970s and 1980s, many congressional Democrats had been uncomfortable with the use of force in U.S. foreign policy. Now, in the early 1990s, just as many liberals were reconverted to the creed of humanitarian intervention, congressional Republicans began to voice their skepticism regarding real or potential military actions overseas.[144] Part of the explanation, of course, was simply partisan politics: having lost the White House in 1992, Republicans in Congress were both free and inclined to criticize the new president across the board. But there was in fact a real difference of philosophy between the administration and its Republican critics on national security policy.[145] Compared to the Clinton foreign policy team, congressional Republicans tended to be significantly more skeptical of peacekeeping, multilateralism, and humanitarian intervention. This was doubly true of the freshman class of 1994, which was more populist, ideological, and antiestablishment than its predecessors.[146] The new Republican Congress was frequently described as "isolationist." In fact, its preferences were not so much isolationist as unilateralist.[147] Republicans were divided during the mid-to-late 1990s between advocates of U.S. primacy, advocates of neoisolationism, and advocates of a hard-nosed realism in strategic affairs. They did not really agree on what sort of grand strategy the United States should follow. They were often divided, as in the case of Kosovo, over the question of whether to authorize the use of force by the president. But they generally agreed that the manner of intervention under Clinton had been ill-advised. This belief—together with partisan incentives—led them to frequently criticize or resist proposals for military action on the part of the administration.[148] In this way, the culture of limited liability expressed itself through Congress as well as public opinion.

A third significant constraint on military action during the Clinton administration came from what some might view as a surprising source: the career military itself. As with public opinion, the legacy of Vietnam weighed heavily on the U.S. armed forces. The reaction within the military had been to reject concepts of "signaling," "calibration," or "limited war" and to return to more of an all-or-nothing approach: that is, to resist calls for military intervention, but to insist that overwhelming force be used once the decision for war had been made.[149] The new approach became known as the "Powell Doctrine," after the Chairman of the Joint Chiefs of Staff in the early 1990s, Colin Powell. In strictly military terms, the doctrine had much to recommend it. But the problem was twofold. First, the military's resistance to the use of force often robbed U.S. foreign policymakers of bargaining power over regional crises. As Madeleine Albright said to Colin Powell, "What's the point of having this superb military that you're always talking about if we can't use it?"[150] Second, in practice, the reluctance to use force often carried over into the conduct of military interventions already underway. During the war over Kosovo, for example, the Pentagon was reluctant to even consider planning for a ground invasion.[151] And in certain cases, such as peacekeeping in Bosnia, commanders admitted that their highest priority was not so much accomplishing the mission as preventing any U.S. casualties.[152] The frustration of local commanders with ambiguous orders and ambiguous missions was certainly understandable. But the rise of a "zero-tolerance" culture within the career military establishment—zero tolerance for casualties, as well as for mistakes—did not empower U.S. diplomacy.

Public opinion, Congress, and the Pentagon all acted as constraints on Clinton's ability to support a liberal internationalist agenda by force. But the truth is that Clinton himself set the tone by refusing to act consistently on strategic matters. Given the aggressive and idealistic foreign policy positions he staked out rhetorically, Clinton was excessively sensitive to the domestic political cost associated with backing them up. Presidents are indeed constrained by domestic political forces, but not entirely so. If they act with energy and clarity, they can to some extent redefine what is politically feasible.[153] But to an unusual degree for any modern president, Clinton simply demurred from courting opposition on questions of military intervention. Instead, his primary concern on such matters seems to have been to "stay out of trouble"—to leave foreign policy to the leading bureaucratic players, and keep it from interfering with his domestic political agenda.[154] In the end, once the threat of complete foreign policy disaster was fully apparent, Clinton would sometimes take courageous and politically risky steps. He did so, for example, in Bosnia in the summer of 1995. But his initial preference for absolute limited liability, politically and strategically, often encouraged these looming disasters in the first place.

One of the inevitable consequences of America's seeming hypersensitivity to casualties was that it reinforced the view overseas that the United States could be successfully coerced, in spite of its immense material power. Groups and nations that opposed the United States were offered a template, a strategy for how to defeat the United States: inflict casualties, impose costs, count on domestic political opposition within the United States to constrain military action, and ultimately wear down the Americans.[155] Indeed, there is evidence to suggest that every one of America's adversaries during this period counted on precisely this weakness to defeat the United States. Mohammed Aideed, for example, the Somali warlord, told U.S. special envoy Robert Oakley that "we know how to get rid of Americans, by killing them so that public opinion will put an end to things."[156] That strategy in fact succeeded, which only emboldened others to do the very same. In his 1996 "declaration of war" against Israel and the United States, for example, Osama bin Laden referred to the way in which the United States had been forced out of Somalia:

> After vigorous propaganda about the power of the United States and its post–Cold War leadership of the new world order—you moved tens of thousands of international forces, including 28,000 American soldiers, into Somalia. However, when tens of your soldiers were killed in minor battles and one American pilot was dragged in the streets of Mogadishu you left the area carrying disappointment, humiliation, defeat, and your dead with you. Clinton appeared in front of the whole world threatening and promising revenge, but these threats were merely a preparation for withdrawal. You have been disgraced by Allah and you withdrew; the extent of your impotence and weaknesses became very clear.[157]

Saddam Hussein and Slobodan Milošević seem to have reached similar conclusions: that the United States could be defeated or outlasted by taking advantage of its great sensitivity to costs and casualties.[158] Given the fact that U.S. foreign policymakers during the 1990s were indeed ultrasensitive to the costs of intervention, this was not an unreasonable conclusion to reach.

Other symptoms of the general U.S. preference for limited liability overseas showed up in U.S. military and international expenditures during the 1990s. Certainly, U.S. defense expenditures remained far greater than those of any other power, at about $300 billion per year. But given the ambitious global mission outlined in the Clinton administration's strategy of "engagement and enlargement," defense expenditures were actually rather low. The "Bottom-Up Review" of the military's force structure, undertaken in 1993, called for cuts in defense spending of approximately 10 percent from Bush's "Base Force" of 1991. It also called for further cuts in personnel, for example by reducing the number of active Army divisions from twelve to ten.[159] The U.S. armed forces were left with about 1.4 million personnel, of whom approximately 200,000 would be stationed in Western Europe and Northeast Asia. It is fair to say that in spite of prior assurances to the contrary, the Bottom-Up Review did not initiate any radical changes in the basic force structure of the U.S. military. Instead, it essentially preserved the existing force structure while reducing it in size.[160] The stated rationale for this new force was the possibility of two major regional contingencies occurring more or less simultaneously, presumably against Iraq and North Korea. But the capabilities necessary for meeting both contingencies with confidence were not actually maintained.[161] Moreover, the accelerated pace of smaller-scale operations, due in part to the new predilection for humanitarian intervention, tended to overstrain the existing armed forces. Expenditures on modernization, procurement, readiness, and salaries were allowed to slide. Already by 1995, the Clinton administration faced considerable pressure from Republicans in Congress to increase spending on defense, and that pressure would continue throughout Clinton's tenure.

Low levels of spending on international affairs were even more striking. For all the talk of promoting a new international order, the United States spent remarkably little on diplomacy and foreign aid during the 1990s: about $20 billion per year. For a country with a gross national product of $10 trillion, this was an astonishingly small amount: 0.2 percent, to be precise, proportionately far less than that spent by other industrialized democracies. This minimal sum was expected to cover, among other things, funding for the State Department, including the maintenance of its many posts and embassies overseas; contributions to the United Nations and its multiple operations; international developmental and hu-

manitarian assistance; democracy promotion; economic and military aid
to American allies; and the securing of nuclear materials in the former
Soviet Union.[162] It is difficult to see how penny-pinching in matters
like the disposal of nuclear waste actually served U.S. interests. Nevertheless, such expenditures were always open to the populist charge, especially from conservatives, that all such money was being wasted. In fact,
the American public seems to have grossly and systematically overestimated the amount actually spent on foreign aid.[163] But the perception of
waste and abuse on this issue—sometimes quite justified—left the Clinton
administration open to criticism, and forced it to keep international expenditures low.

Over time, given its preference for low costs and low risks in national
security policy, the Clinton administration would be forced to tone down
some of the more untenable implications of its liberal internationalist approach. It would be forced, for example, to recognize the limited impact
of the United States on human rights abuses in China. It would be forced
to back off from its earlier ambitions regarding the reinvigoration of the
United Nations. It would be forced to become more cautious with regard
to multilateral interventions. It would be forced to recognize the practical
inevitability, late in 1995, of something like a de facto partition of Bosnia.
It would be forced to negotiate, out of simple necessity, with "rogue
states" such as North Korea, Yugoslavia, and Iran, and eventually to drop
the concept altogether. And it would be forced to increase defense spending in order to support all new strategic commitments abroad. Still, there
would be no fundamental rethinking under Clinton of the basic assumptions behind a national security strategy of "engagement and enlargement." The twin paradigms of primacy and liberal internationalism
would continue to animate U.S. foreign policy behavior throughout the
1990s, just as they had since World War Two, alongside an equally strong
and contradictory preference for limited liability.

CONCLUSION

The collapse of the USSR provided the most dramatic change in the international system since 1945. It seemed to offer the opportunity for a com-
parably radical reorientation of America's diplomatic and strategic role
in the world. Americans could, for example, have disbanded their Cold
War alliances and brought all of their overseas forces home. Or they
could have turned to a strategy of realpolitik, maintaining a military presence in key regions, but acting only to preserve a balance between the
major powers of Europe and Asia. These alternatives were rejected. Instead, under the Clinton administration, the United States embarked

upon a strategy of engagement and enlargement, a liberal internationalist strategy marked by broad continuity with Cold War commitments and assumptions.

Structural realism cannot explain this post–Cold War outcome. There may have been certain international pressures running against strategic disengagement, but there were no such pressures militating in favor of a liberal strategy like engagement and enlargement. That strategy cannot be fully explained without reference to certain cultural legacies that continued to influence U.S. foreign policy behavior during the 1990s. In the absence of any sense of policy failure, U.S. officials were not inclined to question the assumptions that had undergirded U.S. national security policy since World War Two. Instead, these liberal, globalist assumptions continued to shape the thinking of U.S. foreign policymakers. Out of both genuine conviction, and the anticipation of domestic political necessity, candidate and then President Clinton embraced and then encouraged this broad, post–Cold War foreign policy consensus. As a result, any real alternatives to a liberal, globalist strategy—such as strategic disengagement, or a purely balance-of-power approach—were removed from serious consideration. In spite of their potential feasibility, these alternative strategies never had a chance. They were filtered out of public debate, because of the internationalist assumptions that have governed U.S. national security policy since the 1940s, and because of the liberal assumptions that have always helped shape the U.S. approach to international relations. Yet in practice, these liberal internationalist goals were actually pursued through quite limited means. The outcome was a pattern already familiar from our previous postwar cases: a serious and continuing gap between capabilities and commitments in the conduct of U.S. grand strategy.

Conclusion

THE AMERICAN STRATEGIC DILEMMA

IN THIS FINAL AND CONCLUDING chapter, I begin by analyzing recent patterns of strategic adjustment under the George W. Bush administration, using the same conceptual framework as in previous chapters. I then summarize the main theoretical findings of this work, and offer some predictions regarding the future of American grand strategy.

AMERICAN GRAND STRATEGY UNDER THE GEORGE W. BUSH ADMINISTRATION

George W. Bush initially came into office, relative to Clinton, with a somewhat less internationalist and more realist approach toward U.S. grand strategy. To a certain extent, this shift can be explained by referring to the limited strategic overstretch that resulted from the interventions of the 1990s. But the shift toward strategic realism really had more to do with the ideas and assumptions held by the incoming Bush foreign policy team than with any overwhelming international pressures. A modest or second-order strategic adjustment in early 2001 was the result of changes in administration—and changes in the ideas held by each administration—rather than changes in the international system.

After the terrorist attacks of September 11, 2001, the Bush administration moved from a realist approach toward a strategy of American primacy. This shift was the result of a window of opportunity opening after a dramatic external shock. In the wake of that shock, key advocates were able to set the agenda on behalf of a strategic vision of primacy, aggressive democracy-promotion, and military preemption. This particular outcome was not completely predetermined by international pressures; it had more to do with the recurring power of classical liberal ideas in American grand strategy, resurrected in a particularly muscular form by President Bush. The war in Iraq was the most obvious manifestation of the new strategy. But that same war was also informed by limited liability assumptions, in that the Bush administration was initially unwilling to pay the price that would have been necessary to secure a stable postwar Iraq.

The decision for war against Saddam Hussein is sometimes characterized as a kind of conspiracy. It was not a conspiracy, any more than Wilson's League of Nations, Truman's strategy of containment, or Clinton's strategy of democratic enlargement were conspiracies. Rather, the war in Iraq was the result of a pattern of strategic adjustment that has occurred repeatedly and predictably in American history: international shocks and pressures created an opening for new strategic ideas, and leading state officials took the opportunity to put forward their preferred approach, based largely upon their culturally influenced perceptions of the national interest. The strategy that won out after September 11, 2001, was one broadly consistent with traditional American liberal assumptions regarding the benefits of a democratized world order. For better or worse, Bush's post-9/11 strategy of aggressive democracy-promotion overseas was not out of step with historical precedent.[1] On the contrary, it was quite consistent in many ways with America's internationalist and Wilsonian traditions. Also consistent with the Wilsonian tradition was the fact that the means Bush employed—especially in Iraq—did not quite match up to the very ambitious and even idealistic ends that were sought. Apparently, the Bush administration initially hoped to secure a democratic Iraq while avoiding the costs of nation building. In this sense, the two traditional elements of U.S. strategic culture—classical liberalism and limited liability—continued to operate, even as the "war on terror" led to a more assertive grand strategy across the board.

Realism, Limited Liability, and Strategic Adjustment, 2001

Upon taking office in 2001, the Bush administration initiated certain changes in American grand strategy. The new Republican foreign policy team emphasized military preparedness, great-power politics, and concrete national interests. Bush criticized his predecessor's willingness to engage in nation building and humanitarian intervention overseas. He promised to be more selective in relation to the use of force, and he called for a less interventionist approach with regard to the internal affairs of other countries. He was skeptical of multilateralism, and unyielding toward potential adversaries. On balance, these early adjustments under Bush represented a partial movement away from the liberal internationalism of the Clinton years in favor of a somewhat more realist approach. From a more detached and historical perspective, however, one striking fact about the broad contours of American grand strategy under Bush—pre-9/11—is how continuous they were with the broad contours of American grand strategy under Clinton. First, we briefly examine the continuities between Clinton and Bush, then the differences.

Prior to 9/11, the continuities between Clinton and Bush, prior to 9/11, though little discussed, were extensive and significant. Bush clearly rejected any radical version of strategic disengagement. He maintained the forward presence of almost a quarter of a million American troops in Europe, Northeast Asia, and the Middle East. Beyond this, Bush never abandoned the classically liberal and American idea that the United States ought to promote democracy overseas, for example through the promotion of open markets and free trade. As he put it in a speech at Simi Valley, California, in 1999, "economic freedom creates habits of liberty. And habits of liberty create expectations of democracy."[2] Nor did Bush abandon the idea that the United States ought to maintain its political and military predominance in the world. On the contrary, he supported these goals, while arguing that Clinton had pursued them in the wrong manner. In this sense, his criticisms of Clinton were tactical, rather than fundamental.[3] Bush, like his immediate predecessors, was heir to the postwar tradition of American internationalism; he did not propose to abandon that tradition. Nor, in the absence of dramatic alterations in international conditions, did he have any compelling reason to initiate radical changes in American grand strategy. The differences from Clinton were stressed during the 2000 campaign, in part for political reasons: Bush sought to rally Republican support, and to cut into perceived Democratic weaknesses on foreign policy and defense. But in fact, Bush's initial foreign policy approach was a selective form of internationalism, just as Clinton's had been: influenced by liberal assumptions, as well as by considerable concern for limited liability.

Within this broad range of agreement, of course, there were important differences between Clinton and Bush. The foreign policy positions taken by Bush during the 2000 presidential campaign flowed from criticisms that had been made of Clinton over the prior eight years, and specifically from the advice that Bush received from leading foreign policy experts within the Republican Party.[4] Bush argued for an increase in military spending, along with the transformation and modernization of America's armed forces. He was especially critical of what he called the "open-ended deployments and unclear military missions" of the Clinton era, and promised to be much more careful about sending U.S. forces abroad.[5] He called for limited cuts in America's military presence overseas, suggesting, for example, that U.S. peacekeepers in Bosnia could be brought home. In a noteworthy series of comments during the October 2000 presidential debates against Al Gore, Bush underscored his skepticism regarding what he called "nation-building" missions. He suggested that, as president, he would not have intervened in either Haiti or Somalia. And he called for clear criteria surrounding the use of force, based upon "vital national interests," rather than humanitarian objectives. As Bush put it, "I would be guarded in my approach. I don't think we can be all things to all people in the world. I think we've got to be very careful when we commit our troops."[6]

More generally, Bush tried to make the case during the 2000 campaign for a more hard-line and unyielding approach toward potential adversaries of the United States.[7] He and his advisors argued, for example, against any further negotiated "deals" with North Korea. They advocated a somewhat more detached and hard-nosed approach with regard to Russia. They suggested that China be treated as a strategic rival, rather than as a strategic partner.[8] They called for a more concerted effort to engineer the overthrow of Saddam Hussein. They argued unreservedly for the construction of a national missile defense system. And they made clear his concern over any erosion of U.S. sovereignty through potential membership in a variety of new multilateral agreements, such as the International Criminal Court.[9] At the same time, however, then Governor Bush insisted that "the United States must be humble . . . humble in how we treat nations that are figuring out how to chart their own course." So the tone of his comments during the presidential campaign suggested that Bush would be more hard-line than Clinton, but at the same time more modest in intervening in the internal affairs of other countries. The reason was clear: liberal humanitarian concerns would henceforth take a back seat to considerations of U.S. self-interest. As Bush put it during the second presidential debate, "when it comes to foreign policy, that'll be my guiding question: is it in our nation's interests?"[10]

Bush's foreign policy appointments in 2001 were broadly consistent with the tone of his presidential campaign. The leading appointments were Colin Powell as secretary of state, Donald Rumsfeld as secretary of defense, and Condoleezza Rice as national security advisor. Vice-President Dick Cheney would also turn out to be a figure of central importance in foreign policymaking under Bush. Other significant appointments included Paul Wolfowitz and Douglas Feith at the Pentagon; Richard Armitage, John Bolton and Richard Haass at State; Elliot Abrams at the National Security Council; John Negroponte at the UN; and Lewis Libby at the Vice-President's Office. The most popular interpretation of internal divisions within the Bush administration was to point to Powell as the supposed "multilateralist," against Rumsfeld and Cheney as the leading "unilateralists," on almost every issue of significance.[11] There was certainly something to this interpretation, in that Powell was visibly more concerned about preserving good relations with America's allies than, for example, Rumsfeld. But the ideological differences between these men were often overstated in the press. In fact, Powell was hardly a devotee of liberal multilateralism. Rather, he was simply a pragmatic Republican internationalist, in the tradition of Bush's own father.[12] Nor were Rumsfeld and Cheney as reflexively opposed to every single international organization or agreement as their critics often suggested. The really interesting division within the administration—a division that seemed to cut through many individuals internally, including the president himself—was not between unilateralists and multilateralists, but between a realist strategic vision and a more ambitious and idealistic vision of U.S. global primacy.[13]

Referring back to the beliefs of post–Cold War primacists, recall that these authors suggested that the United States act aggressively to "Americanize" the international system, and to perpetuate America's political and military predominance in the world. Certainly there were intimations of this approach even as Bush took office. In fact, many of his leading foreign policy advisors—including Rumsfeld, Cheney, Wolfowitz, Armitage, Feith, Bolton, Abrams, and Libby—had signed on in 1997–1998 to an explicit vision of U.S. primacy laid out by the ubiquitous William Kristol in his "Project for a New American Century."[14] The assumptions of the primacist position influenced U.S. grand strategy during the opening months of the Bush administration on a wide range of issues, from missile defense to China to international organizations to "rogue states." But prior to September 11, the single most important theme in both the strategic thinking and the actual strategic behavior of the Bush team was not so much primacy as realism.

Initially, Bush and his advisors made their skepticism regarding nation building and humanitarian intervention abundantly clear. As Condoleezza Rice put it, "we really don't need to have the 82nd Airborne escorting kids to kindergarten."[15] The Bush foreign policy team called for a refocusing of U.S. national security policy on great power politics and concrete national interests. They suggested that the United States play down its pretensions as an international social engineer, and show, in Bush's words, "humility" toward internal political processes in other states. They called on the United States to be more selective in its use of force abroad.[16] They argued for bringing America's strategic commitments back into balance with its military capabilities. They did not initiate massive increases in military spending.[17] They toned down their adversarial campaign rhetoric against China. They did not, in fact, embrace the concept of "rogue-state rollback." And they did not actually take aggressive actions against particular rogue states such as Iraq. In fact, the overall early tenor of the Bush administration's foreign policy was that of a "return to professionalism."[18] Richard Haass had articulated the new foreign policy pragmatism quite succinctly in a 1999 *Foreign Affairs* article, in which he stated that when it came to world politics, "order is more fundamental than justice."[19] This was about as clear a statement of the realist foreign policy approach as one could imagine. The implication was that the Bush administration would turn its back on the Wilsonian interventions of the Clinton years in favor of a more modest and pragmatic grand strategy.

If we compare these assumptions and positions to the various post–Cold War strategic alternatives outlined earlier, it appears that the initial foreign policy approach of George W. Bush was more realist than anything else. Committed and consistent primacists, such as Paul Wolfowitz, were certainly inside the administration, but they were unable (at first) to reshape U.S. grand strategy in the direction they desired.[20] Bush appointees such as Powell, Rice, and Haass were openly skeptical of any of sort of crusading idealism in foreign affairs.[21] Cheney and Rumsfeld took hard-line stands on a variety of foreign policy issues, but seemed unwilling or unable to press for a comprehensive strategy of primacy across the board. Above all, the new president showed only limited interest in the sweeping, aggressive agenda of primacist foreign policy advocates. His instincts seemed to be hard-nosed and practical, rather than hugely ambitious or idealistic.[22] As long as Bush was uninterested in a more aggressive approach, Cheney and Rumsfeld would lean toward a somewhat intransigent or nationalistic version of strategic realism. Consequently, that remained the predominant tone of Bush's foreign policy team up until the terrorist attacks on Washington and New York.

Terrorism, Primacy, and Strategic Adjustment, 2001–2003

In the weeks and months after the terrorist attacks of September 11, 2001, the Bush administration gravitated toward a new grand strategy, one of American primacy. Certain themes remained constant from before 9/11: an uncompromising stance toward potential adversaries, the belief in the continuing relevance of military power, and skepticism regarding multilateral institutions. But other assumptions underwent a drastic alteration. The administration's new strategy emphasized U.S. preponderance, rather than any equilibrium among the great powers. It called for the worldwide promotion of democracy—by force if necessary. And it also stressed the need for preemptive military action against authoritarian states with ties to terrorist organizations. Gone, too, was the earlier emphasis on realpolitik. Instead, the new strategy embraced a kind of muscular, assertive Wilsonianism. The greatest manifestation of the new approach was in the war against Iraq. But that war was simply the most visible consequence of a general shift in strategic assumptions within the Bush administration.

The Bush administration maintained—and structural realists might agree—that the shift in strategic assumptions was an inevitable response to terrorism. But the causal links between 9/11 and the new grand strategy were actually more complicated, and more interesting, than that. No doubt, the attacks on Washington and New York were catalytic. Yet the particular strategic adjustments undertaken by the Bush administration could not have been predicted simply on the basis of structural or international pressures. From a structural realist perspective—and this represents an obvious weakness of the approach—terrorism is of limited significance. It represents no change in the underlying distribution of power. We would not necessarily expect to see dramatic alterations in any country's grand strategy on the basis of terrorist attacks alone. A tightening up of homeland defense, a more aggressive approach toward counterterrorism—this we would probably expect to see. But the more sweeping strategic changes, such as those actually adopted by the Bush administration, structural theories could not have predicted them. In fact, the United States had a variety of options after 9/11. It could have responded by adopting a tough but restrained response toward terrorism, have turned toward a more multilateral approach, or even have used the attacks as an excuse to withdraw militarily from the Middle East. Indeed, a number of leading realist authors advocated each of these responses and opposed an invasion of Iraq.[23] Clearly, these same realists did not view a war against Iraq as inevitable—and, indeed, it was not.

What actually happened after 9/11 was more consistent with a neoclassical model of strategic adjustment than with any purely structural explanation. The events of that day obviously acted as an intense shock to both the American public and to U.S. foreign policymakers. A dramatic attack on the American homeland stimulated the search for a new strategy that would prevent other such catastrophes. An interesting feature of this process, however, and one consistent with past cases of strategic adjustment, was that the particular strategy chosen was hardly the only one available. Certainly, one might have expected the United States to retaliate against the government of Afghanistan for harboring the terrorists that had planned 9/11. A more aggressive counterterrorist approach was also clearly in the cards. But beyond these changes, it is not self-evident that the United States was compelled to follow any particular grand strategy. The terrorist attacks simply opened up a window of opportunity for advocates of alternative grand strategies to come forward and make their case. What happened in 2001–2002 was that key foreign policy advocates—first within and beyond the administration, and then including the president himself—took advantage of this window of opportunity to set the agenda, and to build support for a new strategy of American primacy. This new strategy—epitomized by the war against Iraq—was both more aggressive, and, in many ways, more idealistic than Bush's previous approach. It tapped into long-standing, classical liberal assumptions within the United States as to how to meet foreign threats. The increased sense of danger among Americans meant that domestic constraints on U.S. grand strategy were somewhat lessened. The overall result was a significant adjustment in the mentality underlying U.S. grand strategy. But concerns over limited liability, while reduced, were not removed altogether. The tension between international pressures, American liberal assumptions, and the preference for limited liability would continue after 9/11 in new and unexpected forms.

The first phase of the war on terror was the least controversial. The administration's initial response to 9/11 was to demand that Afghanistan's Taliban regime turn over the leading members of Al Qaeda. After the Taliban refused this demand, the Bush administration launched U.S. military action in Afghanistan. This was a significant step because it indicated a new and more aggressive counterterrorist approach. As Bush put it in his address to a special joint session of Congress on September 20, 2001, "Any nation that continues to harbor or support terrorism will be regarded by the United States as a hostile regime."[24] This was already a departure from the more restrained counterterrorist approach that the United States had followed, for example, under Clinton. Nevertheless, U.S. military action against the Taliban had broad public and congressional backing, as well as extensive international support.[25] Given that the Taliban had sheltered and supported the authors of the worst terrorist attack in U.S. history, and then refused to hand them over, the administration's response was natural and predictable.

The war itself was fought in a manner that demonstrated a somewhat greater willingness to risk American lives than had been the case with the humanitarian interventions of the 1990s. Special operations forces, in particular, were often put in harm's way.[26] Still, the Bush administration's approach toward Afghanistan actually had much in common with Clinton's approach in cases like those of Bosnia and Kosovo. The basic strategy was to rely upon allied, proxy forces on the ground—in this case, the Northern Alliance—and to support them with air strikes, financial aid, and military advice.[27] Any early, significant ground commitment by regular U.S. troops was conspicuously lacking. At one point during the war, as progress stalled, the Joint Chiefs of Staff were forced to consider the possibility of a U.S. ground invasion involving approximately 50,000 troops.[28] But the sudden collapse of the Taliban in November seemed to obviate the need for any such invasion. As Max Boot of the Council on Foreign Relations put it, the war against the Taliban was won with "the blood and guts of the Northern Alliance, helped by copious quantities of American ordnance and a handful of American advisers."[29] Clearly, the tradition of limited liability was still alive and well in U.S. grand strategic thought.

The manner in which the administration fought the war had fateful consequences for the ability of the United States to meet its wartime goals. The fall of the Taliban was certainly a severe blow to Al Qaeda, but the failure to send U.S. ground forces in earlier meant that many Al Qaeda fighters—including, apparently, Osama Bin Laden—were able to escape and reconstitute along the Pakistani-Afghan border. Instead of actually sending in its own troops to encircle the members of Al Qaeda, the United States had relied upon the Northern Alliance to do so. But there was no reason to expect that these proxy forces would share America's precise political goals beyond victory over the Taliban. Similarly, the administration's continued resistance to nation building—its unwillingness to contribute to a new International Security Assistance Force in Afghanistan, and its unwillingness to contribute very much toward postwar reconstruction—left Afghanistan's friendly new government without effective control over the country outside of Kabul. In short, the U.S. insistence on limited liability left it without the ability to control the political situation in Afghanistan, or even to secure its own self-defined security interests against Al Qaeda.[30]

Nevertheless, the war in Afghanistan was widely viewed as a major success, and, ending as soon as it did, it did not trigger any searching public debate over the basic outlines of U.S. grand strategy. The vast majority of politically significant actors within the United States were on board for military action against the Taliban. Beyond Afghanistan, however, there was still the question of how the United States would reshape its national security policy in response to 9/11. And on this question, there were a number of broad alternatives available. Indeed, the basic alternatives were really the same as they had been since the end of the Cold War. The United States could respond to 9/11 by completely disengaging from its alliances and military deployments overseas.[31] It could respond by deepening its commitment toward cooperative, multilateral engagement abroad.[32] It could respond by following more of a realist approach, playing down Wilsonian pretensions and ambitions.[33] Or it could respond by adopting an aggressive new strategy of U.S. primacy. The actual response of the Bush administration was to move away from its prior realism and toward a strategy of U.S. primacy.

Already in his speech of September to Congress, Bush had declared that the United States would fight a protracted war not only against Al Qaeda but against "every terrorist group of global reach."[34] This goal quickly developed into an even more all-encompassing war on terror. Critics pointed out the practical impossibility of declaring war against an entire form of violence.[35] But the administration's use of sweeping language was deliberate. First, it helped to build public support for the upcoming campaigns in Afghanistan and against Al Qaeda. Equally importantly, however, it reflected a genuine shift in mentality on the part of the administration, and served to notify the public that a fundamental adjustment in U.S. grand strategy was underway. As even the president's critics admit, Bush was truly shocked by the attacks of 9/11. These attacks triggered a willingness on his part to listen to the advocates of a more aggressive strategic approach.[36] They also triggered a willingness on the part of key foreign policy advisors, such as Dick Cheney and Donald Rumsfeld, to press urgently for such an approach.[37] As Rumsfeld put it, September 11 created "the kind of opportunities that World War II offered, to refashion the world."[38] The implication of a rather vague yet sweeping war on terror was precisely that it allowed for the pursuit of a broad new national security agenda, even in areas not directly related to the attacks of 9/11.[39] The leading example of this phenomenon was the war in Iraq.

Before 9/11 Bush had been unconvinced of the need for urgent military action against Iraq.[40] Certainly, he had criticized Clinton for failing to eject Saddam Hussein from power, but once in office, Bush had backed off from his earlier rhetoric, and essentially maintained a strategy of containment. Given a palpable lack of interest on the part of the president, strong advocates of "regime change" like Paul Wolfowitz were simply unable to force the issue. In the days right after 9/11, very little actually changed. Wolfowitz and Rumsfeld raised the possibility of immediately invading Iraq, but in the absence of any evidence linking Saddam Hussein to 9/11, most of the cabinet remained unconvinced of the need for immediate action. Dick Cheney joined with Colin Powell in arguing that the administration first tackle Afghanistan before moving on to Iraq.[41] The president agreed, and the issue was temporarily postponed.

The conclusion of the war in Afghanistan during November–December 2001 provided the opportunity to put Iraq at the top of the president's agenda. Key presidential advisors and hardliners like Cheney joined longtime true believers like Wolfowitz in arguing for a forcible "regime change" in Iraq.[42] Their reasons were several. First, hawks such as Cheney seem to have been truly concerned that if Saddam Hussein continued to maintain and/or develop weapons of mass destruction, he might use them to threaten American interests in the Middle East. Second, these same hawks suggested that Iraqi WMD might eventually be provided to anti-American terrorists. The example of 9/11 only demonstrated, all too vividly, the potential for catastrophic terrorist attacks on the United States. As Bush stated in his September 2002 address before the UN, "Our greatest fear is that terrorists will find a shortcut to their mad ambitions when an outlaw regime supplies them with the technologies to kill on a massive scale."[43] In reality, concern over terrorism was only one reason among several in the decision for war. But even critics of the war, such as John Judis, admit that these concerns were "not just for public consumption."[44] They were genuine. And they seem to have weighed heavily on Bush.

A third argument that clearly gained currency in the wake of 9/11 was the neoconservative idea that a defeated Iraq could be democratized, which would subsequently act as a kind of trigger for democratic changes throughout the region. As Bush put it in a February 2003 address to members of the American Enterprise Institute, "A liberated Iraq can show the power of freedom to transform that vital region, by bringing hope and progress into the lives of millions."[45] This argument was probably secondary to more basic security concerns in terms of its impact on the decision for war. But it did have an effect on the president.[46] And again, 9/11 was the crucial catalyst, since it appeared to demonstrate that U.S. support for authoritarian regimes in the Middle East had only encouraged Islamic extremism along with terrorist organizations like Al Qaeda. Finally, the very fact that Al Qaeda had recruited so many of its leading operatives from Saudi Arabia by playing on resentments against U.S. bases there only highlighted the undesirability of maintaining an extensive U.S. military presence in the Saudi kingdom over the long term. By invading Iraq and overthrowing Saddam Hussein, the United States would be able to shift its military base within the region and remove its unwelcome troop presence from Saudi Arabia. Such were the arguments for war. Many career civil servants in the U.S. military, at the State Department, and in the CIA were by all accounts skeptical of these arguments, skeptical that the costs of war would not outweigh the benefits.[47] But at some point early in 2002, in the words of one administration official, Bush "internalized the idea of regime change," and made the decision to confront Iraq.[48]

The rest of the story leading up to the war in Iraq is well known. Powell, in an August 2002 cabinet meeting, apparently managed to convince the president, along with the rest of the cabinet that Saddam Hussein's disarmament—rather than his overthrow—should be the centrally stated goal of American policy, and that the United States should pursue that goal through the UN rather than unilaterally.[49] This approach had the advantage of gaining some measure of international legitimacy for U.S. policy, which in turn helped build support for action against Iraq within the United States. In September 2002, at America's request, the UN approved resolution 1441, calling for new weapons inspections in Iraq, and stating that the Iraqi regime was already in material breach of prior resolutions; in October, the U.S. Senate authorized the use of force by the president, by a margin of three to one. UN weapons inspectors entered Iraq. At that point, of course, the "nightmare scenario" for administration hawks was that Iraq would respond by completely disarming itself of WMD, and thus rob the United States of its centrally stated reason for military action. But as he had done in 1990–1991, Saddam obliged the hawks by refusing to concede. Serious Iraqi disarmament was not forthcoming. This left only the question of international support for U.S. action. The United States and its leading ally, Great Britain, would have preferred a second UN resolution, giving military action a clear stamp of approval. But the threat of a veto by France as well as opposition from other powers prevented any such resolution. With the diplomatic game played out, on March 17, 2003, Bush issued a final ultimatum, calling on Saddam Hussein to abandon power altogether. Two days later, U.S. and allied forces began the invasion of Iraq.

Bush's decision for war against Iraq would have been remarkable, even if it had been an isolated incident unrelated to any broader strategic vision. But of course this was not the case. The war was justified quite explicitly in terms of a new national security strategy, and was itself only the most visible outcome of this new strategy. In the wake of 9/11, Bush consistently gravitated toward a foreign policy approach that was bold, ambitious, and idealistic.[50] In his September 20, 2001, address, the president had hinted at a broader, global struggle beyond the immediate threat of Al Qaeda. In his January 2002 State of the Union address, Bush was more specific about the administration's new security priority: "To prevent regimes that sponsor terror from threatening America or our friends and allies with weapons of mass destruction." Three regimes, in particular, were singled out as being part of a supposed "axis of evil": Iran, Iraq, and North Korea. Bush indicated a willingness to act preemptively: "I will not wait on events while dangers gather." And he struck a remarkably universalistic and uncompromising tone regarding America's role in the world, saying that "America will lead by defending liberty and justice because they are right and true and unchanging for all people everywhere."[51] Already by January 2002, then, the trend was clear: the war on terror would morph into a broader crusade against rogue states, and, indeed, into a much more assertive and even Wilsonian grand strategy on the part of the United States.

The new strategy was laid out most fully and explicitly in the new National Security Strategy of the United States of America, released by the White House in September 2002. In that document, the administration began by pointing out that "the United States possesses unprecedented— and unequalled—strength and influence in the world." It renounced any purely realpolitik approach in arguing that "the great strength of this nation must be used to promote a balance of power that favors freedom."[52] American classical liberal values were again described, as they had been on the eve of war against the Taliban, as "nonnegotiable demands."[53] The promotion of free trade and market democracy was held up as a central U.S. interest.[54] And interestingly, the possibility of traditional great-power competition was played down. Instead, other powers were urged to join with the United States in affirming the general trend toward democracy and open markets worldwide. "With Russia," the administration stated, "we are already building a new strategic relationship, based on a central reality of the twenty-first century: the United States and Russia are no longer strategic adversaries."[55] And even with China, the new national security strategy emphasized areas of common interest, and hopes for liberalization.[56] Of course, this broad affirmation of classical liberal assumptions was no doubt used in part for reasons of domestic politics and public relations. In the United States, liberal arguments are always employed to bolster strategic adjustments of any kind. But the United States had been no less liberal—broadly speaking—in the year 2000, when the nascent Bush team was stressing the need for realism in foreign affairs. So the new strategy does seem to have reflected a real shift on the part of the administration toward a more deliberately Wilsonian approach.

Within this general affirmation of America's interest in the promotion of market democracy overseas, the new national security strategy painted a stark picture of grave threats to American security. The threat of terrorism was naturally the focus, but the specific danger was drawn in a striking and expansive manner. Most crucially, the administration argued that the proliferation of WMD on the part of state sponsors of terrorism necessitated an entirely new U.S. security strategy. Deterrence and containment would no longer work. The United States would henceforth reserve the right to use force, in a preventive and unilateral fashion if necessary, against rogue states in order to prevent the possibility of weapons transfers to terrorists.[57] As stated in the September 2002 document:

> Given the goals of rogue states and terrorists, the United States can no longer rely solely on a reactive posture as we have done in the past. The inability to deter a potential attacker, the immediacy of today's threats, and the magnitude of potential harm that could be caused by our adversaries' choice of weapons, do not permit that option. . . . We must adapt the concept of imminent threat to the capabilities and objectives of today's adversaries. . . . As was demonstrated by the losses on September 11, 2001, mass civilian casualties is [sic] the specific objective of terrorists and these losses would be exponentially more severe if terrorists acquired and used weapons of mass destruction. . . . To forestall or prevent such hostile acts by our adversaries, the United States will, if necessary, act preemptively.[58]

All of the above arguments—regarding preventive military action as well as a broader Wilsonian vision of world order—were repeated by the president in major addresses at West Point in June 2002, at the United Nations in September of that same year, in Cincinnati that October, in the State of the Union address the following January, and on the eve of war against Iraq in February and March 2003.[59]

Preventive wars are not unknown in American history, but by any standard, to openly embrace the concept of preventive military action as a centerpiece of U.S. grand strategy was a remarkably bold departure. Bush did not suggest that Iraq was the only case in which such action might be required. On the contrary, he argued that an entirely new approach toward national security was called for across the board. As he put it in his West Point address of 2002, "Containment is not possible when unbalanced dictators with weapons of mass destruction can deliver those weapons on missiles or secretly deploy them to terrorist allies. . . . We must take the battle to the enemy, disrupt his plans, and confront the worst threats before they emerge."[60] And Bush actually began to implement this new strategy, piece by piece, in the months after 9/11. Not only was Iraq invaded in the spring of 2003, but the form of the invasion, in itself, was a leading indicator of the administration's new willingness to incur serious risks: a major U.S. force in combat on the ground, involving hundreds of thousands of troops, along with the possibility of many American casualties.[61] In the United States, for the first time in almost twenty years, defense spending was increased dramatically: from $334 billion in fiscal year 2002 to approximately $400 billion in fiscal year 2004.[62] And of course, the war on terror went on, in states as diverse as Pakistan, Djibouti, and the Philippines, rearranging U.S. relations with these countries while introducing an increased U.S. presence in their affairs at the same time.

Given all of these changes, how should the national security strategy of the Bush administration be characterized? In broad terms, the new strategy aggressively affirmed U.S. predominance, rather than any sort of global balance of power. It proposed to liberalize and Americanize the international system, in some cases by force. It embraced the concept of rogue-state rollback. And it called for energetic action to preempt any conceivable threat to U.S. national security. As the administration's own supporters recognized, this was a strategy of U.S. primacy, and a striking shift from Bush's more realist approach prior to 9/11.

Naturally, this new strategy caused intense controversy, just as the war in Iraq caused intense controversy. The administration may have had virtually unanimous domestic support for war against the Taliban, but once they began "phase two" against Iraq, and began to clarify the full scope of their ambitions, important sections of domestic support began to fall away. Most realists, nationalists, and liberal internationalists had supported the war in Afghanistan after 9/11. But important elements of all three subcultures were much more resistant to a preventive war against Saddam Hussein. In fact, it might be said that for the first time since the end of the Cold War, during the debate over Iraq there was a truly widespread and passionate debate within the United States over the appropriateness of some central aspect of U.S. grand strategy.

The most common and searching criticism of the Bush administration's new national security strategy within academic circles was to suggest that it invited all of the classic risks of "imperial overstretch." Authors such as John Ikenberry, Jack Snyder, Robert Litwak, Jeffrey Record, and David Hendrickson argued that this new strategy was bound to be counterproductive, since it would only tend to trigger fierce antagonism and resistance overseas.[63] More specifically, these critics suggested that an openly announced policy of preemption would only invite abuse by other potential aggressors while eroding America's alliances as well as its overall influence in the world. These criticisms had merit. But a more subtle and equally probable danger, which received much less discussion, was in some ways the opposite one: namely, that the Bush administration would fail to make good on its promises of a serious commitment to peace, stability, and democracy overseas.

In this regard, the precedent in Afghanistan was certainly not encouraging. There, after helping to defeat the Taliban, the United States proved unwilling to invest very much, militarily or financially, in postwar stability. The inevitable result was a weak, new Afghan government, unable to secure even minimal control over the countryside outside of Kabul.[64] To be fair, the Bush foreign policy team understood that Saddam Hussein would not be overthrown without a major commitment of U.S. ground troops. But in terms of planning for a post-Saddam Iraq, the administration seems to have based its initial actions upon the most optimistic assumptions: ordinary Iraqis would rise up in support of U.S. forces; these same forces would rapidly transfer authority toward a friendly interim government; the oil would flow, paying for reconstruction efforts; and the great majority of U.S. troops would come home quickly. These were never very likely prospects, and with all of the warnings that it received, the administration should have known better. As Bush himself said during the 2000 presidential campaign, nation building is difficult and expensive. The administration's preference was to avoid nation-building operations—an understandable predilection in itself. But once the administration made the decision to go to war against Saddam Hussein, it was also obliged to prepare for the foreseeable likelihood of major, postwar reconstruction efforts—not only for humanitarian reasons, but in order to secure the political objectives for which it had gone to war in the first place.[65]

The Bush administration's early reluctance to plan for Iraq's postwar reconstruction had serious and deadly consequences. Once Saddam's government was overthrown, a power vacuum was created, and the United States did not initially step in to fill the void. Widespread looting, disorder, and insecurity were the inevitable result. This set the tone for the immediate postwar era. Moreover, because of these insecure conditions, many of Saddam's former operatives were given the opportunity to develop and pursue a dangerous, low-level insurgency against U.S. forces. The subsequent learning curve within the Bush administration has been steep. By necessity, the president has come a long way toward recognizing how expensive this particular process of nation building is going to be. The approval by Congress, in the fall of 2003, of $87 billion for continuing operations in Iraq and Afghanistan was clearly a step in the right direction. Bush has indicated repeatedly, to his credit, that the United States cannot cut and run from its new commitments. But there are also worrying signs, as there were before the war, that U.S. troops may disengage from the counterinsurgency effort within Iraq before they have actually had the opportunity to stabilize the political situation in that country.

Nation-building operations sometimes fail, even under favorable circumstances. But without robust involvement on the part of outside powers, such operations simply cannot succeed. The example of Afghanistan (along with previous efforts in the 1990s) should have demonstrated that nation building on the cheap is impractical and ineffective. It was an illusion to think that a stable, secure, and democratic Iraq could arise without a significant long-term U.S. investment of both blood and treasure.[66] Having defined such an Iraq as a vital U.S. interest, it was only appropriate that the administration pay the price to achieve it. But even after 9/11, the preference for limited liability in strategic affairs continued to weigh heavily on Bush. Postwar reconstruction efforts were delayed until almost too late; it remains to be seen whether this was a fatal mistake, since the final political outcome in Iraq has yet to be determined.

To reiterate: the administration responded to the challenge of 9/11 by devising a more assertive, Wilsonian grand strategy. The stated goal of this strategy was not only to initiate rogue-state rollback but to promote a more open and democratic world order. By all accounts, Bush and his advisors really did believe that 9/11 offered the United States, in the words of Donald Rumsfeld, an "opportunity to refashion the world." The problem was not that President Bush departed from a long tradition of liberal internationalism; it was that he continued some of the worst features of that tradition. Specifically, in Iraq, he continued the tradition of articulating and pursuing a set of extremely ambitious and idealistic foreign policy goals without initially providing the full or proportionate means to achieve those goals. In this sense, it must be said, George W. Bush was very much a Wilsonian.

CONCLUSION

The Bush administration came to power in 2001 determined to tone down the liberal internationalism of the Clinton era, and to bring a new realism to the conduct of U.S. grand strategy. In particular, Bush promised to be more selective with regard to military intervention overseas. At first, this new approach held, in spite of divisions within the administration and among its supporters. The terrorist attacks of September 11, 2001, opened up a window of opportunity for advocates of a more assertive, and, indeed, a more "idealistic" grand strategy, to come to the fore. The war on Iraq was the most visible manifestation of this new strategy. But a change in emphasis took place across the board as the Bush administration made it clear that it would act energetically to preempt threats to U.S. security and to promote a world order more reflective of U.S. preferences.

None of these changes were dictated by international structural pressures per se. In fact, during this entire period, the underlying distribution of power within the international system—a key independent variable for structural realism—never changed. The initial strategic adjustments undertaken by the Bush administration were much more the result of new ideas in the White House than of severe external pressures. And in terms of a strategic response to 9/11, beyond adopting a more vigorous counterterrorism policy, there were any number of ways that the United States might have reacted. A strategy of primacy was not the only one available, and indeed, many realists opposed such a strategy. There is actually nothing within structural realism that would have allowed us to predict exactly how the United States would respond to such terrorist attacks. At the same time, there is very little evidence that domestic economic interests pushed or pulled U.S. grand strategy in one direction or another. Critics of the Bush administration, both at home and abroad, were right to see the influence of neoconservatives as fundamental in shaping the new strategy, but they were wrong to see that influence as essentially venal, economic, or electoral in motivation. The strategists of American primacy believed in what they were doing. The independent influence of ideas was a crucial, missing element in the story. Moreover, the recurrence of certain prevailing ideas and assumptions regarding strategic affairs within the United States points to the continuing existence of a nationally distinctive strategic culture. It can hardly be a coincidence that when Bush and his advisors searched for a way to understand and respond to the events of 9/11, they fell back on classical liberal ideas, just as Clinton had done before them. No U.S. leader is ever entirely free from the influence of liberal ideas regarding international relations. Bush's early realism was never wholehearted, only a corrective in relation to what had come before. But that particular form of realism regarding strategic affairs seems to have disappeared, at least temporarily. Nation building, intervention, and Wilsonian ambitions have returned in earnest, and the doctrine of democratic enlargement has had its revenge.

CASE SUMMARIES AND THEORETICAL FINDINGS

The cases of U.S. strategic adjustment examined in this book show certain similar features. During the great debate of 1918–1921, there were three plausible strategic alternatives open to the United States: membership in a worldwide League of Nations, disengagement from Europe, or a straightforward military alliance with France and Great Britain. Given America's immense material power by 1918, international conditions could not have predicted the return to disengagement. Certainly, domestic politics, presidential leadership, and sheer contingency all had a dramatic effect on the eventual outcome of the League debate. But these patterns of politics and leadership were powerfully conditioned by U.S. strategic culture. Common assumptions of limited liability, together with classical liberal beliefs, acted to shape and constrain new strategic ideas; decision-makers were unable and/or unwilling to build support for any limited and realistic strategic commitment to Europe for what were, essentially, cultural reasons. A simple balance-of-power alliance with France was ruled out by Woodrow Wilson—and many other Americans—because it seemed to violate liberal foreign policy goals. At the same time, member-ship in a strong League of Nations was ruled out by the Senate, because it seemed to violate the American tradition of limited liability in strategic affairs. The culturally influenced result was a return to disengagement, in spite of the fact that the United States was materially ready to assume a larger role in world affairs.

In the case of Harry Truman and U.S. strategic adjustment after 1945, there were four strategic options: a return to strategic disengagement, rollback against the USSR, an explicit sphere-of-influence agreement with Moscow, or the worldwide containment of communism. International conditions at the time ruled out disengagement, as well as rollback, but such conditions by themselves cannot explain why U.S. officials selected containment. If international conditions had been the only significant source of American behavior, U.S. officials could have just as easily settled on an explicit policy of mutual spheres of influence with Moscow. A pure sphere-of-influence arrangement, however, lacked powerful advocates within the United States, because it simply did not resonate with Ameri-cans culturally. U.S. officials would accept an open, liberal sphere, but not a closed Soviet sphere in Eastern Europe. American liberal norms and ideas acted as a filter on strategic options, ruling out a strict sphere-of-influence approach. Containment was adopted not because it was the only strategy that matched international conditions, but because it was the only strategy that matched international conditions as well as American cultural concerns. At the same time, a weakened but persistent preference for limited liability led U.S. officials to select a version of containment that was extremely ambitious but relatively inexpensive—a combination that could not last, and indeed broke down after the outbreak of the Korean War.

After the end of the Cold War, the United States had four basic strategic alternatives: disengagement, balance of power, liberal internationalism, or U.S. primacy. International conditions made disengagement unlikely, but did not rule out any of the other three strategies. The Clinton administration adopted an essentially liberal internationalist strategy—engagement and enlargement—marked by broad continuity with post-1945 commitments and assumptions. That strategy cannot be explained without reference to certain cultural legacies that continued to influence U.S. strategic behavior during the 1990s. As always, given the liberal assumptions of American strategic culture, grand strategies based upon pure realpolitik or balance-of-power assumptions found little favor with U.S. officials. And in the absence of any sense of policy failure, Americans were not inclined to question the internationalist assumptions that had undergirded U.S. national security policy since the 1940s. Hence, out of both conviction and the anticipation of domestic political necessity—and in the absence of any compelling case for change—candidate and then President Clinton embraced and encouraged a broad, post–Cold War strategic consensus. Consequently, any real alternatives to an internationalist grand strategy were removed from serious consideration. At the same time, under the Clinton administration, liberal internationalist goals were pursued through sometimes very limited means. A pervasive concern over limited liability continued to inform American foreign policymaking, especially on questions of military intervention.

The George W. Bush administration came to power in 2001 with a somewhat less liberal internationalist and more realist approach toward U.S. grand strategy. In particular, Bush promised to be more selective with regard to military interventions overseas. This shift toward strategic realism had more to do with the ideas and assumptions held by the incoming Bush foreign policy team than with any overwhelming international pressures. The terrorist attacks of September 11, 2001, opened a window of opportunity for advocates of a more assertive, and more idealistic, grand strategy to come to the fore. This particular outcome was not completely predetermined by international pressures; it had more to do with the recurring power of classical liberal ideas in U.S. grand strategy, resurrected in a particularly muscular form by President Bush. The war in Iraq was the most visible manifestation of a new strategy of U.S. primacy. But assumptions of limited liability continued to inform U.S. strategic behavior in that the Bush administration was initially unwilling to pay the price that would have been necessary to secure a stable postwar Iraq.

Looking back at U.S. strategic adjustment under Wilson, Truman, and Clinton, as well as Bush, what are the main theoretical findings to be drawn from these cases of change (or potential change) in U.S. grand strategy? First, structural realist theories that refer only to international pressures cannot, by themselves, explain patterns of strategic adjustment. Such models do explain a certain amount of variance in U.S. grand strategy, but they leave out crucial aspects of each policy outcome, and are ultimately unsatisfying as explanatory models. Only by adding a cultural and ideational account of strategic change do we begin to have an adequate explanation of strategic outcomes.

Our main finding was that cultural and ideational legacies have a powerful impact on grand strategy, independent of international pressures. In early twentieth-century America, the tradition of limited liability and strategic disengagement—together with a heritage of classical liberal thought on foreign policy matters—acted as a sharp constraint on new strategic ideas. Certain plausible strategic choices—such as a Franco-American alliance after World War One—were ruled out of consideration, in spite of their material advantages, for what were essentially cultural reasons. In effect, the United States began to act as a world power much later than one would have expected, given its material interests outside the Western Hemisphere. And when, in the late 1940s, U.S. officials did finally adopt a new set of peacetime strategic commitments, they did so in a way that was strongly influenced by U.S. strategic culture: not by agreeing to a sphere-of-influence deal, but by embarking on a worldwide struggle against communism, without initially creating the military capabilities to fully support such an ambitious strategy. International pressures, alone, simply cannot account for these peculiar strategic outcomes.

It is important to note here, however, that cultural and ideational factors cannot be taken as a *substitute* for a structural realist account of strategic change. International pressures are real, and have a significant impact on strategic outcomes. By referring to changes in the international distribution of power, structural realism provides a compelling long-term explanation of America's rise to world power. But this is true only *over the long term*. With respect to the timing and the precise nature of strategic adjustment, structural realism is inadequate as an explanatory model.

A neoclassical realist model provides a more complete and convincing explanation for changes in U.S. grand strategy. According to such a model, international material pressures are the single most important long-term cause behind strategic adjustment. This is where neoclassical realists differ from constructivists. We need not refer to any variation in U.S. strategic culture in order to explain America's adoption of a global grand strategy after either 1945 or 1991. Changes in the international distribution of power are sufficient to do that. But according to a neoclassical realist model, changes in international conditions are not sufficient to explain precise changes in grand strategy. Here, strategic culture can and must be brought in as a permissive cause, or filter, that shapes the final choices made by foreign policymakers.

International pressures are real and constraining; they are not entirely subjective; this is a crucial realist insight. But international pressures are also filtered through the lens of domestic cultural beliefs and perceptions. Viable strategic options can be ruled out as inappropriate or unacceptable for domestic cultural reasons, in spite of international pressures to the contrary. Strategic cultures may eventually change under the strain of international conditions. But domestic cultural influences are not necessarily washed out by the pressures of international competition: this is the neoclassical realist concession to constructivism. Certainly, U.S. policymakers rejected neoisolationism after 1945, and again after 1991 and 2001, in large part because of international conditions. But the particular strategies adopted in lieu of disengagement have always been informed by American cultural—which is to say, liberal—assumptions. In this sense, the United States has never been completely "socialized"—as a structural realist would expect—into the practices and assumptions of realpolitik. Interestingly, this is exactly what classical realists like George Kennan and Hans Morgenthau used to argue: that American liberal "idealism" has a real impact on U.S. foreign policy behavior.[67] Contemporary realists would gain by drawing on the insights of Kennan and Morgenthau in recognizing the causal power of domestic culture on foreign policy outcomes.

In terms of other findings, the effect of domestic political competition on U.S. grand strategy turned out to be quite significant. We found, in every one of these cases, that the desire to win election or re-election often played a crucial part in leading presidents, senators, and congressmen to support or oppose particular strategic ideas. The need to build winning coalitions had a critical impact on the substance of proposed strategic alternatives. This seems to have been especially true in the case of politicians whose party was out of power. In 1951, for example, many Republicans attacked Truman's foreign policy and supported a kind of Asia-first unilateralism, in large part out of simple frustration with the entire Democratic agenda of the previous eighteen years. The aim of these attacks was not simply to implement a different national security policy, but to inflict a political defeat upon the opposing party. Even in this case, however, there was a real and substantive disagreement between Republicans and Democrats over the proper course of U.S. grand strategy. Domestic political interests and domestic political competition were thus fused, as always, with genuine differences of opinion over foreign policy. And for those individuals in the executive branch, who were actually responsible for directing foreign policy—such as Wilson and Truman—domestic political motives were usually of secondary importance.

Finally, one of the main findings of this study was the critical importance of presidential leadership and presidential choice in shaping strate-

gic behavior. In the months after 9/11, George W. Bush made crucial decisions in favor of war in Iraq that another president might not have made.
Bill Clinton likewise played a leading, but less dramatic, role during the
1990s, working to maintain domestic support for a liberal internationalist
strategic approach. In 1945–1951, it is true that a number of deep underlying causes—some international and some cultural—all pointed toward
a rough bipartisan consensus in favor of containment. Nevertheless, this
consensus actually had to be constructed by human beings, and the Truman administration did so with great skill. And in the earlier case, during
1918–1921, contingent patterns of agenda setting by one man, Woodrow
Wilson, made a tremendous difference in the final outcome. As we saw
in that case, in is quite conceivable that a different president would have
built a winning coalition in favor of a U.S. entry into the League of Nations had he been willing to adopt a more modest conception of what
that commitment entailed. Such a commitment could also have included
a quiet, but immensely consequential, alliance with France and Great Britain. But Wilson chose not to build such a coalition, because it would not
have supported his own conception of the League of Nations. As a result,
internationalists were divided, and the U.S. legacy of nonentanglement
once again came to the fore. Of course, we cannot know whether a different leader could have overcome the widespread distrust among Americans
of so-called entangling alliances. What we do know is that Wilson made
crucial, peculiar choices that doomed any such effort to failure. It is surely
worth noting that these choices were not forced on him by structural
pressures; presidential leadership, in itself, was a crucial source of the
final outcome.

In spite of the similarities between these four cases, they each evince
differences, as well. The role of international, structural pressures was
especially obvious in the period immediately after World War Two. The
role of domestic politics and presidential leadership was especially apparent in the League of Nations debate. The exact, relative weight of these
various factors—international pressures, strategic culture, domestic politics, and individual leadership—obviously varies from case to case in determining patterns of strategic adjustment; no monocausal explanation
can satisfactorily explain strategic choice. But the precise role of domestic
politics in particular deserves further examination. Future studies should
address in more detail the question of exactly *how* domestic political pressures shape strategic adjustment. Specifically, we still need a more thorough and systematic investigation of the extent to which partisan competition influences patterns of strategic choice.

Several other questions remain that point the way toward potential
future research. First, to what extent is the neoclassical realist model of
strategic adjustment applicable to other countries? In chapter 2, I devel-

oped an emphasis on U.S.-specific patterns of agenda setting and coalition building. There is no reason to believe that these particular domestic political patterns are the same from one country to the next. But the basic neoclassical realist framework from chapter 1—of international pressures interacting with nationally specific strategic cultures—ought to and can be tested with relation to other countries. We might very well find that a similar tug of war between international pressure and domestic strategic culture exists for other nations, too.

Second, in the course of these case studies, I did not examine the causal impact of shifting sectional or sectoral interests in determining patterns of strategic adjustment. Yet this sort of economic-interest approach is one of the most powerful and popular in international relations.[68] It seems entirely possible that economic interests might help explain why one strategic subculture wins out over another. But can such outcomes be thought of as *primarily* the result of shifting coalition interests? It would be useful to know how far such arguments can go, relative to the model developed within this book, and how much causal weight they can actually carry in comparison with a neoclassical realist framework.

Finally, I found that certain cultural legacies—specifically, liberalism and limited liability—have had a persistent, and even a dysfunctional, effect on the conduct of U.S. grand strategy. But this is not to deny that these same cultural legacies have also had certain *positive* effects on U.S. grand strategy over time. The positive contributions of the American liberal tradition upon U.S. grand strategy are fairly well understood; the world would be a less democratic, less peaceful, and less prosperous place without it.[69] Has the U.S. preference for limited liability in strategic affairs—although weaker than it once was—had any similar positive effects—for example, in making the United States seem less threatening to other countries, or in allowing the United States to husband its strength in difficult times? And is it possible that democratic *institutions* play a corrective role in mitigating the impact of strategic culture?

THE FUTURE OF U.S. GRAND STRATEGY

What predictions would these findings suggest in relation to future cases of strategic adjustment? Simply put, we can expect that the United States—like other countries—will be most likely to adopt new grand strategies because of significant changes in the level of external threat, and/or changes in the international distribution of power. At the same time, such international pressures will be filtered through the lens of domestic cultural assumptions, allowing the United States to adopt a grand strategy consistent with its own strategic culture. It is precisely for this reason that the United States is unlikely to adopt the recommendations of realists like Henry Kissinger for a more modest and pure balance-of-power strategy as a substitute for either primacy or liberal internationalism. Such a strict balance-of-power strategy is not well suited to America's strategic culture, or to American liberal assumptions regarding the nature of international relations. A more probable outcome, unfortunately, is that if America's relative power within the international system decreases significantly—and in the absence of pressing external threats—the United States will eventually reject both primacy and liberal internationalism by turning back to a grand strategy resembling the pristine disengagement of the interwar era. Such a strategy resonates with Americans culturally—with both conservative nationalists and liberal progressives—in a way that no balance-of-power strategy ever could. A strategically disengaged United States could at least convince itself that it was being true to its own liberal democratic traditions. Such a neoisolationist turn would be a disaster for the United States, as it would be for the rest of the world. But if history is any indication, then U.S. strategic culture will probably not allow for primacy and/or liberal internationalism to be replaced by anything other than liberal isolationism. At the same time, however, given America's very high and seemingly stable share of the current distribution of power within the international system, there is no reason to believe that U.S. foreign policymakers will adopt a strategy of neoisolationism at any time in the foreseeable future. Cultural theory leads us to expect that Americans will reject any pure balance-of-power approach to international affairs. But realism tells us that Americans will also reject neoisolationism, since no great power ever gives up its predominant position in the world unless it is forced to do so.

America's foreign policy elites are not likely to retreat into isolationism, or to abandon their longstanding ambition to create an "Americanized" international order. What is more probable, and therefore more dangerous, is that they will continue to oscillate between various forms of globalism, and to press for a more open and democratic international system without willing the means to sustain it. This would certainly be in keeping with the past, and with the tensions inherent in U.S. strategic culture. As we have seen, Woodrow Wilson thought that he could promote a liberal world order through the League of Nations without making any specific strategic commitments that might prove costly to the United States. The Truman administration, while it learned many lessons from Wilson's failure, thought at first that it could pursue the worldwide containment of the Soviet Union without imposing a heavy burden of rearmament on the American people. The Clinton administration hoped and believed that it could promote democratic enlargement in an ever-widening circle of nations without really risking U.S. money or U.S. lives. And even the Bush administration, for all the talk of its imperial ambitions, has proven reluctant to invest the bare minimum in any of the nonmilitary instruments of U.S. influence abroad. In this sense, the choice between a strategy of primacy and a strategy of liberal internationalism, which currently seems to characterize public debate over U.S. foreign policy, is almost beside the point. Neither strategy will work if Americans are unwilling to incur the full costs and risks that are implied in either case.

A preference for limited liability is a part of the U.S. strategic tradition just as much as is the desire to promote a liberal international order. On many occasions, that preference has proven to be a worthwhile check on potentially costly initiatives and adventures. But an excessive emphasis on limited liability is unsuited to a country that claims to be, in Madeleine Albright's words, the world's leading champion for freedom. In fact, it is not only unsuitable, but simply impossible to promote the kind of international system that Americans say they want without paying a heavy price for it. Ironically, it is here, as a prescription, rather than as an explanation for U.S. foreign policy, that realism has the most to offer. Classical realists like Walter Lippmann and Hans Morgenthau offered a similar warning over fifty years ago. To pursue a global grand strategy without providing the means—military, political, and economic—for it is to invite not only humiliation, but disaster. The United States, together with its allies, can either take up the burden of truly acting on its own internationalist rhetoric, or it can keep the costs and risks of foreign policy to a minimum. It cannot do both. That is the U.S. strategic dilemma.

NOTES

CHAPTER ONE
POWER, CULTURE AND GRAND STRATEGY

1. B. H. Liddell Hart, *Strategy* (New York: Praeger, 1954), p. 31.
2. Ibid., pp. 335–36.
3. Eric Nordlinger, *Isolationism Reconfigured* (Princeton: Princeton University Press, 1995), pp. 9–10.
4. Barry Posen, *The Sources of Military Doctrine: France, Britain and Germany Between the World Wars* (Ithaca: Cornell University Press, 1985), p. 13.
5. Charles Kupchan, *Vulnerability of Empire* (Ithaca: Cornell University Press, 1994), p. 3, n. 4.
6. Thomas Christensen, *Useful Adversaries: Grand Strategy, Domestic Mobilization, and Sino-American Conflict, 1947–1958* (Princeton: Princeton University Press, 1996), p. 7.
7. Robert Art, "A Defensible Defense: America's Grand Strategy After the Cold War," in Sean Lynn-Jones and Steven Miller, eds., *America's Strategic Choices: An International Security Reader* (Cambridge, Mass.: The MIT Press, 1997), p. 79.
8. Samuel Huntington, "The Evolution of National Strategy," in Daniel Kaufman et al, eds., *U.S. National Security Strategy for the 1990s* (Baltimore: Johns Hopkins University Press, 1991), pp. 11–12.
9. Edward Luttwak, *Strategy: The Logic of War and Peace* (Cambridge, Mass.: Belknap Press of Harvard University Press, 1987), p. 180.
10. Paul Kennedy, ed., *Grand Strategies in War and Peace* (New Haven: Yale University Press, 1991), pp. 2–4.
11. Robert Art, "Defensible Defense," pp. 51–52.
12. Michael Desch, *When the Third World Matters: Latin America and United States Grand Strategy* (Baltimore: Johns Hopkins University Press, 1993), p. 2; John L. Gaddis, *Strategies of Containment* (New York: Oxford University Press, 1982), p. ix.
13. Huntington, "Evolution of National Strategy," p. 11; Luttwak, *Strategy*, p. 235.
14. Luttwak, *Strategy*, p. 182.
15. Kupchan, *Vulnerability of Empire*, pp. 67–68.
16. Alastair Iain Johnston, *Cultural Realism: Strategic Culture and Grand Strategy in Chinese History* (Princeton: Princeton University Press, 1995), p. 115.
17. As these three authors themselves admit.
18. Peter Trubowitz and Edward Rhodes, "Explaining American Strategic Adjustment," in Peter Trubowitz, Emily Goldman, and Edward Rhodes, eds., *The Politics of Strategic Adjustment: Ideas, Institutions and Interests* (New York: Columbia University Press, 1999), pp. 3–25.

19. See, for example, Thomas Berger, *Cultures of Antimilitarism: National Security in Germany and Japan* (Baltimore: Johns Hopkins University Press, 1998); and Alastair Iain Johnston, *Cultural Realism.*

20. Fareed Zakaria, "Realism and Domestic Politics," *International Security* 17, no. 1 (Summer 1992): 177–98.

21. I do not claim that the list of generalizable causes of strategic adjustment is exhausted by these two factors alone. There is, for example, a very worthwhile literature on sectional and sectoral economic interests as a crucial source of strategic choice. Their relative causal weight in the process of strategic adjustment is beyond the scope of this book. For a work that emphasizes the centrality of economic interests in the formation of U.S. grand strategy, see Peter Trubowitz, *Defining the National Interest* (Chicago: University of Chicago Press, 1998).

22. A point made by Stephen Brooks and William Wohlforth in "Power, Globalization and the Cold War: Reevaluating a Landmark Case for Ideas," *International Security* 25, no. 3 (Winter 2000–2001): 6–7.

23. Michael Desch, "Culture Clash," *International Security* 23, no. 1 (Summer 1998): 141–70.

24. Berger, *Cultures of Antimilitarism*, p. 9; Johnston, *Cultural Realism*, pp. 1–4; Elizabeth Kier, *Imagining War: French and British Military Doctrines Between the Wars* (Princeton: Princeton University Press, 1997), pp. 3–5.

25. Robert Jervis, *Perception and Misperception in International Politics* (Princeton: Princeton University Press, 1976), pp. 32–57, 117–287; Jerel Rosati, "The Power of Human Cognition in the Study of World Politics," *International Studies Review* 2, no. 3 (Fall 2000): 56–57.

26. Berger, *Cultures of Antimilitarism*, p. 9; John Duffield, "Political Culture and State Behavior: Why Germany Confounds Neorealism," *International Organization* 53, no. 4 (Autumn 1999): 765–70; David Elkins and Richard Simeon, "A Cause in Search of Effects, or What Does Political Culture Explain?" *Comparative Politics* 11, no. 2 (1979): 127–29; Johnston, *Cultural Realism*, pp. 34–36; Peter Katzenstein, ed., *The Culture of National Security: Norms and Identity in World Politics* (New York: Columbia University Press, 1996), pp. 6–7; Richard Wilson, "The Many Voices of Political Culture," *World Politics* 52, no. 2 (January 2000): 246–73.

27. Kupchan, *Vulnerability of Empire*, p. 5; Albert Yee, "The Causal Effects of Ideas on Politics," *International Organization* 50, no. 1 (Winter 1996): 86–88.

28. It is of course possible to conceive of cultural factors as also operating at the international or systemic level, and a variety of constructivist authors such as Alexander Wendt have made the case for such a conception. I do not deny the potential contributions of such an approach, but in the current discussion I am primarily interested in culture as a unit or state-level variable.

29. Berger, *Cultures of Antimilitarism*, pp. 9, 12; Kier, *Imagining War*, pp. 3–5.

30. Judith Goldstein and Robert Keohane, eds., *Ideas and Foreign Policy: Beliefs, Institutions and Political Change* (Ithaca: Cornell University Press, 1993), pp. 13–17.

31. Emanuel Adler, "Seizing the Middle Ground: Constructivism in World Politics," *European Journal of International Relations* 3, no. 3 (September 1997):

330, 337; Berger, *Cultures of Antimilitarism*, pp. 16–19; Kier, *Imagining War,* pp. 3–5.

32. Berger, *Cultures of Antimilitarism*, pp. 14–16; Katzenstein, *The Culture of National Security*, p. 17.

33. Michael Barnett, "Identity and Alliances in the Middle East," in Katzenstein, ed., *The Culture of National Security*, pp. 400–447; Mlada Bukovansky, "American Identity and Neutral Rights from Independence to the War of 1812," *International Organization* 51, no.2 (Spring 1997): 217–18.

34. Richard Price and Nina Tannenwald, "Norms and Deterrence: The Nuclear and Chemical Weapons Taboo," in Katzenstein, ed., *The Culture of National Security*, pp. 114–52.

35. Berger, *Cultures of Antimilitarism*, p. 21.

36. Duffield, "Political Culture and State Behavior," p. 772; Elkins and Simeon, "A Cause in Search of its Effects," p. 128; Johnston, *Cultural Realism,* p. 35.

37. Sheri Berman, "Ideas, Norms and Culture in Political Analysis," *Comparative Politics* 33, no. 2 (January 2001): 38; Goldstein and Keohane, *Ideas and Foreign Policy*, pp. 20–24.

38. Yee, "The Causal Effects of Ideas on Politics," pp. 95–101.

39. Johnston, *Cultural Realism,* p. 1.

40. Ibid., pp. 61–154.

41. A good example of such an argument is in Posen, *Sources of Military Doctrine,* pp. 7–8, 239.

42. For a summary of core realist assumptions, see Michael Doyle, *Ways of War and Peace* (New York: W. W. Norton, 1997), pp. 41–201; and Robert Gilpin, "The Richness of the Political Theory of Realism," *International Organization* 38, no. 2 (Spring 1984): 287–304.

43. Kenneth Waltz, *Theory of International Politics* (Reading: Addison-Wesley, 1979), pp. 74–77, 93–97, 127–28.

44. Kenneth Waltz, "International Politics is Not Foreign Policy," *Security Studies* 6, no. 1 (Autumn 1996): 54–55; Waltz, *Theory of International Politics*, pp. 70–72, 116–28.

45. See especially Colin Elman, "Why Not Neorealist Theories of Foreign Policy?" *Security Studies* 6, no. 1 (Autumn 1996): 7–53.

46. Eric Labs, "Beyond Victory: Offensive Realism and the Expansion of War Aims," *Security Studies* 6, no. 4 (Summer 1997): 1–49; John Mearsheimer, *The Tragedy of Great Power Politics* (New York: W. W. Norton, 2001), pp. 21–22, 31–39.

47. Robert Gilpin, *War and Change in World Politics* (New York: Cambridge University Press, 1981), p. 23; Martin Wight, *Power Politics* (London: Leicester University Press, 1978), p. 144.

48. John Mearsheimer, "The False Promise of International Institutions," in Michael Brown, Sean Lynn-Jones, and Steven Miller, eds., *The Perils of Anarchy: Contemporary Realism and International Security* (Cambridge, Mass.: MIT Press, 1995), pp. 369–70.

49. Hans Morgenthau, *Politics Among Nations: The Struggle for Power and Peace* (New York: McGraw Hill, 1993), pp. 99–102.

50. Waltz, *Theory of International Politics*, pp. 70–73.

51. Raymond Aron, *Peace and War* (New York: Praeger, 1966), pp. 90–91; Charles Glaser, "The Security Dilemma Revisited," *World Politics* 50, no. 1 (October 1997): 171–201; Andrew Kydd, "Sheep in Sheep's Clothing: Why Security Seekers Do Not Fight Each Other," *Security Studies* 7, no. 1 (Autumn 1997): 114–55.

52. Randall Schweller, "Neorealism's Status Quo Bias: What Security Dilemma?" *Security Studies* 5, no. 3 (Spring 1996): 90–121; Arnold Wolfers, *Discord and Collaboration* (Baltimore: Johns Hopkins University Press, 1962), p. 156.

53. Another version of realism that claims to explain changes in grand strategy is "defensive realism." Defensive realists start from the premise that international pressures by themselves rarely force states into aggressive behavior; aggressive grand strategies are typically best explained by domestic political pathologies, such as the formation of rent-seeking cartels within a particular state. Defensive realists certainly do not make the mistake of overemphasizing systemic pressures, but there are questions as to whether such an approach is really consistent with realism as a research program. For leading defensive realist works, see Jack Snyder, *Myths of Empire: Domestic Politics and International Ambition* (Ithaca: Cornell University Press, 1991), and Stephen Van Evera, *Causes of War: Power and the Roots of Conflict* (Ithaca: Cornell University Press, 1999). For a penetrating critique of defensive realism, see Zakaria, "Realism and Domestic Politics."

54. Christensen, *Useful Adversaries*; Aaron Friedberg, *In the Shadow of the Garrison State: America's Anti-Statism and its Cold War Grand Strategy* (Princeton: Princeton University Press, 2000); Randall Schweller, *Deadly Imbalances* (New York: Columbia University Press, 1998); Stephen Walt, *Revolution and War* (Ithaca: Cornell University Press, 1996); William Wohlforth, *The Elusive Balance: Power and Perceptions during the Cold War* (Ithaca: Cornell University Press, 1993); Fareed Zakaria, *From Wealth to Power: The Unusual Origins of America's World Role* (Princeton: Princeton University Press, 1998).

55. Gideon Rose, "Neoclassical Realism and Theories of Foreign Policy," *World Politics* 51, no. 1 (October 1998): 144–72.

56. Ibid., pp. 146–47, 154. See also Jeffrey Taliaferro, "Security Seeking Under Anarchy," *International Security* 25, no. 3 (Winter 2000/2001): 132–35, 142–43.

57. Christensen, *Useful Adversaries*, p. 15; Gilpin, *War and Change in World Politics*, p. 96; Posen, *The Sources of Military Doctrine*, pp. 7–8, 239.

58. Raymond Aron, *Peace and War* (New York: Praeger, 1966), pp. 90–91; Randall Schweller, "The Progressiveness of Neoclassical Realism," in Colin Elman and Miriam Fendius Elman, eds., *Progress in International Relations Theory* (Cambridge, Mass.: MIT Press, 2003), p. 336; Jennifer Sterling-Folker, "Realist Environment, Liberal Process, and Domestic-Level Variables," *International Studies Quarterly* 41, no. 1 (March 1997): 9, 16–23.

59. Christensen, *Useful Adversaries*, p. 11.

60. Alexander George, "Domestic Constraints on Regime Change in U.S. Foreign Policy: The Need for Policy Legitimacy," in John Ikenberry, ed., *American Foreign Policy: Theoretical Essays* (New York: Longman, 1999), pp. 336–60.

61. Kupchan, *Vulnerability of Empire*, pp. 61–63.

62. Desch, "Culture Clash," pp. 166–69.

63. Jeffrey Legro, *Cooperation Under Fire* (Ithaca: Cornell University Press, 1995), p. 231.

64. Jeffrey Lantis, "The Moral Imperative of Force: The Evolution of German Strategic Culture," *Comparative Strategy* 21, no. 1 (January–March 2002): 21–46.

65. Desch, "Culture Clash," pp. 166–69; Kurt Jacobsen, "Much Ado About Ideas," *World Politics* 47, no. 2 (January 1995): 285.

66. Schweller, "The Progressiveness of Neoclassical Realism," pp. 340–41; Sterling-Folker, "Realist Environment, Liberal Process, and Domestic-Level Variables," p. 20.

CHAPTER TWO
STRATEGIC CULTURE AND STRATEGIC ADJUSTMENT IN THE UNITED STATES

1. Louis Hartz, *The Liberal Tradition in America* (New York: Harcourt Brace, 1955), pp. 4–11; Samuel Huntington, *American Politics: The Promise of Disharmony* (Cambridge, Mass.: Belknap Press of Harvard University Press, 1981), chap. 2; Seymour Lipset, *American Exceptionalism: A Double-Edged Sword* (New York: W. W. Norton, 1997), pp. 31–52.

2. Daniel Rodgers, *Contested Truths: Keywords in American Politics Since Independence* (Cambridge, Mass.: Harvard University Press, 1987).

3. Bernard Bailyn, *The Ideological Origins of the American Revolution, Enlarged Edition* (Cambridge. Mass.: Belknap Press of Harvard University Press, 1992); Gordon Wood, *The American Revolution* (New York: The Modern Library, 2002), pp. 91–135.

4. On the liberal tradition and its implications for international relations, see Michael Doyle, *Ways of War and Peace* (New York: W. W. Norton, 1997), pp. 205–311; Michael Howard, *War and the Liberal Conscience* (Oxford: Oxford University Press, 1989); and John Owen, *Liberal Peace, Liberal War: American Politics and International Security* (Ithaca: Cornell University Press, 1997), pp. 22–50.

5. "Democratic peace theory" represents an important modification of classical liberal assumptions. According to democratic peace theory, liberal democracies are *not* necessarily any less warlike than nondemocracies. Rather, liberal democracies simply do not go to war with one another. Even this more limited claim has invited skeptical responses. For an excellent summary of the arguments for and against democratic peace theory, see Michael Brown, Sean Lynn-Jones and Steven Miller, eds., *Debating the Democratic Peace* (Cambridge, Mass.: MIT Press, 1996).

6. Felix Gilbert, *To the Farewell Address* (Princeton: Princeton University Press, 1961), pp. 16–17; Gordon Wood, *American Revolution*, pp. 106–8.

7. Michael Hunt, *Ideology and U.S. Foreign Policy* (New Haven: Yale University Press, 1987), pp. 17–18.

8. In his very fine survey of American diplomatic history, Walter McDougall suggests that the "crusader" tradition in U.S. foreign policy begins only with the

Progressive era, circa 1898. But the emphasis on creating an "empire of liberty"—through force, if necessary—dates back to the very founding of the United States. The key distinction between the period before and after the Spanish-American War is that the United States began to act militarily beyond the confines of the American mainland. The crusading tradition certainly existed before the 1890s, as evidenced by periodic and popular support throughout the nineteenth century for U.S. expansion westward across the American continent. See Walter McDougall, *Promised Land, Crusader State* (New York: Houghton Mifflin, 1997), pp. 36–37, 59–75, 84, 117–18.

9. H. W. Brands, *What America Owes the World* (New York: Cambridge University Press, 1998), pp. vii–ix; Christopher Coker, *Reflections on American Foreign Policy Since 1945* (New York: Palgrave Macmillan, 1990), pp. 20–23.

10. Cecil Crabb, *American Diplomacy and the Pragmatic Tradition* (Baton Rouge: Louisiana State University Press, 1989), p. 3.

11. Ibid., pp. 290–96.

12. Hunt, *Ideology and U.S. Foreign Policy*, p. 15.

13. The internalization of culturally conditioned rhetoric, whereupon policymakers come to actually hold certain beliefs that they might have originally espoused for instrumental reasons, is referred to by Jack Snyder as "blowback." See Jack Snyder, *Myths of Empire: Domestic Politics and International Ambition* (Ithaca: Cornell University Press, 1991), pp. 41–42, 49.

14. David Elkins and Richard Simeon, "A Cause in Search of Effects, or What Does Political Culture Explain?" *Comparative Politics* 11, no. 2 (1979): 127–29.

15. A classic critique of these tendencies is in George Kennan, *American Diplomacy* (Chicago: University of Chicago Press, 1951), pp. 95–101.

16. Samuel Huntington, *American Politics*, pp. 236–45.

17. McDougall, *Promised Land, Crusader State*, p. 5.

18. Colin Gray, *The Geopolitics of Superpower* (Lexington: University of Kentucky Press, 1988), pp. 42–43.

19. The concept of "limited liability" in strategic affairs was developed by B. H. Liddell Hart during the 1930s. Liddell Hart argued that British interests would be well served—and had been well served in the past—by avoiding any major ground commitments on the European continent. Subsequent authors have demonstrated quite convincingly that Britain frequently relied upon substantial ground commitments abroad in order to achieve its foreign policy goals. See Brian Bond, *Liddell Hart: A Study of His Military Thought* (London: Cassell, 1977); Michael Howard, *The Causes of Wars* (Cambridge: Howard University Press, 1983); Paul Kennedy, *The Rise and Fall of British Naval Mastery* (London: Ashfield Press, 1986); and John Mearsheimer, *Liddell Hart and the Weight of History* (Ithaca: Cornell University Press, 1989).

20. John Gaddis, *The United States and the End of the Cold War* (New York: Oxford University Press, 1992), pp. 5–9.

21. Washington's address is in Thomas Paterson, ed., *Major Problems in American Foreign Policy*, vol. 1 (Lexington, Ky.: D.C. Heath, 1989), pp. 74–77.

22. McDougall, *Promised Land, Crusader State*, pp. 44–49.

23. For evidence of widespread assumptions of limited liability within the United States before 1941, see Selig Adler, *The Isolationist Impulse: Its Twentieth*

Century Reaction (New York: Free Press, 1957), pp. 219–90; Wayne Cole, *Roosevelt and the Isolationists* (Lincoln: University of Nebraska Press, 1983); and Thomas Guinsburg, *The Pursuit of Isolationism in the United States Senate from Versailles to Pearl Harbor* (New York, 1983).

24. Kent Greenfield, *American Strategy in World War II: A Reconsideration* (New York: Krieger Publishing Co., 1982).

25. Aaron Friedberg, *In the Shadow of the Garrison State: America's Anti-Statism and its Cold War Grand Strategy* (Princeton: Princeton University Press, 2000); John Gaddis, *Strategies of Containment* (New York: Oxford University Press, 1982).

26. Gray, *Geopolitics of Superpower*, p. 45.

27. Stephen Krasner, *Defending the National Interest* (Princeton: Princeton University Press, 1978), pp. 61–70.

28. Kurt Gaubatz, *Elections and War* (Stanford: Stanford University Press, 1997); Ole Holsti, *Public Opinion and American Foreign Policy*, rev. ed. (Ann Arbor: University of Michigan Press, 2004).

29. This is not to say that the impact of these domestic political factors and institutions is, on balance, dysfunctional or irrational. In order to determine that, one would need to examine *all* of the effects upon U.S. foreign policy—both positive and negative—of elections, Congress, and public opinion. One would also need to weigh and consider the inherent value apart from their utility in foreign affairs, of democratic institutions. The only contention here is that domestic political factors and institutions tend, most of the time, to act as a constraint rather than as a stimulus on costly strategic initiatives. For a spirited defense of congressional and popular influence on American foreign policy, see Miroslav Nincic, *Democracy and Foreign Policy: The Fallacy of Political Realism* (New York: Columbia University Press, 1992).

30. For a relevant and compelling analysis of what he calls "normal internationalism" in American diplomacy prior to Woodrow Wilson, see Frank Ninkovich, *The Wilsonian Century* (Chicago: University of Chicago Press, 1999), pp. 17–47.

31. Holsti, *Public Opinion and American Foreign Policy*, pp. 52, 130–61.

32. Warren Cohen, *Empire Without Tears* (New York: McGraw Hill, 1987); Herbert Hoover, *American Individualism* (New York: Best Books, 1922).

33. As already suggested, a given administration might choose to pursue limited liability in some of these areas but not others.

34. These four strategic subcultures correspond, to some extent, to the schools described by Walter Russell Mead: Wilsonian (internationalist), Jacksonian (nationalist), Jeffersonian (progressive), and Hamiltonian (realist). See Walter Russell Mead, *Special Providence: American Foreign Policy and How it Changed the World* (New York: Knopf, 2001). See also Henry Nau, *At Home Abroad: Identity and Power in American Foreign Policy* (Ithaca: Cornell University Press, 2002). On the subject of strategic subcultures, see Elizabeth Kier, "Culture and French Military Doctrine Before World War II," in Peter Katzenstein, ed., *The Culture of National Security* (New York: Columbia University Press, 1996), pp. 201–2. On the subject of American political subcultures more generally, see David H. Fischer, *Albion's Seed: Four British Folkways in America* (New York: Oxford University Press, 1989).

35. Mead, *Special Providence*, pp. 218–63.

36. Ibid., p. 127.

37. For a multicausal framework to which this author is indebted, see Richard Herrmann and Richard Ned Lebow, eds., *Ending The Cold War: Interpretations, Causation and the Study of International Relations* (New York: Palgrave Macmillan, 2004), pp. 7–8, 14–16.

38. Gaddis, *Strategies of Containment*, pp. 336–44; Raymond Garthoff, *Détente and Confrontation: American-Soviet Relations from Nixon to Reagan* (Washington, D.C.: Brookings Institution Press, 1985), pp. 409–13, 453–63, 538–52.

39. Gaddis, *Strategies of Containment*, pp. 355–56.

40. There is some debate over the extent to which American voters select presidential candidates due to foreign policy preferences. Certainly it would be inaccurate to suggest that the public does not consider foreign policy at all when voting in presidential elections. There is considerable evidence that many voters—particularly attentive ones—do have coherent preferences on foreign policy issues, for example, for or against cooperative internationalism. But when one considers the many reasons that people vote in presidential elections—party identification, economic conditions, preferences on social issues, the candidate's personality—one can hardly interpret electoral outcomes as simple referendums on existing foreign policies.

41. To paraphrase Max Weber, political actors may be motivated primarily by interests, rather than ideas, but ideas are "switchmen" that determine the tracks along which those actors pursue their self-interest. See Weber, "The Social Psychology of the World Religions," in C. Wright Mills, *From Max Weber* (New York: Oxford University Press, 1980), p. 280. On the role of ideas in foreign policy, specifically, see Jeffrey Checkel, *Ideas and International Political Change* (New York: Yale University Press, 1998); Alexander George, "The Operational Code: A Neglected Approach to the Study of Political Leaders and Decision-Making," *International Studies Quarterly* 13 (1969): 190–222; Judith Goldstein, *Ideas, Interests and American Trade Policy* (Ithaca: Cornell University Press, 1993); Judith Goldstein and Robert Keohane, eds., *Ideas and Foreign Policy: Beliefs, Institutions and Political Change* (Ithaca: Cornell University Press, 1993); Robert Jervis, *Perception and Misperception in International Politics* (Princeton: Princeton University Press, 1976), chap. 4; Yuen Khong, *Analogies at War* (Princeton: Princeton University Press, 1992); Richard Little and Steve Smith, eds., *Belief Systems and International Relations* (New York: Blackwell, 1988); and Kathleen McNamara, *The Currency of Ideas: Monetary Politics in the European Union* (Ithaca: Cornell University Press, 1998).

42. Goldstein and Keohane, *Ideas and Foreign Policy*, pp. 20–24; Albert Yee, "The Causal Effects of Ideas on Politics," *International Organization* 50, no. 1 (Winter 1996): 95. Goldstein and Keohane suggest that ideas become a powerful constraint once institutionalized. Yee points out that such institutionalization can be informal in nature. Ideas have a constraining influence on policy outcomes simply by shaping policy discourse and by making a number of alternative options literally unthinkable. Leading institutionalist works include James March and

Johan Olsen, "The New Institutionalism: Organizational Factors in Political Life," *APSR* 78 (1984): 734–49; Paul DiMaggio and Walter Powell, eds., *The New Institutionalism in Organizational Analysis* (Chicago: University of Chicago Press, 1991); Sven Steinmo, Kathleen Thelen, and Frank Longstreth, eds., *Structuring Politics* (New York: Cambridge University Press, 1992).

43. This process can be contrasted with that of domestic policy adjustments, where policy failures may be triggered by a wide variety of events, and where there is usually greater room for political leaders to determine what constitutes "failure." Foreign policy problems or failures tend to be more pronounced than in the domestic realm. See John Kingdon, *Agendas, Alternatives, and Public Policies* (New York: HarperCollins, 1995), p. 227.

44. The phrase "punctuated equilibrium" is originally Stephen Jay Gould's. See also Aaron Friedberg, *The Weary Titan* (Princeton: Princeton University Press, 1988), pp. 14–17; and Goldstein, *Ideas, Interests, and American Trade Policy*, pp. 13–14.

45. Goldstein, *Ideas, Interests, and American Trade Policy*, pp. 252–54.

46. It seems likely that if civil servants or bureaucratic actors are to have any great influence over strategic outcomes, it will be here, at this initial stage of informal and invisible agenda setting. See Kingdon, *Agendas, Alternatives, and Public Policies*, pp. 68–70.

47. On the role of "change agents" in bringing new strategic alternatives forward, see Friedberg, *The Weary Titan*, pp. 285–88. On the role of such policy entrepreneurs in American domestic politics, see Frank Baumgartner and Bryan Jones, *Agendas and Instability in American Politics* (Chicago: University of Chicago Press, 1993), and Kingdon, *Agendas, Alternatives and Public Policies*.

48. Goldstein, *Ideas, Interests, and American Trade Policy*, pp. 14–15.

49. For an excellent discussion of agenda setting, see William Riker, *The Art of Political Manipulation* (New Haven: Yale University Press, 1986).

50. Fred Greenstein, *Personality and Politics* (Princeton: Princeton University Press, 1987), pp. 33–46.

51. Barbara Farnham, *Roosevelt and the Munich Crisis* (Princeton: Princeton University Press, 1997), p. 24; Robert Putnam, "The Logic of Two-Level Games," *International Organization* 42 (Summer 1988): 427–60.

52. On the trade-off between political feasibility and policy feasibility, see Peter Hall, *The Political Power of Economic Ideas* (Princeton: Princeton University Press, 1989), pp. 374–75.

53. Gary King, Robert Keohane, and Sidney Verba, *Designing Social Inquiry: Scientific Inference in Qualitative Research* (Princeton: Princeton University Press, 1994), p. 227.

54. As King, Keohane, and Verba point out, small-N studies actually benefit from a careful, nonrandom selection of cases.

55. Yuen Khong, *Analogies At War*, pp. 53–57; Philip Tetlock and Aaron Belkin, *Counterfactual Thought Experiments in World Politics: Logical, Methodological, and Psychological Perspectives* (Princeton: Princeton University Press, 1996), pp. 3–4, 10–12.

CHAPTER THREE
THE LOST ALLIANCE: IDEAS AND ALTERNATIVES IN
AMERICAN GRAND STRATEGY, 1918–1921

1. Interpretations of the League debate have fallen into three broad schools of thought over the years: realist, revisionist, and liberal. Classical realists in the 1950s such as George Kennan maintained that Wilson's vision for the League was overly idealistic and bound to fail internationally, regardless of domestic opposition. Vietnam-era revisionists such as N. Gordon Levin suggested that both Wilson and his Republican opponents were mainly interested in promoting capitalism internationally; the details of the League debate are therefore secondary to revisionists. Liberals have generally argued that Wilson had a compelling and attractive vision for world peace, and that its rejection by the Senate was a tragedy. The liberal interpretation has been the dominant one in American historiography for many years; its greatest exponent was Arthur Link, and it has been recently restated by historians such as Thomas Knock and John Milton Cooper. An important counter to all three interpretations—liberal, realist, and revisionist—is the work of Lloyd Ambrosius, who argues that Wilson searched for universal control in the face of international pluralism. As to why Wilson failed to win over the Senate, several arguments are common. The first stresses partisan opposition on the part of Senate Republicans; this is Knock's argument. The second argument, which owes a great deal to the work of Edwin Weinstein, emphasizes Wilson's failing health over the course of 1919—an issue that looms large in both Link and Cooper. Finally, political psychologists such as Alexander George point to the peculiar impact of Wilson's stubborn personality. My own interpretation of the League debate within this chapter is closer to Kennan's than any other, but I modify and supplement his interpretation by showing precisely how and why domestic cultural considerations, via patterns of presidential agenda setting and coalition building, determined the final outcome. I also suggest that the deadlock between Wilson and the Senate had as much to do with genuine and principled differences of opinion over America's role in the world as with issues of health, partisanship, or psychology. See George Kennan, *American Diplomacy* (Chicago: University of Chicago Press, 1951), pp. 55–73; N. Gordon Levin, *Woodrow Wilson and World Politics: America's Response to War and Revolution* (New York: Oxford University Press, 1968); Arthur Link, *Woodrow Wilson: Revolution, War and Peace* (Arlington Heights, Ill.: H. Davidson, 1979), pp. 72–128; Thomas Knock, *To End All Wars: Woodrow Wilson and the Quest for a New World Order* (New York: Oxford University Press, 1992); John Milton Cooper, *Breaking the Heart of the World: Woodrow Wilson and the Fight for the League of Nations* (New York: Cambridge University Press, 2001); Lloyd Ambrosius, *Woodrow Wilson and the American Diplomatic Tradition: The Treaty Fight in Perspective* (New York: Cambridge University Press, 1987); Edwin Weinstein, *Woodrow Wilson: A Medical and Psychological Biography* (Princeton: Princeton University Press, 1981); Alexander George and Juliette George, *Woodrow Wilson and Colonel House: A Personality Study* (New York: J. Day Co., 1956); and David Steigerwald, "The Reclamation of Woodrow Wilson?" in Michael Hogan, ed., *Paths to Power: The*

Historiography of American Foreign Relations to 1941 (New York: Cambridge University Press, 2000), pp. 148–75.

2. Exceptions include David Lake, *Entangling Relations* (Princeton: Princeton University Press, 1999), pp. 78–127; and Jeffrey Legro, "Whence American Internationalism," *International Organization* 54, no. 2 (Spring 2000): 253–89.

3. Frank Ninkovich, *The Wilsonian Century: U.S. Foreign Policy since 1900* (Chicago: University of Chicago Press, 1999), pp. 17–47.

4. Emily Rosenberg, *Spreading the American Dream: American Economic and Cultural Expansion, 1890–1945* (New York: Hill and Wang, 1982), pp. 3–62.

5. William Widenor, *Henry Cabot Lodge and the Search for an American Foreign Policy* (Berkeley: University of California Press, 1980), pp. 221–65.

6. Knock, *To End All Wars*, pp. 105–47; Link, *Woodrow Wilson*, pp. 47–71.

7. Allan Millett and Peter Maslowski, *For the Common Defense: A Military History of the United States of America* (New York: Free Press, 1984), p. 375.

8. Ralph Levering, *The Public and American Foreign Policy, 1918–1978* (New York: Morrow, 1978), pp. 43–45.

9. An address in Washington to the League to Enforce Peace, May 27, 1916, *Papers of Woodrow Wilson*, [hereafter *PWW*,] ed. Arthur Link (Princeton: Princeton University Press, 1966–1994), vol. 37, p. 113. Wilson used almost the very same words in his famous "Fourteen Points" address to Congress on January 8, 1918. See *Public Papers of Woodrow Wilson*, [hereafter *PPWW*,] ed. Ray Stannard Baker and William Dodd (New York: Harper and Brothers, 1925–1927), vol. 1, p. 161.

10. *PPWW*, vol. 1, p. 426.

11. Gilbert Close, Confidential Secretary to Wilson, to Admiral William Benson, January 27, 1919, Woodrow Wilson Papers, Library of Congress, Washington, D.C., [hereafter *WW Papers*,] Series 8A; Phillips O'Brien, *British and American Naval Power: Politics and Policy, 1900–1936* (Westport, Conn.: Praeger, 1998), pp. 137–39.

12. Akira Iriye, *After Imperialism: The Search for a New Order in the Far East, 1921–1931* (Cambridge, Mass.: Harvard University Press, 1965), pp. 13–21.

13. *Papers Relating to the Foreign Relations of the United States, 1919: The Paris Peace Conference* [hereafter *FR: PPC*], Department of State (1942–1946), vol. 3, p. 1002. See also Klaus Schwabe, *Woodrow Wilson, Revolutionary Germany and Peacemaking, 1918–1919* (Chapel Hill: University of North Carolina Press, 1985), pp. 395–402.

14. Betty Miller Unterberger, "Woodrow Wilson and the Bolsheviks: The Acid Test of Soviet-American Relations," *Diplomatic History* 11, no. 2 (Spring 1987): 71–90; Levin, *Woodrow Wilson and World Politics*, p. 204.

15. Newspaper column, November 17, 1918, *The Works of Theodore Roosevelt*, Hermann Hagedorn, ed. (New York: C. Scribner's Sons, 1925), vol. 19, pp. 400–403.

16. *Congressional Record* [hereafter *CR*], 65th Congress, 3rd session, vol. 57 (Dec. 21, 1918), p. 728.

17. Lodge to Henry White, December 2, 1918, cited in William Widenor, *Henry Cabot Lodge and the Search for an American Foreign Policy*, p. 298.

18. *CR*, 65th Congress, 3rd session, December 18, 1918, vol. 57, pp. 603–8; 66th Congress, 1st session (June 10, 1919), vol. 58, p. 894.

19. Ralph Stone, *The Irreconcilables: The Fight Against the League of Nations* (Lexington: University Press of Kentucky, 1970), pp. 5–12.

20. Ibid., p. 261.

21. *New York Times*, March 20, 1919.

22. The unwillingness of the United States (and the inability of Britain) to assume a "hegemonic" role during the interwar years is central to the work of realists such as Robert Gilpin and E. H. Carr, but these authors do not explain America's unwillingness to play such a role. See Robert Gilpin, *War and Change in World Politics* (New York: Cambridge University Press, 1981), p. 234; Charles Kindleberger, *A Financial History of Western Europe* (Boston: Allen and Unwin, 1984), pt. 4; E. H. Carr, *The Twenty Years' Crisis, 1919–1939* (London: Macmillan and Co., 1940). For a contrary view of America's interwar disengagement given from a structural realist perspective, see John Mearsheimer, *The Tragedy of Great Power Politics* (New York: W. W. Norton, 2001), pp. 252–59.

23. Paul Kennedy, *The Rise and Fall of the Great Powers* (New York: Random House, 1987), p. 277.

24. A restatement of the realist case against Wilson is contained in Henry Kissinger, *Diplomacy* (New York: Simon and Schuster, 1994), pp. 221–49.

25. A classic critique is F. H. Hinsley, *Power and the Pursuit of Peace* (Cambridge: Cambridge University Press, 1963).

26. Address to the Italian Parliament, January 3, 1919, *PWW*, vol. 53, 599; address at Guildhall, December 28, 1918, *PWW*, vol. 53, p. 532.

27. Address to the Senate, January 17, 1917, *PWW*, vol. 40, pp. 533–39.

28. *PPWW*, vol. 1, p. 343.

29. Game theoretic analysis has also confirmed that collective security systems are more likely to function effectively under the leadership of a hegemon or oligopoly of powers. See George Downs and Kenneth Iida, eds., *Collective Security Beyond the Cold War* (Ann Arbor: University of Michigan Press, 1994), pp. 21, 29.

30. *New York Times*, February 27, 1919.

31. Frank Costigliola, *Awkward Dominion: American Political, Economic and Cultural Relations with Europe, 1919–1933* (Ithaca: Cornell University Press, 1984), p. 35; Michael Hogan, *Informal Entente: The Private Structure of Cooperation in Anglo-American Economic Diplomacy, 1918–1928* (Columbia: University of Missouri Press, 1977), pp. 21–22; Melvyn Leffler, *The Elusive Quest: America's Pursuit of European Stability and French Security, 1919–1933* (Chapel Hill: University of North Carolina Press, 1979); and Carl Parrini, *Heir to Empire: United States Economic Diplomacy, 1916–1923* (Pittsburgh: University of Pittsburgh Press, 1969), pp. 69–70.

32. *PPWW*, vol. 1, pp. 620–45.

33. Theodore Roosevelt, "An International Posse Comitatus," *New York Times*, November 8, 1914.

34. Theodore Roosevelt, *America and the World War* (New York: C. Scribner's Sons, 1915), pp. 102–3, 136.

35. Edward House, *Philip Dru: Administrator* (New York: B. W. Huebsch, 1912), p. 273.

36. Knock, *To End All Wars*, pp. 50–54.

37. Knock, *To End All Wars*, pp. 55–57, 128.

38. On this point I differ from Thomas Knock. Knock states that there were two versions of the League, a conservative one and a progressive one, but he argues that Wilson was essentially in agreement with the progressive version. I argue that Wilson's version of the League differed significantly from both the conservative and the progressive versions.

39. Ninkovich, *The Wilsonian Century*, pp. 22–23.

40. Wilson to Edward House, December 24, 1915, *PWW*, vol. 35, pp. 387–88.

41. Wilson to House, May 16, 1916, *PWW*, vol. 32, pp. 57–58.

42. An address in Washington to the League to Enforce Peace, May 27, 1916, *PWW*, vol. 32, pp. 113–16.

43. Address in Omaha, Nebraska, October 5, 1916, *PWW*, vol. 38, p. 348.

44. Wilson to Theodore Marburg, chairman of the committee on foreign organizations of the League to Enforce Peace, March 5, 1918, *WW Papers*, Series 4, File 297.

45. William Wiseman, head of British intelligence operations in the United States, to Lord Reading, British ambassador to the United States, August 16, 1918, *PWW*, vol. 49, p. 273.

46. George Egerton, *Great Britain and the Creation of the League of Nations* (Chapel Hill: University of North Carolina Press, 1978), pp. 66–69.

47. Address to Joint Sessions of Congress, April 2, 1917, January 8, 1918, and an address at the Metropolitan House, September 27, 1918, *PWW*, vol. 41, pp. 519–27, vol. 45, pp. 534–39, and vol. 51, pp. 127–33, respectively.

48. Address to the Senate, January 22, 1917, *PWW*, vol. 40, pp. 533–39.

49. Knock, *To End All Wars*, pp. 146, 163–65.

50. "Clash of French and American Peace Plans," *Literary Digest* 60:9–11.

51. Ambrosius, *Woodrow Wilson and the American Diplomatic Tradition*, pp. 47–49, 85–86. Of all the Republican internationalists, Theodore Roosevelt offered the most far-reaching public criticisms of Wilson's program, emphasizing the need for a strong military and a weakened Germany.

52. *PPWW*, vol. 5, pp. 352–56.

53. No such bargaining was necessary with the Germans, who were temporarily incapable of resisting Allied dictates.

54. Lloyd George, January 31, 1919, cited in George Egerton, "Ideology, Diplomacy, and International Organization: Wilson and the League of Nations in Anglo-American Relations, 1918–1920," in *Woodrow Wilson and a Revolutionary World, 1913–1921*, Arthur Link, ed. (Chapel Hill: University of North Carolina Press, 1982), p. 35.

55. John Ferris, "The Symbol and Substance of Seapower: Great Britain, the United States, and the One-Power Standard," in *Anglo-American Relations in the 1920s: The Struggle for Supremacy*, ed. Brian McKercher (Edmonton: University of Alberta Press, 1990), pp. 55–80.

56. George Baer, *One Hundred Years of Sea Power: The U.S. Navy, 1890–1990* (Stanford: Stanford University Press, 1994), p. 89; Seth Tillman, *Anglo-American Relations at the Paris Peace Conference of 1919* (Princeton: Princeton University Press, 1961), pp. 45–51.

57. Cited in Ambrosius, *Woodrow Wilson and the American Diplomatic Tradition*, p. 52.

58. *FR: PPC*, pp. 785–817.

59. See Walter McDougall, *France's Rhineland Diplomacy, 1914–1924* (Princeton: Princeton University Press, 1978); David Stevenson, *French War Aims Against Germany, 1914–1919* (Oxford: Clarendon Press, 1982); and Andre Tardieu, *The Truth About the Treaty* (London: Hudder and Stoughton, 1921).

60. Leon Bourgeois to Wilson, January 31, 1919; Stephen Pinchon to Wilson, February 4, 1919, *WW Papers*, Series 5B, Box 13.

61. Tardieu, *The Truth About the Treaty*, pp. 139–40, 176–78, 186.

62. Woodrow Wilson, Memorandum on the Amendments Proposed by France, April 8, 1919, *WW Papers*, Series 5B, Reel 400.

63. House Diary, March 27, 1919, in Charles Seymour, ed., *The Intimate Papers of Colonel House* (Boston and New York: Houghton Mifflin, 1926–1928), vol. 4, p. 395.

64. This was the argument of John Maynard Keynes, a British Treasury official at the time. See John Maynard Keynes, *The Economic Consequences of the Peace* (London: The Labour Research Department, 1920), pp. 147–48.

65. Levin, *Woodrow Wilson and World Politics*, p. 146.

66. Costigliola, *Awkward Dominion*, p. 35; Hogan, *Informal Entente*, pp. 21–22; Leffler, *The Elusive Quest*, pp. 24, 28; Rosenberg, *Spreading the American Dream*, p. 144.

67. Parrini, *Heir to Empire*, p. 246.

68. See Marc Trachtenberg, *Reparations in World Politics* (New York: Columbia University Press, 1980).

69. Wilson to James Phelan, April 7, 1919, *WW Papers*, Series 5B, Reel 399.

70. Ray Stannard Baker, *Woodrow Wilson and World Settlement* (Garden City, N.Y.: Doubleday, Page and Co., 1922), vol. 2, p. 266.

71. Wilson to George Herron, April 28, 1919, *WW Papers*, Series 5B, Reel 403.

72. Other significant reservations on Lodge's list were that the United States would be the sole judge of whether it had fulfilled its obligations to the League, that the United States would accept no League mandates without congressional approval, and that the United States would tolerate no outside interference in the Western Hemisphere contrary to the Monroe Doctrine. For the full text of Lodge's final reservations, see *CR*, 66th Cong., 2nd session, vol. 59 (March 19, 1920), p. 4599.

73. Ralph Stone, *The Irreconcilables*, p. 115.

74. George and George, *Woodrow Wilson and Colonel House*. The Georges recently restated their case in *Presidential Personality and Performance* (Boulder, Colo.: Westview Press, 1998). Similar interpretations of Wilson's behavior are made in James David Barber, *The Presidential Character* (Englewood Cliffs, N.J.: Prentice-Hall, 1977), pp. 12, 46, 68.

75. Weinstein, *Woodrow Wilson: A Medical and Psychological Biography*, pp. 355–63.

76. Link, *Woodrow Wilson*, p. 119.

77. Knock, *To End All Wars*, p. 240; Arno Mayer, *Politics and Diplomacy of Peacemaking: Containment and Counterrevolution at Versailles, 1918–1919* (New York: Knopf, 1967), pp. 120–29.

78. Robert Higgs, *Crisis and Leviathan: Critical Episodes in the Growth of American Government* (New York: Oxford University Press, 1987), p. 123.

79. Lodge to Charnwood, January 24, February 25, April 16, 1920, cited in Ambrosius, *Woodrow Wilson and the American Diplomatic Tradition*, pp. 259–60.

80. Beveridge to Lodge, January 28, 1919, cited in Widenor, *Henry Cabot Lodge and the Search for an American Foreign Policy*, p. 301.

81. Root to Lodge, June 19, 1919, cited in ibid., p. 331.

82. *CR*, 66th Cong., 1st session, vol. 57 (Feb. 21, 1919), pp. 3911–15. For more on Borah's opposition to the League, see Robert Maddox, *William E. Borah and American Foreign Policy* (Baton Rouge: Louisiana State University Press, 1969), pp. 50–72.

83. *CR*, 66th Congress, 1st sess., vol. 58 (Aug. 12, 1919), pp. 3778–84.

84. Ambrosius, *Woodrow Wilson and the American Diplomatic Tradition*, p. 102.

85. Ibid., p. 101.

86. Herbert Margulies, *The Mild Reservationists and the League of Nations Controversy in the Senate* (Columbia: University of Missouri Press, 1989), p. xii.

87. Tumulty to McCormick, September 25, 1919, *WW Papers*, Series 4, File 3211.

88. John Milton Cooper, "Fool's Errand or Finest Hour? Woodrow's Wilson's Speaking Tour in September 1919," in *The Wilson Era*, ed. John Milton Cooper and Charles Neu (Arlington Heights, Ill.: Harlan Davidson, 1991), pp. 198–220.

89. Croly to Wilson, January 23, 1917, and Lippmann to Wilson, January 31, 1917, *PWW*, vol. 40, p. 559, and vol. 41, p. 83.

90. *CR*, 66th Congress, 1st session, vol. 58 (June 2, 1919), pp. 501–9.

91. Robert Johnson, *The Peace Progressives and American Foreign Relations* (Cambridge, Mass.: Harvard University Press, 1995), pp. 3–9, 86–104; Knock, *To End All Wars*, p. 257; Stone, *The Irreconcilables*, p. 180.

92. Karen Miller, *Populist Nationalism: Republican Insurgency and American Foreign Policy Making, 1918–1925* (Westport, Conn.: Greenwood Press, 1999), pp. 55–72.

93. Ibid., pp. 73–117.

94. Kendrick Clements, *The Presidency of Woodrow Wilson* (Lawrence: University Press of Kansas,) pp. 205–6.

95. Johnson, *The Peace Progressives*, pp. 81–86; Knock, *To End All Wars*, pp. 236, 267–68.

96. U.S. Senate, *Treaty of Peace with Germany: Hearings before the Committee on Foreign Relations* (Washington, D.C.: G.P.O., 1919), pp. 757–933.

97. Cited in Ambrosius, *Woodrow Wilson and the American Diplomatic Tradition*, pp. 99–100.

98. U.S. Senate, *Treaty of Peace with Germany*, pp. 139–378, 1161–1292. As a sitting Secretary of State, Lansing did not actually testify against the treaty, but his Senate testimony on August 6 and 11 was so half-hearted that politically it

represented a blow to Wilson. On September 12, Bullitt revealed Lansing's private doubts regarding the League. Lansing had long been skeptical of the central element in Wilson's approach to the League: a positive guarantee of political independence and territorial integrity under Article 10. The secretary of state also shared the feeling common among liberals that Germany had been treated too harshly at Versailles, and that the United States was regressing into balance-of-power behavior by cooperating too closely with Britain and France. By 1919, however, Lansing was marginalized by Wilson, and had very little influence over foreign policy decision making. Bullitt's revelations before the Senate only confirmed Wilson's alienation from his secretary of state. Lansing resigned on February 12, 1920.

99. Ambrosius, *Woodrow Wilson and the American Diplomatic Tradition*, pp. 143, 168–70.

100. Beth McKillen, "The Corporatist Model, World War One, and the Public Debate over the League of Nations," *Diplomatic History* 15, no. 2 (Spring 1991): 171–98.

101. Ambrosius, *Woodrow Wilson and the American Diplomatic Tradition*, p. 155.

102. *CR*, 66th Congress, 1st sess., vol. 58 (November 19, 1919), pp. 9767–9804.

103. Underwood to Wilson, November 21, 1919, and Hitchcock to Wilson, November 22, 24, 1919, *WW Papers*, Series 2, Box 193.

104. Jusserand to Polk, March 11, 1920, *WW Papers*, Series 2, Box 196.

105. *PPWW*, vol. 6, pp. 453–56.

106. *CR*, 66th Congress, 2nd sess., vol. 59 (Mar. 19, 1920), pp. 4567–4604.

107. On American public opinion during the League debate, see Cooper, *Breaking the Heart of the World*, pp. 424–25.

108. Lodge to Bryce, April 20, 1920, cited in Ambrosius, *Woodrow Wilson and the American Diplomatic Tradition*, p. 252.

109. Harding to Hiram Johnson, July 27, September 6, 1920, cited in Ambrosius, *Woodrow Wilson and the American Diplomatic Tradition*, pp. 273, 276.

110. Harding straddled the League issue quite effectively in 1920, promising in vague terms to work toward some sort of international organization for peace. This position helped keep Republican internationalists on board going into the 1920 election. See Cooper, *Breaking the Heart of the World*, pp. 376–98.

111. Joseph Tumulty to Edith Wilson, August 1, 1920 [Cox's speech], *WW Papers*, Series 2, Box 197.

112. Lodge to Root, May 17, 1920, cited in Ambrosius, *Woodrow Wilson and the American Diplomatic Tradition*, p. 263.

113. For an account that emphasizes Republican internationalists' concern over intraparty unity, see Miller, *Populist Nationalism*, pp. 73–96.

114. John Milton Cooper, *The Warrior and the Priest: Woodrow Wilson and Theodore Roosevelt* (Cambridge, Mass.: Belknap Press of Harvard University Press, 1983), pp. 331–35.

115. James Sundquist, *Dynamics of the Party System* (Washington, D.C.: Brookings Institution, 1983), p. 181; Ralph Levering, *The Public and American Foreign Policy, 1918–1978*, p. 46.

116. Lodge to Ellis Loring Dresel, American Commissioner in Berlin, April 18, 1921, cited in Widenor, *Henry Cabot Lodge and the Search for an American Foreign Policy*, p. 347.

117. Miller, *Populist Nationalism*, pp. 97–117.

118. Speech in Des Moines, October 7, 1920, cited in Ambrosius, *Woodrow Wilson and the American Diplomatic Tradition*, p. 282.

119. Hogan, *Informal Entente*, pp. 4–5; Rosenberg, *Spreading the American Dream*, p. 12.

120. Leffler, *The Elusive Quest*, pp. 32–42.

121. Iriye, *After Imperialism*, pp. 19–20.

122. Allan Millett and Peter Maslowski, *For the Common Defense*, pp. 366, 378.

123. William Braisted, *The United States Navy in the Pacific, 1900–1922* (Austin: University of Texas Press, 1971), p. 595.

124. It is sometimes suggested that even if the League had won Senate approval, it would have made little difference, in that the United States would have reverted to strategic disengagement by the 1930s, regardless. This view, however, underestimates the lasting difference that a successful conclusion of the League debate might have had upon American public opinion. As John Milton Cooper has argued, "the critical consideration here [was] not so much League membership or Article X in itself but, as Wilson insisted, the American public's frame of mind. . . . The critical time for creating the proper frame of mind was during and just after the League fight." See Cooper, *Breaking the Heart of the World*, p. 427.

CHAPTER FOUR
CONCEIVING CONTAINMENT: IDEAS AND
ALTERNATIVES IN AMERICAN GRAND STRATEGY, 1945–1951

1. Historical interpretations of America's adoption of containment have gone through several phases: traditionalist, revisionist, and postrevisionist. Traditionalist historians, such as Herbert Feis, maintained that containment was the reluctant, but inevitable and appropriate, American response to determined Soviet aggression. In the 1960s and 1970s, revisionists, such as William Appleman Williams and Gabriel Kolko, turned the traditionalist interpretation on its head. They argued that it was the United States that had acted most aggressively after World War Two; that the desire for open markets had impelled U.S. officials to create a kind of informal empire around the borders of the USSR; and that Moscow had reacted defensively, out of justifiable concern for its own national security. Beginning in the 1970s, and up to the present, a number of eclectic postrevisionist works by authors like John Gaddis, Melvyn Leffler, and Marc Trachtenberg have tended to moderate or rebut the more extreme claims of the revisionists, to emphasize geopolitical causes of Cold War conflict, and to deny that narrow economic interests were paramount in the minds of U.S. officials. Post–Cold War archival revelations have also given new life to what might be called a "neotraditionalist" interpretation, of which Gaddis has been a leading convert and advocate. Updated versions of revisionist arguments live on in the

work of authors like Bruce Cumings and Arnold Offner. See Herbert Feis, *From Trust to Terror: The Onset of the Cold War, 1947–1950* (New York: W. W. Norton, 1970); William Appleman Williams, *The Tragedy of American Diplomacy* (New York: Dell Publishing, 1962), pp. 202–76; Joyce Kolko and Gabriel Kolko, *The Limits of Power: The World and United States Foreign Policy, 1945–1954* (New York: Harper and Row, 1972); John Gaddis, *The United States and the Origins of the Cold War, 1941–1947* (New York: Columbia University Press, 1972); idem, "The Emerging Post-Revisionist Synthesis on the Origins of the Cold War," *Diplomatic History* 7 (Summer 1983): 171–90; and idem, *We Now Know: Rethinking Cold War History* (New York: Oxford University Press, 1997); Melvyn Leffler, *A Preponderance of Power: National Security, the Truman Administration, and the Cold War* (Stanford: Stanford University Press, 1992); Marc Trachtenberg, *A Constructed Peace: The Making of the European Settlement, 1945–1963* (Princeton: Princeton University Press, 1999); Bruce Cumings, *The Origins of the Korean War*, 2 vols. (Princeton: Princeton University Press, 1981–1990); and Arnold Offner, *Another Such Victory: President Truman and the Cold War, 1945–1953* (Stanford: Stanford University Press, 2002).

2. Herbert Hoover, December 20, 1950, in *Addresses Upon the American Road: 1950–1955* (Stanford: Stanford University Press, 1955), pp. 3–10.

3. Robert Taft, *A Foreign Policy for Americans* (Garden City, N.Y.: Doubleday, 1951), pp. 18–20, 75, 100.

4. Michael Hogan, *A Cross of Iron* (New York: Cambridge University Press, 1999), pp. 7–9, 20–21, 120–21; Leroy Rieselbach, *The Roots of Isolationism* (Indianapolis: Bobbs-Merrill, 1966), pp. 64, 106–20, 122, 136, 150–56.

5. Henry Wallace, *Toward World Peace* (New York: Reynal and Hitchcock, 1948), pp. 40–41, 67.

6. Murray Rothbard, "The Foreign Policy of the Old Right," *Journal of Libertarian Studies* 2, no. 1 (1978): 85–96; Karl Schmidt, *Henry Wallace, Quixotic Crusade 1948* (Syracuse, N.Y.: Syracuse University Press, 1960), pp. 84–85.

7. For a complete examination of the way in which antistatist sentiment in the United States acted as a check on the creation of more expensive grand strategies, see Aaron Friedberg, *In the Shadow of the Garrison State* (Princeton: Princeton University Press, 2000).

8. Taft, *A Foreign Policy for Americans*, pp. 103–13.

9. James Burnham, *Containment or Liberation?* (New York: J. Day, 1953), pp. 34–36, 43, 251–52.

10. Ibid., pp. 128–40.

11. Richard Betts, *Soldiers, Statesmen and Cold War Crises* (New York: Columbia University Press, 1991), p. 87; Russell Buhite and Christopher Hamel, "War for Peace: The Question of an American Preventive War against the Soviet Union, 1945–1955," *Diplomatic History* 14, no. 3 (Summer 1990): 367–84; Marc Trachtenberg, *History and Strategy* (Princeton: Princeton University Press, 1991), pp. 100–118.

12. Rosemary Foot, *The Wrong War: American Policy and the Dimensions of the Korean Conflict* (Ithaca: Cornell University Press, 1985), pp. 67–87; Michael Schaller, *Douglas MacArthur: The Far Eastern General* (Oxford: Oxford University Press, 1989), pp. 223–27.

13. Conflicting economic interests also seem to have made a partition of Germany inevitable: the USSR wanted an immediate transfer of massive war reparations from the Germans, while Britain and the United States opposed such transfers in favor of a partial rehabilitation of the German economy. In practical terms, the only mutually acceptable solution was to allow the USSR to take reparations from its own zone, while reconstructing a West German sphere—free from Soviet influence, but dependent on the United States. See Avi Shlaim, "The Partition of Germany and the Origins of the Cold War," *Review of International Studies* 11, no. 2 (1985): 123–37.

14. A.W. DePorte, *Europe between the Superpowers* (New Haven: Yale University Press, 1986), pp. 115–65; John Gaddis, *The Long Peace: Inquiries Into the History of the Cold War* (New York: Oxford University Press, 1987), pp. 215–45; Trachtenberg, *A Constructed Peace*, pp. 3–65, 398–402.

15. John Gaddis, *Strategies of Containment* (New York: Oxford University Press, 1982), pp. 274–344; Raymond Garthoff, *Détente and Confrontation: American-Soviet Relations from Nixon to Reagan* (Washington, D.C.: Brookings Institution Press, 1985), pp. 25–32.

16. Mike Bowker and Phil Williams, *Superpower Détente: A Reappraisal* (London: Sage Publications, 1988); Garthoff, *Détente and Confrontation*, pp. 24–52, 1069–72.

17. Hedley Bull, *The Anarchical Society* (New York: Columbia University Press, 1995 edition), pp. 207–18.

18. George Kennan to Charles E. Bohlen [hereafter CEB] January 26, 1945, Charles Bohlen Papers, Box 1, "Personal Correspondence 1944–46," General Records of the Department of State, Record Group [hereafter RG] 59, National Archives [hereafter NA].

19. Bohlen memorandum, October 18, 1945, Bohlen Papers, Box 3, Memos (CEB) 1945, RG 59, NA.

20. Walter Lippmann, "Today and Tomorrow," *Washington Post*, November 27, 1945.

21. Trachtenberg, *A Constructed Peace*, pp. 4–33.

22. Diane Clemens, *Yalta* (Oxford: Oxford University Press, 1970), pp. 247–55, 287–89; Robert Dallek, *Franklin D. Roosevelt and American Foreign Policy* (Oxford: Oxford University Press, 1979), pp. 507–8.

23. Deborah Larson, *Origins of Containment: A Psychological Explanation* (Princeton: Princeton University Press, 1985), pp. 177, 185.

24. James Byrnes, "Neighboring Nations in One World," *Department of State Bulletin* 13 (November 4, 1945): 709–11.

25. Eduard Mark, "American Policy Toward Eastern Europe and the Origins of the Cold War: An Alternative Interpretation," *Journal of American History* 68 (September 1981): 313–36.

26. Gaddis, *Strategies of Containment*, p. 359.

27. Leffler, *A Preponderance of Power*, pp. 100–140. See note 78 for further references.

28. Ibid., pp. 8–9, 15–18.

29. "Mr. X" [George Kennan], "The Sources of Soviet Conduct," *Foreign Affairs* 25 (July 1947): 580–82.

30. Clark Clifford, "American Relations with the Soviet Union: A Report to the President by the Special Counsel to the President," September 24, 1946, in Thomas Etzold and John Gaddis, eds., *Containment: Documents on American Policy and Strategy, 1945–1950* (New York: Columbia University Press, 1978), pp. 70–71.

31. This is *not* necessarily to say that a sphere-of-influence approach would have been superior to containment, morally or practically speaking. One of the multiple virtues of containment was that it never gave a stamp of legitimacy to Soviet rule in Eastern Europe. I only argue that as a matter of description, containment was not a purely "realpolitik" strategy, and that its adoption cannot be explained with reference to international pressures alone.

32. The anti-Communist assumptions behind containment may seem obvious to the reader, but several Cold War scholars over the years have portrayed this strategy in its early phases as strictly geopolitical, geared toward Soviet power rather than communism per se. I therefore spell out the anti-Communist assumptions behind the thinking of leading U.S. architects of containment, including George Kennan himself. For a primarily geopolitical interpretation of early U.S. containment strategy (1946–1948), see Thomas Christensen, *Useful Adversaries: Grand Strategy, Domestic Mobilization, and Sino-American Conflict, 1947–1958* (Princeton: Princeton University Press, 1996), pp. 32–76; Gaddis, *Strategies of Containment*, pp. 25–71; and Charles Kupchan, *Vulnerability of Empire* (Ithaca: Cornell University Press, 1994), pp. 418–85.

33. George Kennan to James Byrnes, February 22, 1946, *Foreign Relations of the United States* [hereafter *FR*], *1946*, vol. 6 (Washington, D.C.: GPO, 1969), pp. 703–4.

34. Ibid., pp. 706–8.

35. Clifford, "American Relations with the Soviet Union," p. 66.

36. As Walter Lippmann put it, "For a diplomat to think that rival and unfriendly powers cannot be brought to a settlement is to forget what diplomacy is all about." Lippmann, *The Cold War: A Study in U.S. Foreign Policy* (New York: Harper and Brothers, 1947), p. 60.

37. Anders Stephanson, "Ideology and Neorealist Mirrors," *Diplomatic History* 17, no. 2 (Spring 1993): 293.

38. Leffler, *A Preponderance of Power*, pp. 8–9.

39. Walter Hixson, *George Kennan: Cold War Iconoclast* (New York: Columbia University Press, 1989), pp. 44, 47–72, 222–23.

40. George Marshall to Jefferson Caffery, February 3, 1947, *FR*, *1947*, vol. 6, pp. 77–78.

41. Lloyd Gardner, *Approaching Vietnam: From World War Two Through Dienbienphu, 1941–1954* (New York: W. W. Norton, 1988), pp. 62–66.

42. Hixson, *George Kennan*, 151–52.

43. William Stueck, *The Road to Confrontation: American Policy Toward China and Korea, 1945–1950* (Chapel Hill: University of North Carolina Press, 1981), p. 255.

44. Report on the Ad Hoc Committee on Korea, August 4, 1947, *FR*, *1947*, vol. 6, pp. 738–41. See also Barton Bernstein, "The Truman Administration and

the Korean War," in Michael Lacey, ed., *The Truman Presidency* (New York: Cambridge University Press, 1991), p. 416.

45. Gregory Mitrovich, *Undermining the Kremlin: America's Strategy to Subvert the Soviet Bloc, 1947–1956* (Ithaca: Cornell University Press, 2000), pp. 1–14.

46. George Kennan, NSC 20/1, "U.S. Objectives with Respect to Russia," August 18, 1948, in Etzold and Gaddis, *Containment,* p. 184.

47. Leffler, *A Preponderance of Power,* pp. 15–19.

48. For a more thorough discussion of this point, see the section on domestic coalition building, below.

49. A.W. DePorte, *Europe Between the Superpowers,* pp. 58–59; Paul Kennedy, *The Rise and Fall of the Great Powers: Economic Change and Military Conflict from 1500 to 2000* (London: Unwin Hyman, 1988), pp. 365–69.

50. Donald White, "The Nature of World Power in American History: An Evaluation at the End of World War Two," *Diplomatic History* 11, no. 3 (Summer 1987): 188–91.

51. Kennedy, *The Rise and Fall of the Great Powers,* p. 355.

52. Cited in Marc Trachtenberg, *History and Strategy,* p. 119.

53. Russell Buhite and Christopher Hamel, "War for Peace," pp. 382–84; *McGeorge Bundy, Danger and Survival: Choices About the Bomb in the First Fifty Years* (New York: Vintage, 1988), p. 202.

54. JCS 1953/1, Report of the Ad Hoc Committee, "Evaluation of the Effect of Soviet War Effort Resulting from the Strategic Air Offensive," May 12, 1949, CCS 373 (10–23–48), Bulky Package, part 1, Records of the United States Joint Chiefs of Staff, RG 218, NA. See also Samuel Williamson and Steven Rearden, *The Origins of U.S. Nuclear Strategy, 1945–1953* (New York: St. Martin's, 1993), pp. 140–41.

55. See, for example, British concerns in M. L. Dockrill, "The Foreign Office, Anglo-American Relations and the Korean War, June 1950–June 1951," *International Affairs* 3 (Summer 1986): 459–76.

56. Regarding Soviet strategic culture and its varieties, see David Jones, "Soviet Strategic Culture," in Carl Jacobsen, ed., *Strategic Power: USA/USSR* (London: St. Martin's Press, 1990), pp. 35–49; and Jack Snyder, *Myths of Empire: Domestic Politics and International Ambition* (Ithaca: Cornell University Press, 1991), pp. 230–33.

57. On Marxist Leninism as a motivating factor behind Soviet expansionism, see Dwight Macdonald, "Communist Bloc Expansion in the Early Cold War: Challenging Realism, Refuting Revisionism," *International Security* 20, no. 3 (Winter 1995–1996): 185; and Martin Malia, *The Soviet Tragedy: A History of Socialism in Russia, 1917–1991* (New York: Free Press, 1994), p. 298.

58. Milovan Djilas, *Conversations with Stalin* (New York: Harcourt Brace, 1962), p. 114.

59. Roy Medvedev, *Let History Judge,* trans. Colleen Taylor (New York: Knopf, 1971), pp. 474–75.

60. Archival revelations and scholarly works over the past twenty years have tended to undermine earlier, revisionist interpretations of Stalin's foreign policy as essentially defensive. In the new literature, while Stalin certainly comes across

as frequently reactive and pragmatic, the overarching cultural, personal, and domestic political influences on his grand strategy are undeniable. Specifically, Stalin was (1) convinced of an inevitable conflict between the USSR and capitalist powers, (2) inclined to utilize the prospect of such conflict in order to tighten his control over Soviet society, (3) determined to promote the expansion of the Soviet socialist bloc wherever practicable, and, (4) paranoid to an extent that baffles the imagination. It is impossible not to conclude that these combined traits made some degree of postwar conflict with the United States inevitable. As to the viability of a limited postwar security arrangement based upon closed spheres of influence, the evidence is more equivocal; Stalin appears to have been attracted to this alternative in 1945 and even later. See Robert Conquest, *Stalin: Breaker of Nations* (New York: Viking Press, 1991), pp. 268–95; Gaddis, *We Now Know*, pp. 13–31, 289–92; David Holloway, *Stalin and the Bomb: The Soviet Union and Atomic Energy* (New Haven: Yale University Press, 1994), pp. 134–71, 252–72; Vojtech Mastny, *The Cold War and Soviet Insecurity: The Stalin Years* (New York: Oxford University Press, 1996); R.C. Raack, *Stalin's Drive to the West, 1938–1945* (Stanford: Stanford University Press, 1995), pp. 140–68; Dmitri Volkogonov, *Stalin: Triumph and Tragedy*, ed. and trans. Harold Shukman (New York: Grove Weidenfeld, 1991), pp. 483–541; William Wohlforth, *The Elusive Balance: Power and Perceptions during the Cold War* (Ithaca: Cornell University Press, 1993), pp. 40–87, 94–120; and Vladislav Zubok and Constantine Pleshakov, *Inside the Kremlin's Cold War: From Stalin to Khrushchev* (Cambridge, Mass.: Harvard University Press, 1996), pp. 3–77. For a somewhat different interpretation of the new evidence, which emphasizes Soviet defensive concerns rather than the peculiar nature of Stalin's regime, see Melvyn Leffler, "Inside Enemy Archives," *Foreign Affairs* 75, no. 4 (July–August 1996): 120–35.

61. Vojtech Mastny, *Russia's Road to the Cold War: Diplomacy, Warfare, and the Politics of Communism, 1941–1945* (New York: Columbia University Press, 1979), pp. 107–8; and idem, *The Cold War and Soviet Insecurity*, p. 20; Albert Resis, *Stalin, The Politburo, and the Onset of the Cold War: 1945–1946* (Pittsburgh: University of Pittsburgh Center for Russian and East European Studies, 1988) pp. 1–31; Vladislav Zubok and Constantine Pleshakov, *Inside the Kremlin's Cold War*, pp. 26–35.

62. Winston Churchill, *The Second World War, Volume VI: Triumph and Tragedy* (Boston: Houghton Mifflin, 1953), pp. 227–28.

63. Ibid., pp. 292–93.

64. Medvedev, *Let History Judge*, pp. 478–79.

65. Vladimir O. Pechatnov, "The Big Three after World War Two: New Documents on Soviet Thinking about Post War Relations with the United States and Great Britain," Cold War International History Project Working Paper 13 (July 1995).

66. James Byrnes, *Speaking Frankly* (New York: Harper and Brothers, 1947), pp. 280–81.

67. Franklin Roosevelt, in Samuel Rosenman, ed., *Public Papers and Addresses of Franklin Delano Roosevelt: 1945*, vol. 12 (New York: Harper and Brothers, 1950), p. 261.

68. Warren Kimball, *The Juggler: Franklin Roosevelt as Wartime Statesman* (Princeton: Princeton University Press, 1991), pp. 13, 18–19, 168–74.

69. Robert Sherwood, *Roosevelt and Hopkins: An Intimate History* (New York: Harper and Brothers, 1948), p. 266.

70. Kimball, *The Juggler*, pp. 63–81, 127–57; Randall Bennett Woods, *A Changing of the Guard: Anglo-American Relations, 1941–1946* (Chapel Hill: University of North Carolina Press, 1990), p. 240.

71. Leffler, *A Preponderance of Power*, pp. 19–20.

72. Mark, "American Policy Toward Eastern Europe and the Origins of the Cold War," pp. 313–36.

73. Lloyd Gardner, *Spheres of Influence: The Great Powers Partition Europe, from Munich to Yalta* (Chicago: I. R. Dee, 1993), pp. x–xiii, 265; Kimball, *The Juggler*, pp. 95, 103–4, 107–25, 182, 191; John Ruggie, *Winning the Peace: America and World Order in the New Era* (New York: Columbia University Press, 1996), pp. 30–34.

74. Gaddis, *The United States and the Origins of the Cold War, 1941–1947*, pp. 152–53.

75. Ibid., pp. 356–58.

76. See, for example, Charles Bohlen's comments to George Kennan, undated but early 1945, box 28, Kennan papers, Princeton University, Princeton, New Jersey.

77. Leffler, *A Preponderance of Power*, pp. 34–36.

78. Cited in Graham Ross, *The Foreign Office and the Kremlin* (New York: Cambridge University Press, 1984), p. 202.

79. Alonzo Hamby, "The Mind and Character of Harry S. Truman," in Michael Lacey, ed., *The Truman Presidency* (New York: Cambridge University Press, 1991), pp. 48–49.

80. Robert Ferrell, ed., *Off the Record: The Private Papers of Harry S. Truman* (New York: Harper and Row, 1980), pp. 21–22, 25, 30–32, 35; Leffler, *A Preponderance of Power*, pp. 25–26, 30, 40–47, 104–5.

81. Harry Truman, *Memoirs: 1945, Year of Decisions* (New York: Signet, 1955), p. 87.

82. Leffler, *A Preponderance of Power*, pp. 34–36; Robert Messer, *The End of An Alliance: James F. Byrnes, Roosevelt, Truman, and the Origins of the Cold War* (Chapel Hill: University of North Carolina Press, 1982), pp. 115–80; Truman, *Year of Decisions*, pp. 551–52.

83. See, for example, Averell Harriman to Edward Stenninius, January 10, 1945, *FR: The Conferences at Malta and Yalta, 1945* (Washington, D.C.: GPO, 1955), pp. 450–51.

84. Leahy Diary, April 23, December 26, 28, 1945, Leahy Papers, RG 48, NA; James Forrestal, in Walter Millis, ed., *The Forrestal Diaries* (New York: Viking, 1951), pp. 49–51, 127–28.

85. Gaddis, *Strategies of Containment*, p. 55; Larson, *Origins of Containment*, pp. 256–57. For Kennan's own interpretation of the long telegram's reception, which also stresses the good fortune of its timing, see George Kennan, *Memoirs: 1925–1950* (Boston: Little, Brown, 1967), p. 295. For the full text of the long

telegram, see Kennan to James Byrnes, February 22, 1946, *FR, 1946,* vol. 6, pp. 696–709.

86. Gaddis, *The United States and the Origins of the Cold War,* pp. 260, 267, 291, 294–96; Truman, *Year of Decisions,* pp. 551–52.

87. Robert Beisner, "Pattern of Peril: Dean Acheson Joins the Cold Warriors, 1945–46," *Diplomatic History* 20, no. 3 (Summer 1996): 321–55; Robert Donovan, *Conflict and Crisis: The Presidency of Harry S. Truman, 1949–1953* (New York: W. W. Norton, 1982), pp. 222–28.

88. Deborah Larson argues that the assumptions behind containment became entrenched in 1947, rather than 1946. But most historians of the period agree that the definitive shift toward containment in the minds of U.S. officials took place early in 1946. See Gaddis, *Strategies of Containment,* p. 21; Larson, *Origins of Containment,* pp. 342–49; Leffler, *A Preponderance of Power,* pp. 100, 131, 137–38; Daniel Yergin, *Shattered Peace: The Origins of the Cold War* (New York: Penguin, 1990), p. 100.

89. For the best expression of those new assumptions, see the Clifford-Elsey report of September 1946, which drew on the views and expertise of virtually every interested bureaucratic agency. Excerpts of that report are printed in Etzold and Gaddis, *Containment,* pp. 64–71.

90. See, for example, Truman's inaugural address of 1949, in *Public Papers of the Presidents: Harry S. Truman* [hereafter *PPS:HST*], *1949* (Washington, D.C.: GPO, 1964), pp. 112–26. See also Hogan, *A Cross of Iron,* pp. 18–19, 157–58; and Leffler, *A Preponderance of Power,* pp. 162–63.

91. Leffler, *A Preponderance of Power,* pp. 13–14, 53.

92. Hogan, *A Cross of Iron,* pp. 426–33.

93. For evidence of broad popular support for containment in the late 1940s, see Benjamin Page and Robert Shapiro, *The Rational Public: Fifty Years of Trends in Americans' Policy Preferences* (Chicago: University of Chicago Press, 1992), pp. 200–202; and Eugene Wittkopf and James McCormick, "The Cold War Consensus: Did it Exist?" *Polity* 22, no. 4 (Summer 1990): 631–41.

94. Geir Lundestad, *The American "Empire"* (New York: Oxford University Press, 1990), pp. 54–61.

95. Gaddis, *Strategies of Containment,* pp. 58–63.

96. Terry Anderson, *The United States, Great Britain and the Cold War, 1944–1947* (Columbia: University of Missouri Press, 1981), pp. 209–11; Victor Rothwell, *Britain and the Cold War, 1941–1947* (London: J. Cape, 1982), pp. 259, 411–42, 454–55.

97. Donald Sassoon, "The Rise and Fall of Western European Communism, 1939–1948," *Contemporary European History* 1 (1992): 139–69.

98. SWNCC 360, "Policies, Procedures, and Costs of Assistance," April 24, 1947, RG 319, ABC 400.336 (March 20, 1947), section 1-A, NA; "Rewrite of JWPC Paper 'Political Trends in Western and Northern European Countries,' " June 5, 1947, RG 319, P and O, 350.05 TS, NA.

99. Dunn to Marshall, May 3, 1947, *FR, 1947,* vol. 3, pp. 89–92; Kennan to Marshall, January 20, 1948, *FR, 1948,* vol. 3, p. 7; Marshall to Douglas, February 28 and March 4, 1948, *FR, 1948,* vol. 2, pp. 101, 123; Marshall to Dunn, May 20 and June 6, 1947, *FR, 1947,* vol. 3, pp. 909–10, 917. See also John Lamberton

Harper, *America and the Reconstruction of Italy, 1945–1948* (New York: Cambridge University Press, 1986), pp. 118–54; Michael Hogan, *The Marshall Plan* (New York: Cambridge University Press, 1987), pp. 60–87; and Edward Rice-Maximim, "The United States and the French Left, 1945–1949: The View From the State Department," *Journal of Contemporary History* 19 (October 1984): 734–35.

100. Hogan, *The Marshall Plan*, pp. 238–92; Alan Milward, *The Reconstruction of Western Europe, 1945–1951* (London: Methuen, 1984), pp. 282–98; William Wallace, *The Transformation of Western Europe* (London: Royal Institute of International Affairs, 1990), p. 68.

101. John Young, *Britain, France and the Unity of Europe* (Leicester: Leicester University Press, 1984), pp. 62–69.

102. Douglas to Marshall, February 25, 26, 28 and March 2, 1948, *FR, 1948*, vol. 2, pp. 87–89, 92–95, 98–100, 110–11.

103. John Baylis, "Britain and the Formation of NATO," in Joseph Smith, ed., *The Origins of NATO* (Exeter: University of Exeter, 1990), pp. 3–32; Irwin Wall, "France and the North Atlantic Alliance," in Francis Heller and John Gillingham, eds., *NATO: The Founding of the Atlantic Alliance and the Integration of Europe* (New York: St. Martin's Press, 1992), pp. 45–56.

104. Marshall to Truman, February 11, 1948, *FR, 1948*, vol. 2, pp. 61–63; JCS 1868/11, "Guidance for United States Military Representatives for London Military Talks on the Western Union of Nations," July 8, 1948, RG 319, P and O, 092 TS, NA.

105. Gaddis, *Strategies of Containment*, pp. 73–74.

106. Acheson memorandum of conversation with Senators Tom Connally and Arthur Vandenberg, February 14, 1949, *FR, 1949*, vol. 4, p. 109.

107. Milward, *Reconstruction of Western Europe*, pp. 362–407.

108. Cited in Trachtenberg, *History and Strategy*, pp. 157–58.

109. Ernest May, "The American Commitment to Germany, 1949–55," *Diplomatic History* 13, no. 4 (Fall 1989): 443–44.

110. On, for example, the German desire for a U.S. troop presence, see Thomas Schwartz, *America's Germany: John McCloy and the Federal Republic of Germany* (Cambridge, Mass.: Harvard University Press, 1991), pp. 299–300.

111. NSC 82, "United States Position Regarding Strengthening the Defense of Europe and the Nature of Germany's Contribution Thereto," September 8, 1950, *FR, 1950*, vol. 3, pp. 273–78.

112. Roger Dingman, "Strategic Planning and the Policy Process: American Plans for War in East Asia, 1945–1950," *Naval War College Review* 32 (November–December 1979): 4–21; Michael Schaller, *The American Occupation of Japan* (New York: Oxford University Press, 1985), p. 51; Howard Schonberger, "U.S. Policy in Postwar Japan: The Retreat from Liberalism," *Science and Society* 46 (Spring 1982): 39–60.

113. JCS 2180/2, "United States Policy Toward Japan," December 28, 1950, *FR, 1950*, vol. 6, pp. 1389–90.

114. Memo by Acheson, May 28, 1951, *FR, 1951*, vol. 6, pp. 1050–51.

115. CIA, "Feasibility of Japanese Rearmament in Association with the United States," April 20, 1951, ibid., pp. 993–1001.

116. John Dower, *Embracing Defeat* (New York: W. W. Norton, 1999), pp. 547–52.

117. Warren Cohen, "China in Japanese-American Relations," in Akira Iriye and Warren Cohen, eds., *The United States and Japan in the Postwar World* (Lexington: University Press of Kentucky, 1989), pp. 36–43.

118. John Dower, *Empire and Aftermath* (Cambridge, Mass.: Harvard University Press, 1979), pp. 369–400.

119. The rehabilitation of Japan also indirectly led to an unintended set of military commitments between the United States, Australia, New Zealand, and the Philippines. These last three countries resisted the rehabilitation of Japan and opposed a lenient peace treaty. Failing that, they asked for American security guarantees against Japan. The United States agreed to offer such military guarantees—bilaterally, in the case of the Philippines, and through the ANZAC alliance in the case of Australia and New Zealand. Unlike NATO, however, these alliances did not indicate any real degree of political reconciliation or economic integration within the region, and for that reason they did not include Japan. See H. W. Brands, "From ANZUS to SEATO: United States Strategic Policy Toward Australia and New Zealand," *International History Review* 9 (May 1987): 250–55; Roger Dingman, "The Diplomacy of Dependency: The Philippines and Peacemaking with Japan," *Journal of Southeast Asian Studies* 27 (September 1986): 314–21.

120. Acheson to Embassy in Iran, April 8, 18, and May 16, 1949, *FR, 1949*, vol. 6, pp. 501, 503, 519–21.

121. NSC 42, "US Objectives with Respect to Greece and Turkey to Counter Soviet Threats to U.S. Security," March 4, 1949, RG 273, NSC, NA.

122. Harry Truman, *Memoirs: Years of Trial and Hope, 1946–52* (New York: Doubleday, 1956), pp. 124–25.

123. Meeting of the Secretaries of State, War, and Navy, March 12, 1947, *FR, 1947*, vol. 5, pp. 109–10.

124. Report Prepared in the Bureau of Near Eastern, South Asian, and African Affairs, "Regional Security Arrangements in the Eastern Mediterranean and Near Eastern Areas," May 11, 1950, *FR, 1950*, vol. 5, pp. 152–56.

125. For an essay that emphasizes the initial desire of American officials to limit U.S. military commitments on the Asian mainland, see "Drawing Lines: the Defensive Perimeter Strategy in East Asia, 1947–1951," in Gaddis, *The Long Peace*, pp. 72–103.

126. NSC 22/1, "Possible Courses of Action with Respect to the Critical Situation in China," August 6, 1948, *FR, 1948*, vol. 8, 133–34; SWNCC, Special Ad Hoc Committee, "Indochina," RG 165, ABC 400.336 (March 20, 1947), section 1-B, NA.

127. William Duiker, *U.S. Containment Policy and the Conflict in Indochina* (Stanford: Stanford University Press, 1994), pp. 90–95.

128. Robert Blum, *Drawing the Line: The Origin of American Containment Policy in East Asia* (New York: W. W. Norton, 1982), pp. 118–23; Gary Hess, *The United States' Emergence as a Southeast Asian Power, 1940–1950* (New York: Columbia University Press, 1987), pp. 322–28.

129. Acheson to Douglas, July 10, 28, 1950, *FR, 1950*, vol. 6, pp. 350, 397–98.

130. Charles Dobbs, *The Unwanted Symbol: American Foreign Policy, the Cold War and Korea, 1945–1950* (Kent, Ohio: Kent State University Press, 1981), pp. 160–92; Burton Kaufman, *The Korean War: Challenges in Crisis, Credibility, and Command* (New York: Knopf, 1986), pp. 23–24; William Stueck, *The Korean War: An International History* (Princeton: Princeton University Press, 1995), p. 43.

131. Cited in Lacey, *The Truman Presidency*, p. 423.

132. Christensen, *Useful Adversaries*, pp. 7–8; Gaddis, *Strategies of Containment*, pp. 25–126; Kupchan, *Vulnerability of Empire*, pp. 418–85; Walter LaFeber, *America, Russia and the Cold War, 1945–1992* (New York: McGraw-Hill, 1993), pp. 53–57, 68–69, 93–98; Snyder, *Myths of Empire*, pp. 255–304; Yergin, *Shattered Peace*, pp. 282–86.

133. For the argument that Western analysts overestimated Soviet military capabilities during the late 1940s, see Matthew Evangelista, "Stalin's Postwar Army Reappraised," *International Security* 7, no. 3 (Winter 1982–1983): 110–38. For the argument that Western analysts *under*estimated Soviet military capabilities after 1948, see Phillip Karber and Jerald Combs, "The United States, NATO and the Soviet Threat to Western Europe: Military Estimates and Policy Options, 1945–1963," *Diplomatic History* 22, no. 3 (Summer 1998): 402, 413, 417–23, 429. For information on the scale of the Soviet military buildup during Stalin's final years in power, see M. Mackintosh, *Juggernaut: A History of the Soviet Armed Forces* (London: Secker and Warburg, 1967), pp. 272–73.

134. For war plan FROLIC, see JCS 1844 and 1844/1, March 9, 17, 1948, RG 218, CCS 381 USSR (3-2-46), section 12, NA; for war plan OFFTACKLE, see JCS 1844/46, "Joint Emergency War Plan," November 8, 1949, ibid., section 41. See also Steven Reardon, *History of the Office of the Secretary of Defense: The Formative Years, 1947–1950* (Washington, D.C.: GPO, 1984), pp. 347–53, 371–76, and Steven Ross, *American War Plans, 1945–1950* (New York: Garland, 1988), pp. 53–75, 94–98, 109–32.

135. JCS 1953/1, Report of the Ad Hoc Committee, "Evaluation of Effect of Soviet War Effort Resulting from the Strategic Air Offensive," May 12, 1949, RG 218, CCS 373 (10-23-48), Bulky Package, part 1, NA.

136. Truman to Acheson, January 31, 1950, *FR, 1950*, vol. 1, p. 142; memos by Paul Nitze, December 19, 1949 and January 17, 1950, *FR, 1949*, vol. 1, p. 611, and *FR, 1950*, vol. 1, pp. 13–16; NSC-68, April 14, 1950, *FR, 1950*, vol. 1, pp. 249–53, 264, 267–69, 273–74, 283, 290.

137. Robert Donovan, *Conflict and Crisis: The Presidency of Harry S. Truman, 1945–1948* (New York: W. W. Norton, 1977), pp. 143, 200, 261; Friedberg, *In the Shadow of the Garrison State*, pp. 174–75; Alonzo Hamby, *Man of the People: A Life of Harry S. Truman* (New York: Oxford University Press, 1995), p. 399; *PPS:HST* (1948), pp. 406–10, 416–22; Truman to Souers, July 1, 1949, *FR, 1949*, vol. 1, pp. 350–52.

138. David Kepley, *The Collapse of the Middle Way: Senate Republicans and Bipartisan Foreign Policy, 1948–52* (New York: Greenwood Press, 1988), pp. 3–4.

139. Friedberg, *In the Shadow of the Garrison State*, pp. 74–115, 146–74; Robert Griffith, "Forging America's postwar order: domestic politics and political

economy in the age of Truman," in Lacey, ed., *The Truman Presidency*, pp. 63–67.

140. Arthur Stein, "Domestic Constraints, Extended Deterrence, and the Incoherence of Grand Strategy: The United States, 1938–1950," in Richard Rosecrance and Arthur Stein, eds., *The Domestic Bases of Grand Strategy* (Ithaca: Cornell University Press, 1993), pp. 97, 119–22.

141. Gaddis, *Strategies of Containment*, p. 359.

142. Souers to NSC, NSC 52, July 5, 1949, and Truman to Souers, July 1, 1949, *FR, 1949*, vol. 1, pp. 350–52.

143. Rearden, *The Formative Years*, pp. 532–36.

144. Friedberg, *In the Shadow of the Garrison State*, pp. 206–44; Gaddis, *Strategies of Containment*, p. 109; Leffler, *A Preponderance of Power*, pp. 371–73.

145. Acheson report to cabinet meeting, July 14, 1950, *FR, 1950*, vol. 1, p. 345.

146. Hogan, *A Cross of Iron*, pp. 266, 313.

147. George Gallup, *The Gallup Poll: Public Opinion, 1935–1971*, vol. 2 (New York: Random House, 1972), pp. 962, 964, 998–99.

148. Paul Hammond, "NSC-68: Prologue to Rearmament," in Warner Schilling, Paul Hammond, and Glenn Snyder, eds., *Strategy, Politics and Defense Budgets* (New York: Columbia University Press, 1962), pp. 351–59.

149. Robert Divine, *Foreign Policy and U.S. Presidential Elections, 1940–1948* (New York: New Viewpoints, 1974), pp. 188–90; Justus Doenecke, *Not to the Swift: The Old Isolationists in the Cold War Era* (Lewisburg, Pa.: Bucknell University Press, 1979), pp. 74–75; H. Bradford Westerfield, *Foreign Policy and Party Politics: Pearl Harbor to Korea* (New Haven: Yale University Press, 1955), pp. 269–95.

150. Kepley, *The Collapse of the Middle Way*, pp. 77–82; Westerfield, *Foreign Policy and Party Politics*, pp. 325–69.

151. William White, *The Taft Story* (New York: Harper and Brothers, 1954), pp. 159–60.

152. Doenecke, *Not to the Swift*, pp. 179–84.

153. Westerfield, *Foreign Policy and Party Politics*, pp. 240–68; White, *The Taft Story*, pp. 167–68.

154. Kepley, *The Collapse of the Middle Way*, pp. 53–61.

155. Hogan, *A Cross of Iron*, pp. 343–44; David Reinhard, *The Republican Right Since 1945* (Lexington: University Press of Kentucky, 1983), pp. 67–73.

156. Ronald Caridi, *The Korean War and American Politics* (Philadelphia: University of Pennsylvania Press, 1968), pp. 116, 119; Taft, *A Foreign Policy for Americans*, pp. 74, 77.

157. Caridi, *The Korean War and American Politics*, pp. 75, 84, 116, 131–37, 154–57; Ronald Radosh, *Prophets on the Right: Profiles of Conservative Critics of American Globalism* (New York: Simon and Schuster, 1975), p. 186.

158. Page and Shapiro, *The Rational Public*, p. 212.

159. Ted Galen Carpenter, "United States NATO Policy at the Crossroads: The Great Debate of 1950–51," *International History Review* 8 (August 1986): 395–414.

CHAPTER FIVE
HEGEMONY ON THE CHEAP: IDEAS AND
ALTERNATIVES IN AMERICAN GRAND STRATEGY, 1992–2000

1. For other, similar attempts to categorize America's post–Cold War grand strategic alternatives, see Richard Haass, "Paradigm Lost," *Foreign Affairs* 74, no. 1 (January–February 1995): 43–58; John Kohout, Steven Lambakis, Keith Payne, Robert Rudney, Willis Stanley, Bernard Victory, and Linda Vlahos, "Alternative Grand Strategy Options for the United States," *Comparative Strategy* 14, no. 4 (1995): 361–420; Alexander Nacht, "U.S. Foreign Policy Strategies," *Washington Quarterly* 18, no. 3 (Summer 1995): 195–210; Henry Nau, *At Home Abroad: Identity and Power in American Foreign Policy* (Ithaca: Cornell University Press, 2002), pp. 43–59; and Barry Posen and Andrew Ross, "Competing Visions for U.S. Grand Strategy," *International Security* 21, no. 3 (Winter 1996–1997): 5–53.

2. Eugene Wittkopf finds that isolationism tends to have disproportionate support on ideological extremes, among both ultraliberals and ultraconservatives. See Eugene Wittkopf, "What Americans Really Think About Foreign Policy," *Washington Quarterly* 19, no. 3 (Summer 1996): 103.

3. Pat Buchanan, *A Republic Not an Empire* (Washington, D.C.: Regnery Press, 2002).

4. Eric Nordlinger, *Isolationism Reconfigured* (Princeton: Princeton University Press, 1995); Christopher Layne, "From Preponderance to Offshore Balancing," *International Security* 22, no. 1 (Summer 1997): 86–124; Ted Galen Carpenter, *Peace and Freedom: Foreign Policy for a Constitutional Republic* (Washington, D.C.: Cato Institute, 2002); Eugene Gholz, Daryl Press, and Harvey Sapolsky, "Come Home, America: The Strategy of Restraint in the Face of Temptation," *International Security* 21, no. 4 (Spring 1997): 5–48.

5. Gholz et al., "Come Home, America," p. 6.

6. Layne, "From Preponderance to Offshore Balancing," p. 113.

7. Gholz et al., pp. 32–33.

8. Layne, "From Preponderance to Offshore Balancing," pp. 112–113.

9. Nordlinger, *Isolationism Reconfigured*, p. 46; Gholz et al., "Come Home, America," p. 13.

10. Earl Ravenal, "The Case for Adjustment," *Foreign Policy* 81 (Winter 1990–1991): 15–19.

11. Layne, "From Preponderance to Offshore Balancing," p. 124.

12. Jack Citrin, "Is American Nationalism Changing? Implications for Foreign Policy," *International Studies Quarterly* 38, no. 1 (March 1994): 1–32; Ole Holsti and James Rosenau, "The Structure of Foreign Policy Beliefs Among Opinion Leaders—After the Cold War," *Millenium* 22, no. 2 (Summer 1993): 258; Wittkopf, "What Americans Really Think About Foreign Policy," p. 93.

13. William Schneider in Robert Lieber, ed., *Eagle Adrift: American Foreign Policy at the End of the Century* (New York: Longmor, 1997), pp. 27–28.

14. Wittkopf, "What Americans Really Think About Foreign Policy," p. 103.

15. Walter McDougall, *Promised Land, Crusader State* (Boston, Mass.: Houghton Mifflin, 1999), p. 211.

16. Samuel Huntington, "America's Changing Strategic Interests," *Survival* 33, no. 1 (January–February 1991): 8; Henry Kissinger, *Does America Need a Foreign Policy?* (New York: Touchstone, 2002); James Kurth, "America's Grand Strategy: A Pattern of History," *National Interest* 43 (Spring 1996): 3–16; James Schlesinger, "Quest for a Post–Cold War Foreign Policy," *Foreign Affairs* 72, no. 1 (Winter 1992–1993): 17–28; Alan Tonelson, "What is the National Interest?" *Atlantic Monthly* 268, no. 1 (July 1991): 35–52.

17. Samuel Huntington, "The Lonely Superpower," *Foreign Affairs* 78, no. 2 (March–April 1999): 48.

18. David Calleo, "The United States and the Great Powers," *World Policy Journal* 16, no. 3 (Fall 1999): 11–19.

19. Josef Joffe, "Bismarck or Britain? Toward an American Grand Strategy after Bipolarity," *International Security* 19, no. 4 (Spring 1995): 94–117.

20. Haass, "Paradigm Lost?" p. 48.

21. Hans Morgenthau, *Politics Among Nations* abridged ed. (New York: McGraw-Hill, 1993), pp. 382–83.

22. William Kristol and Robert Kagan, "Introduction: National Interest and Global Responsibility," in Robert Kagan and William Kristol, eds., *Present Dangers: Crisis and Opportunity in American Foreign and Defense Policy* (San Francisco: Encounter Books, 2000), p. 6.

23. William Kristol and Robert Kagan, "Toward a Neo-Reaganite Foreign Policy," *Foreign Affairs* 75, no. 4 (July–August 1996): 18–32; Charles Krauthammer, "The Unipolar Moment Revisited," *National Interest* 70 (Winter 2002–2003): 5–17; Richard Perle, "Iraq: Saddam Unbound," in Kagan and Kristol, *Present Dangers*, pp. 99–110; Joshua Muravchik, *The Imperative of American Leadership* (Washington, D.C.: AEI Press, 1996); Zalmay Khalilzad, "Losing the Moment? The United States and the World After the Cold War," *Washington Quarterly* 18, no. 2 (Spring 1995): 87–107; Paul Wolfowitz, "Remembering the Future," *National Interest* 59 (Spring 2000): 35–45.

24. Zalmay Khalilzad, *From Containment to Global Leadership? America and the World After the Cold War* (Santa Monica: RAND, 1995), 30; Krauthammer, "The Unipolar Moment," pp. 31–32.

25. Kristol and Kagan, "Introduction: National Interest and Global Responsibility," pp. 4–12.

26. Quoted in Michael Gordon, "Joint Chiefs Warn Congress Against More Military Cuts," *New York Times*, May 20, 1993.

27. Muravchik, *The Imperative of American Leadership*, pp. 36–50.

28. Charles Krauthammer, "The Unipolar Moment," *Foreign Affairs* 70, no. 1 (1990–1991): 23–34.

29. Richard Bernstein and Ross Munro, *The Coming Conflict with China* (New York: Knopf, 1997).

30. Zbigniew Brzezinski, "Living With Russia," *National Interest* 61 (Fall 2000): 5–16.

31. Jeffrey Gedmin, "Europe and NATO: Saving the Alliance," in Kagan and Kristol, *Present Dangers*, pp. 179–96.

32. Kristol and Kagan, "Toward a Neo-Reaganite Foreign Policy," pp. 18–32.

33. Robert Kagan, "The Case for Global Activism," *Commentary* 98, no. 3 (September 1994): 40–44.

34. Muravchik, *The Imperative of American Leadership*, p. 138.

35. Ibid., pp. 71–82.

36. Posen and Ross, "Competing Visions for U.S. Grand Strategy," pp. 28–39.

37. The most famous statement of this goal came in the form of a draft planning document from the Defense Department, which was leaked to the press in March 1992. The document suggested that the United States prevent any potential strategic competitors from forming—for example, in Europe or Japan—by continuing to provide broad security guarantees to America's traditional Cold War allies. It also suggested that the United States act to prevent the emergence of any hostile power in Europe or Asia comparable to the Soviet Union. See Patrick Tyler, "U.S. Strategy Plans for Insuring No Rivals Develop," *New York Times*, March 8, 1992.

38. Nau, *At Home Abroad*, pp. 48–55.

39. Graham Allison and Gregory Treverton, *Rethinking America's Security* (New York: W. W. Norton, 1992); David Callahan, *Between Two Worlds: Realism, Idealism, and American Foreign Policy After the Cold War* (New York: HarperCollins, 1994); John Ikenberry, "Institutions, Strategic Restraint, and the Persistence of America's Postwar Order," *International Security* 23, no. 3 (Winter 1998–1999): 43–78; Joseph Nye, *The Paradox of American Power* (New York: Oxford University Press, 2002); John Ruggie, *Winning the Peace* (New York: Columbia University Press, 1996).

40. Ashton Carter, William Perry, and John Steinbruner, *A New Concept of Cooperative Security* (Washington, D.C.: Brookings Institution, 1992), p. 4; Ole Holsti and James Rosenau, "The Structure of Foreign Policy Beliefs Among American Opinion Leaders—After the Cold War," *Millenium* 22, no. 2 (Summer 1993): 261–63.

41. Nye, *The Paradox of American Power*, pp. 15–16, 141–47.

42. Ikenberry, "Institutions, Strategic Restraint, and the Persistence of America's Postwar Order," pp. 43–44.

43. Ruggie, *Winning the Peace*, p. 25.

44. Nye, *The Paradox of American Power*, pp. 16–17, 154–63; Ruggie, pp. 4–5, 22.

45. James Mayall, "Nationalism and International Security After the Cold War," *Survival* 34, no. 1 (Spring 1992): 19–35; Stephen John Stedman, "The New Interventionists," *Foreign Affairs* 72, no. 1 (Spring 1993): 1–16.

46. Jon Western, "Sources of Humanitarian Intervention: Beliefs, Information and Advocacy in the U.S. Decisions on Somalia and Bosnia," *International Security* 26, no. 4 (Spring 2002): 117–18, 124–27, 135.

47. Allison and Treverton, *Rethinking America's Security*, pp. 36–56; Carter, Perry, and Steinbruner, *A New Concept of Cooperative Security*, p. 25; Nye, *The Paradox of American Power*, pp. 4–17, 143.

48. Carnegie Endowment National Commission, *Changing Our Ways: America and the World* (Washington, D.C.: Brookings Institution, 1992); Lee Hamilton, "A Democrat Looks at Foreign Policy," *Foreign Affairs* 71, no. 3 (Sum-

mer 1993): 32–51; William Kaufman and John Steinbruner, *Decisions for Defense* (Washington, D.C.: Brookings Institution, 1991), pp. 67–76.

49. Posen and Ross, "Competing Visions for U.S. Grand Strategy," pp. 24–25.

50. Carnegie Endowment, *Changing Our Ways*, pp. 73–75.

51. Carter, Perry, and Steinbruner, *A New Concept of Cooperative Security.*

52. Ibid., p. 6.

53. Morton Halperin, "Guaranteeing Democracy," *Foreign Policy* 91 (Summer 1993): 105–22; Nye, *The Paradox of American Power*, pp. 148–53; Tony Smith, *America's Mission: The United States and the Worldwide Struggle for Democracy in the Twentieth Century* (Princeton: Princeton University Press, 1994).

54. Bruce Russett, *Grasping the Democratic Peace* (Princeton: Princeton University Press, 1992).

55. See, for example, Joseph Nye, "The Case for Deep Engagement," *Foreign Affairs* 74, no. 4 (July–August 1995): 90–102.

56. See, for example, Callahan, *Between Two Worlds.*

57. Ole Holsti, *American Leadership in World Affairs: Vietnam and the Breakdown of Consensus* (Boston, Mass.: Allen and Unwin, 1984).

58. John Kohout et al., "Alternative Grand Strategy Options for the United States," *Comparative Strategy* 14, no. 4 (1995): 402–4; Nau, *At Home Abroad*, p. 55.

59. John Mearsheimer, "Back to the Future: Instability in Europe after the Cold War," *International Security* 15, no. 1 (Summer 1990): 5–56; Kenneth Waltz, "The Emerging Structure of International Politics," in Michael Brown et al., eds., *The Perils of Anarchy: Contemporary Realism and International Security* (Cambridge, Mass.: MIT Press, 1995), pp. 42–77.

60. A similar argument was made recently by Charles Kupchan in *The End of the American Era* (New York: Knopf, 2002), pp. 28–29, 62–64.

61. Mearsheimer's prediction of U.S. strategic disengagement is conditional; he expects that the United States will disengage from its overseas commitments unless some potential regional hegemon, such as China, arises in Asia or Europe. See John Mearsheimer, *The Tragedy of Great Power Politics* (New York: W. W. Norton, 2001), pp. 385–400.

62. Ibid., pp. 114–28, 381–82.

63. Ibid., pp. 21–22, 29–40.

64. Kenneth Waltz, *Theory of International Politics* (New York: McGraw-Hill, 1979), pp. 121–22.

65. Waltz, "The Emerging Structure of International Politics," pp. 53–67.

66. Kenneth Waltz, "Structural Realism after the Cold War," in John Ikenberry, ed., *America Unrivaled: The Future of the Balance of Power* (Ithaca: Cornell University Press, 2002), pp. 48, 63.

67. Ibid., pp. 53, 64.

68. Waltz, "The Emerging Structure of International Politics," p. 77.

69. Mearsheimer, *The Tragedy of Great Power Politics*, pp. 40–41, 381–82; Waltz, "Structural Realism after the Cold War," p. 52.

70. Robert Gilpin, *War and Change in World Politics* (New York: Cambridge University Press, 1981); A.F.K. Organski, *World Politics* (New York: Knopf, 1968); Ronald Tammen et al., *Power Transitions* (New York: Chatham House

Publishers, 2000); Adam Watson, *The Evolution of International Society* (London: Routledge, 1992).

71. See William Wohlforth, "The Stability of a Unipolar World," *International Security* 24, no. 1 (Summer 1999): 5–41; and Stephen Brooks and William Wohlforth, "American Primacy in Perspective," *Foreign Affairs* 81, no. 4 (July–August 2002): 20–33.

72. International Institute of Strategic Studies, *The Military Balance 2002/2003* (Oxford: Oxford University Press).

73. Central Intelligence Agency, *World Factbook, 2002.*

74. Nye, *The Paradox of American Power*, pp. 4–16.

75. Michael Mastanduno and Ethan Kapstein, "Realism and State Strategies After the Cold War," in Kapstein and Mastanduno, eds., *Unipolar Politics* (New York: Columbia University Press, 1999), pp. 4–6; Wohlforth, "The Stability of a Unipolar World," pp. 23–37.

76. Michael Mastanduno, "Preserving the Unipolar Moment: Realist Theories and U.S. Grand Strategy After the Cold War," in Michael Brown et al., eds., *America's Strategic Choices* (Cambridge, Mass.: MIT Press, 1997), p. 134.

77. Robert Kagan, "Power and Weakness," *Policy Review* 113 (June–July 2002): 9, 13.

78. Gilpin, *War and Change in World Politics*, pp. 191–94.

79. Mastanduno, "Preserving the Unipolar Moment," p. 137.

80. Carnegie Endowment National Commission, *Changing Our Ways*; Allison and Treverton, *Rethinking America's Security*, pp. 36–56; Kaufmann and Steinbruner, *Decisions for Defense*, pp. 67–76; John Rielly, *American Public Opinion and United States Foreign Policy* (Chicago: Chicago Council on Foreign Relations, 1999), p. 24.

81. For the original and influential argument regarding "imperial overstretch," see Kennedy, *The Rise and Fall of the Great Powers*, pp. 514–15.

82. William Hyland, *Clinton's World: Remaking American Foreign Policy* (Westport, Conn.: Praeger, 1999), p. 12.

83. Elizabeth Drew, *On the Edge: The Clinton Presidency* (New York: Simon and Schuster, 1994), p. 138.

84. T. H. Henriksen, *Clinton's Foreign Policy in Somalia, Bosnia, Haiti, and North Korea* (Stanford: Hoover Institution, 1996), p. 22; Western, "Sources of Humanitarian Intervention," p. 127.

85. Stephen John Stedman, "The New Interventionists," *Foreign Affairs* 72, no. 1 (Spring 1993): 4–5.

86. Bert Rockman, "The Presidency and Bureaucratic Change After the Cold War," in Randall Ripley and James Lindsay, eds., *U.S. Foreign Policy After the Cold War* (Pittsburgh: University of Pittsburgh Press, 1997), p. 29. Clinton's first State of the Union address barely mentioned foreign policy issues. See Clinton's State of the Union, 1993, delivered to the Joint Session of Congress, February 17, 1993, in *Vital Speeches of the Day* 59, no. 11 (March 15, 1993): 322–25.

87. Robert Lieber, "Eagle Without a Cause: Making Foreign Policy Without the Soviet Threat," in Lieber, *Eagle Adrift*, pp. 3–25.

88. David Halberstam, *War in a Time of Peace: Bush, Clinton, and the Generals* (New York: Scribner, 2001), pp. 167–68; Hyland, *Clinton's World*, pp. 18–26.

89. See Warren Christopher, *In the Stream of History: Shaping Foreign Policy for a New Era* (Stanford: Stanford University Press, 1998); Michael Dobbs, *Madeleine Albright* (New York: Henry Holt and Co., 1999); and Thomas Lippmann, *Madeleine Albright and the New American Diplomacy* (Boulder, Colo.: Westview Press, 2000).

90. Anthony Lake, "Defining Missions, Setting Deadlines: Meeting New Security Challenges in the Post-Cold War World," remarks delivered at George Washington University, March 6, 1996, cited in Richard Haass, *Intervention* (Washington, D.C.: Brookings Institution, 1999), pp. 247–48.

91. Drew, *On the Edge*, p. 112.

92. John Ikenberry, *After Victory* (Princeton: Princeton University Press, 2000), pp. 241–45.

93. Ivo Daalder, "The Clinton Administration and Multilateral Peace Operations," in Pew Case Studies in International Affairs, Case 462A (1994), p. 3.

94. John Dumbrell, *American Foreign Policy* (New York: St. Martin's Press, 1997), p. 185.

95. Douglas Brinkley, "Democratic Enlargement: The Clinton Doctrine," *Foreign Policy* 106 (Spring 1997): 117, 120–21, 125; Michael Cox, *United States Foreign Policy After the Cold War: Superpower Without a Mission?* (London, Pinter, 1995), p. 36.

96. See, for example, Clinton's address at George Washington University on February 26, 1993, "Liberal Internationalism: America and the Global Economy," contained in Alvin Rubinstein et al., eds., *The Clinton Foreign Policy Reader* (Armonk, N.Y.: M. E. Sharpe, 2000), pp. 8–13.

97. See, for example, an address by Anthony Lake, assistant to the president for national security affairs, at Johns Hopkins University, September 21, 1993, in *Vital Speeches* 60, no. 1 (1993): 15; an address by Warren Christopher, secretary of state, at Harvard University, January 20, 1995, in *Vital Speeches* 61, no. 10 (1995): 292; and the 1997 State of the Union address by President Bill Clinton, February 4, 1997, in *Vital Speeches* 63, no. 10 (1997): 294.

98. *A National Security Strategy for a New Century*, p. 2.

99. Anthony Lake at Johns Hopkins University, September 21, 1993, *Vital Speeches* 60, no. 1: 15.

100. See, for example, an address by Madeleine Albright, secretary of state, at Rice University, February 7, 1997, in *Vital Speeches* 63, no. 13 (1997): 388. See also *A National Security Strategy for a New Century*, published by the White House in May 1997, pp. 1–2.

101. *A National Security Strategy for a New Century*, p. 8.

102. State of the Union address by President Bill Clinton, February 17, 1993, in *Vital Speeches* 59, no. 11 (1993): 322.

103. Warren Christopher at Harvard University, January 20, 1995, *Vital Speeches* 61, no. 10: 291.

104. For a similar assessment, see Posen and Ross, "Competing Visions for U.S. Grand Strategy," p. 44.

105. Hyland, *Clinton's World*, p. 12.

106. Ibid., p. 16.

107. Halberstam, *War in a Time of Peace*, p. 23.

108. Pat Buchanan, "America First—and Second, and Third," *National Interest*, 19 (1990): 77–82.

109. For an interpretation that stresses the underlying continuity between the foreign policies of Bush Sr. and Clinton, see Andrew Bacevich, *The American Empire: The Realities and Consequences of U.S. Diplomacy* (Cambridge, Mass.: Harvard University Press, 2002), p. 3.

110. Rielly, *American Public Opinion and United States Foreign Policy*, pp. 25–26.

111. Ibid., 4, 12; Steven Kull, I. M. Destler and Clay Ramsay, *The Foreign Policy Gap: How Policymakers Misread the Public* (College Park: Center for International and Security Studies at the University of Maryland, 1997), pp. 23, 133.

112. Both of these Republican leaders, for example, ultimately supported Clinton in his late 1995 decision to deploy American peacekeeping troops to Bosnia. See Elizabeth Drew, *Showdown: The Struggle Between the Gingrich Congress and the Clinton White House* (New York: Simon and Schuster, 1996), pp. 346–47.

113. Stedman, "The New Interventionists," pp. 4–5.

114. Gideon Rose, "Democracy Promotion and American Foreign Policy," *International Security* 25, no. 3 (Winter 2000–2001): 186–203.

115. James Goldgeier, "NATO Expansion: The Anatomy of a Decision," *Washington Quarterly* 21, no. 1 (Winter 1998): 86, 89, 101.

116. In Somalia, for example, in August 1993 Madeleine Albright declared that American troops would "stay as long as needed to lift the country and its people from the category of a failed state into that of an emerging democracy." See Madeleine Albright, "Yes, There is a Reason to Be in Somalia," *Washington Post*, August 10, 1993. On Somalia, see John Bolton, "Wrong Turn in Somalia," *Foreign Affairs* 73, no. 1 (January February 1994): 56–66; Haass, *Intervention*, p. 45; and Karin von Hippel, *Democracy by Force: U.S. Military Intervention in the Post–Cold War World* (New York: Cambridge University Press, 2000), pp. 64, 73, 77. On Bosnia, see idem, pp. 127–67.

117. See Clinton's speech to the nation on November 27, 1995, in which he used the word "leadership" fifteen times in a brief television address. The subject of his address was the need for American soldiers to be sent to Bosnia as peacekeepers. *Vital Speeches* 52, no. 5 (1995): 130–32.

118. von Hippel, *Democracy by Force*, pp. 154–55.

119. Security Council Resolution 814, March 26, 1993.

120. Robert Oakley and John Hirsch, *Somalia and Operation Restore Hope* (Washington, D.C.: United States Institute of Peace, 1995), p. 111.

121. Donatella Lorch, "What Began as a Mission of Mercy Closes with Little Ceremony," *New York Times*, March 26, 1994.

122. Barry Blechman and Tamara Cofman Wittes, "Defining Moment: The Threat and Use of Force in American Foreign Policy," *Political Science Quarterly* 114 (Spring 1999): 21.

123. Mark Danner, "Clinton, the UN, and the Bosnian Disaster," *New York Review of Books*, December 18, 1997: 68, 75–76; James Gow, *Triumph of the Lack of Will: International Diplomacy and the Yugoslav War* (New York: Columbia University Press, 1997), pp. 208, 218.

124. Halberstam, *War in a Time of Peace*, pp. 302, 360; Bob Woodward, *The Choice* (New York: Simon and Schuster, 1996), pp. 256–57, 267.

125. Benjamin Lambeth, *The Transformation of American Airpower* (Ithaca: Cornell University Press, 2000), pp. 174–78; David Shearer, *Private Armies and Military Intervention: Adelphi Paper 316* (Oxford: Oxford University Press, 1998), pp. 58–62.

126. Wesley Clark, *Waging Modern War* (New York: Public Affairs, 2001), p. 206.

127. Daniel Byman and Matthew Waxman, "Kosovo and the Great Air Power Debate," *International Security* 24, no. 4 (Spring 2000): 5–38; Stephen Hosmer, *The Conflict over Kosovo: Why Milosevic Decided to Settle When He Did* (Santa Monica: RAND, 2001).

128. Clark, *Waging Modern War*, pp. 438–40.

129. Halberstam, *War in a Time of Peace*, p. 475.

130. Scholars differ on the relative importance of (1) the NATO air campaign, (2) action by the KLA, (3) the threat of U.S. and/or British ground troops, and (4) Russian diplomatic pressure in forcing Milosevic to finally concede. But it seems fair to say that an air campaign without either proxy forces on the ground or the threat of a ground invasion would have had little success. See Wesley Clark, *Waging Modern War*, pp. 327–29, 332–37; and Ivo Daalder and Michael O'Hanlon, *Winning Ugly: NATO's War to Save Kosovo* (Washington, D.C.: Brookings Institution, 2000), pp. 151–53, 171. For a different interpretation, stressing the importance of the air campaign, see Benjamin Lambeth, *NATO's Air War for Kosovo* (Santa Monica: RAND, 2001).

131. Eliot Cohen, "Kosovo and the New American Way of War," in Andrew Bacevich and Eliot Cohen, eds., *War Over Kosovo: Politics and Strategy in a Global Age* (New York: Columbia University Press, 2001), pp. 38–62; Michael Noonan and John Hillen, "The Promise of Decisive Action," *Orbis* 46, no. 2 (Spring 2002): 229–46.

132. Bacevich, *The American Empire*, pp. 147–66.

133. Daniel Byman and Matthew Waxman, *The Dynamics of Coercion* (New York: Cambridge University Press, 2002), p. 131.

134. Rielly, *American Public Opinion and United States Foreign Policy*, pp. 4, 12.

135. Ibid., p. 26.

136. John Mueller, *War, Presidents and Public Opinion* (New York: John Wiley and Sons, 1973), chap. 3.

137. Blechman and Wittes, "Defining Moment," p. 35.

138. James Burk, "Public Support for Peacekeeping in Lebanon and Somalia: Assessing the Casualties Hypothesis," *Political Science Quarterly* 114 (Spring 1999): 53–78; Andrew Kohut, "Arms and the People," *Foreign Affairs* 73, no. 6 (November–December 1994): 47–61.

139. Peter D. Feaver and Christopher Gelpi, "A Look at Casualty Aversion: How Many Deaths Are Acceptable? A Surprising Answer," *Washington Post*, November 7, 1999.

140. Bruce Russett, *Controlling the Sword* (Cambridge, Mass.: Harvard University Press, 1990), pp. 34–38.

141. Benjamin Page and Robert Shapiro, *The Rational Public* (Chicago: University of Chicago Press, 1992), chaps. 5–6.

142. Kull et al., *The Foreign Policy Gap*, p. 82; Eric Larson, *Casualties and Consensus* (Santa Monica: RAND, 1996).

143. Bruce Jentleson, "The Pretty Prudent Public: Post–Cold War American Public Opinion on the Use of Force," *International Studies Quarterly* 36 (March 1992): 49–74.

144. Alan Tonelson, "Beyond Left and Right," *National Interest* 34 (Winter 1993–1994): 3–18.

145. Eugene Wittkopf, "What Americans Really Think About Foreign Policy," pp. 91–106.

146. William Schneider, "The New Isolationism," in Lieber, *Eagle Adrift*, pp. 33–37.

147. Ibid., p. 26.

148. Andrew Bennett, "Who Rules the Roost? Congressional-Executive Relations on Foreign Policy After the Cold War," in Robert Lieber, ed., *Eagle Rules? Foreign Policy and American Primacy in the Twenty-First Century* (Upper Saddle River, N.J.: Prentice-Hall, 2002), pp. 47–69; Cox, *United States Foreign Policy after the Cold War*, pp. 4, 12–13.

149. Christopher Gacek, *The Logic of Force: The Dilemma of Limited War in American Policy* (New York: Columbia University Press, 1994).

150. Powell's response was equally representative of the post-Vietnam military mindset: "I thought I would have an aneurysm." See Colin Powell, *My American Journey* (New York: Random House, 1995), p. 576.

151. Clark, *Waging Modern War*, pp. 436–40.

152. Tom Bowman, "Debating a No-Casualty Order," *Boston Globe*, April 9, 2000.

153. Russett, *Controlling the Sword*, p. 88.

154. Drew, *Showdown*, pp. 112, 138; Bert Rockman, "The Presidency and Bureaucratic Change after the Cold War," in Ripley and Lindsay, *U.S. Foreign Policy After the Cold War*, pp. 27–29.

155. Byman and Waxman, *The Dynamics of Coercion*, p. 143.

156. Cited in Blechman and Wittes, "Defining Moment," p. 13.

157. Osama Bin Ladin, "Declaration of War (August 1996)," in Barry Rubin and Judith Colp Rubin, eds., *Anti-American Terrorism and the Middle East: A Documentary Reader* (New York: Oxford University Press, 2002), p. 140.

158. Blechman and Wittes, "Defining Moment," p. 25; Barry Posen, "The War for Kosovo: Serbia's Political-Military Strategy," *International Security* 24, no. 4 (Spring 2000); 39–84.

159. Les Aspin, *Report on the Bottom-Up Review* (Washington, D.C.: United States Department of Defense, 1993), p. 28.

160. Lawrence Korb, "Shock Therapy for the Pentagon," *New York Times*, February 15, 1994; Paul Stockton, "When the Bear Leaves the Woods: Department of Defense Reorganization in the Post–Cold War Era," in Ripley and Lindsay, *U.S. Foreign Policy After the Cold War*, p. 109.

161. Andrew Krepinevich, *The Bottom-Up Review: An Assessment* (Washington, D.C.: Defense Budget Project, 1994).

162. Richard Gardner, "The One Percent Solution," *Foreign Affairs* 79, no. 4 (July–August 2000): 2–11. See also Duncan Clarke and Daniel O'Connor, "Security Assistance Policy After the Cold War," in Ripley and Lindsay *U.S. Foreign Policy After the Cold War*, pp. 215–34.

163. Kull et al., *The Foreign Policy Gap*, p. 16.

CONCLUSION
THE AMERICAN STRATEGIC DILEMMA

1. For a stimulating discussion of precedents within American history for Bush's post-9/11 grand strategy, see John Gaddis, *Surprise, Security, and the American Experience* (Cambridge, Mass.: Harvard University Press, 2004).

2. Governor George W. Bush, "A Distinctly American Internationalism," November 19, 1999, Simi Valley, California (www.georgebush.com/speeches/foreignpolicy/foreignpolicy.asp).

3. Andrew Bacevich, *The American Empire* (Cambridge, Mass.: Harvard University Press, 2002), pp. 206–8, 215–23.

4. James Mann, *Rise of the Vulcans: The History of Bush's War Cabinet* (New York: Viking, 2004), pp. 234–60.

5. Governor George W. Bush, "A Period of Consequences," September 23, 1999, The Citadel, South Carolina (www.citadel.edu/pao/addresses/pres_bush.html).

6. Presidential Debate, October 3, 2000, Boston, Massachusetts (www.foreignpolicy2000.org/debate/candidate/candidate.html).

7. George W. Bush, *A Charge to Keep* (New York, William Morrow, 1999), p. 239.

8. Condoleezza Rice, "Promoting the National Interest," *Foreign Affairs* 79, no. 1 (January–February 2000): 55–58.

9. For a representative statement by one of Bush's foreign policy advisors, see John Bolton, "Should We Take Global Governance Seriously?" *Chicago Journal of International Law*, 1, no. 2 (2000): 205–22.

10. Presidential debate, October 11, 2000, Salem, North Carolina (www.foreignpolicy2000.org/debate/candidate/candidate2.html).

11. See, for example, Stewart Patrick, "Don't Fence Me In: The Perils of Going It Alone," *World Policy Journal* 18, no. 3 (Fall 2001): 2–14.

12. Colin Powell, *My American Journey* (New York: Ballantine Books, 1995), pp. 242–43, 328–29, 438, 474.

13. In their book *America Unbound*, Ivo Daalder and James Lindsay describe this division as being between "democratic imperialists" such as Paul Wolfowitz, and "assertive nationalists," such as Dick Cheney and Donald Rumsfeld. See

Daalder and Lindsay, *America Unbound: The Bush Revolution in Foreign Policy* (Washington, D.C.: Brookings Institution Press, 2003), pp. 15–16.

14. See the project for a New American Century's June 3, 1997, "Statement of Principles" (www.newamericancentury.org/statementofprinciples.html), as well as its January 26, 1998, letter to President Clinton regarding Iraq (www.newamericancentury.org/iraqclintonletter.html).

15. Quoted in Michael Gordon, "Bush would stop U.S. Peacekeeping in Balkan Fights," *New York Times*, October 21, 2000.

16. See, for example, the quadrennial defense review of 2001, in which the Bush administration argued for de-emphasizing smaller-scale contingency operations in favor of core missions, such as homeland security, deterrence, and defense. Donald Rumsfeld, *Quadrennial Defense Review Report* (Washington, D.C.: The Department of Defense, 2001), pp. 14, 17, 21.

17. Steven Lee Myers and James Dao, "Bush Plans Modest Increase for the Pentagon," *New York Times*, February 1, 2001.

18. Jonathan Clarke of the Cato Institute, quoted in Lawrence Kaplan and William Kristol, *The War over Iraq* (San Francisco: Encounter Books, 2003), p. 68.

19. Richard Haass, "What to do With American Primacy," *Foreign Affairs*, 78, no. 5 (September–October 1999): 48.

20. Daalder and Lindsay, *America Unbound*, pp. 15, 46–47.

21. See Jacob Heilbrunn, "Condoleezza Rice: George W.'s Realist," *World Policy Journal* 16, no. 4 (Winter 1999–2000): 61; Powell, *My American Journey*, pp. 143–45, 562.

22. Daalder and Lindsay, *America Unbound*, pp. 48–49, 62–71.

23. John Mearsheimer and Stephen Walt, "Keeping Saddam Hussein in a Box," *New York Times*, February 2, 2003; Barry Posen, "The Struggle against Terrorism: Grand Strategy, Strategy, and Tactics," *International Security* 26, no. 3 (Winter 2001–2002): 54; Jack Snyder, "Imperial Temptations," *National Interest* 71 (Spring 2003): 29–40.

24. President Bush, Address to a Joint Session of Congress, September 20, 2001 (www.whitehouse.gov/news/releases/2001/09/20010920-8.html).

25. Leonie Huddy et al., "Trends: Reactions to the Terrorist Attacks of September 11, 2001," *Public Opinion Quarterly* 66, no. 3 (Fall 2002): 423–24.

26. Michael Noonan and John Hillen, "The Promise of Decisive Action," *Orbis* 46, no. 2 (Spring 2002): 229–46.

27. Michael Gordon, "Gains and Limits in New Low-Risk War," *New York Times*, December 29, 2001.

28. Bob Woodward, *Bush at War* (New York: Simon and Schuster, 2002), pp. 257, 291.

29. Max Boot, "This Victory May Haunt Us," *Wall Street Journal*, November 14, 2001.

30. Frederick Kagan, "Did We Fail in Afghanistan?" *Commentary* 115, no. 3 (March 2003): 39–45; Michael O'Hanlon, "A Flawed Masterpiece," *Foreign Affairs* 81, no. 3 (May–June 2002): 47–63.

31. Pat Buchanan, *A Republic, Not An Empire* (Washington, D.C.: Regnery Press, 2002), pp. ix, 46; Christopher Layne, "Offshore Balancing Revisited," *Washington Quarterly* 25, no. 2 (Spring 2002): 233–48.

32. John Ikenberry, "American Grand Strategy in the Age of Terror," *Survival* 43, no. 4 (Winter 2001): 19–34; Joseph Nye, *The Paradox of American Power* (New York: Oxford University Press, 2002), pp. 15, 39, 141–63.

33. Owen Harries, "An End to Nonsense," *National Interest* 65-S (Thanksgiving 2001): 117–20; Henry Kissinger, *Does America Need a Foreign Policy?* (New York: Touchstone, 2002), pp. 74–78, 116, 251–73, 287–88; Barry Posen, "The Struggle against Terrorism: Grand Strategy, Strategy, and Tactics," *International Security* 26, no. 3 (Winter 2001–2002): 39–55.

34. See note 24.

35. Michael Howard, "What's in a Name? How to Fight Terrorism," *Foreign Affairs* 81, no. 1 (January–February 2002): 8–13.

36. Frank Bruni, "For President, A Mission and a Role in History," *New York Times*, September 22, 2001; Michael Hirsh, "Bush and the World," *Foreign Affairs* 81, no. 5 (September–October 2002): 18–19; John Judis, "Why Iraq?" *American Prospect* 14, no. 3 (March 2003): 12–13.

37. Daalder and Lindsay, *America Unbound,* pp. 132–39.

38. "Secretary Rumsfeld Interview," *New York Times*, October 12, 2001.

39. Michael Kinsley, "Defining Terrorism," *Washington Post*, October 5, 2001.

40. Nicholas Lemann, "How It Came to War," *New Yorker* (March 31, 2003): 37–38.

41. *The 9/11 Commission Report: Final Report of the National Commission on Terrorist Attacks Upon the United States* (New York: W. W. Norton, 2004), pp. 334–36; Woodward, *Bush at War*, pp. 49, 61, 83, 87, 91.

42. Bob Woodward, *Plan of Attack* (New York: Simon and Schuster, 2004), pp. 1–8, 29–66. In his remarkably candid memoir, David Frum describes how he was asked in December 2001 to draft a State of the Union address that would make the case for war against Iraq. It was Frum who subsequently helped coin the phrase "axis of evil." See David Frum, *The Right Man: An Inside Account of the Bush White House* (New York: Random House, 2003), pp. 224–45.

43. President Bush at the United Nations General Assembly, September 12, 2002 (www.whitehouse.gov/news/releases/2002/09/20020912–1.html).

44. Judis, "Why Iraq?" pp. 12–13.

45. President Bush, address at the Washington Hilton Hotel, February 26, 2003 (www.whitehouse.gov/news/releases/2003/20030226–11.html).

46. Thomas Carothers, "Promoting Democracy and Fighting Terror," *Foreign Affairs* 82, no. 1 (January–February 2003): 92; George Packer, "Dreaming of Democracy," *New York Times Magazine* (March 2, 2003): 46–49.

47. Joshua Micah Marshall, "Bomb Saddam?" *Washington Monthly* 34, no. 6 (June 2002): 19–25.

48. Lemann, "How It Came to War," 37; Woodward, *Plan of Attack*, pp. 72–136.

49. Woodward, *Bush at War*, pp. 332–36.

50. Nicholas Lemann, "Without a Doubt," *New Yorker* (October 14 and 21, 2002): 177.

51. President Bush, State of the Union Address, January 29, 2002 (www.whitehouse.gov/news/releases/2002/01/20020129–11.html).

52. The White House, *The National Security Strategy of the United States of America* (Washington, D.C.: GPO, September 2002), p. 1.

53. Ibid., p. 3.

54. Ibid., pp. 4, 17–18.

55. Ibid., pp. 26–27.

56. Ibid., pp. 27–28.

57. Ibid., pp. 6, 13–15.

58. Ibid., p. 15.

59. President Bush, speech in Cincinnati, Ohio, October 7, 2002 (www.whitehouse.gov/news/releases/2002/10/20021007–8.html); State of the Union address, January 28, 2003 (www.whitehouse.gov/news/releases/2003/20030128–19.html); Address to the Nation, March 17, 2003 (www.whitehouse.gov/news/releases/2003/20030317–7.html).

60. President Bush at West Point, New York, June 1, 2002 (www.whitehouse.gov/news/releases/2002/06/20020601–3.html).

61. Michael Noonan and John Hillen, "The Promise of Decisive Action," *Orbis* 46, no. 2 (Spring 2002): 229–46.

62. Michael O'Hanlon, *Defense Policy Choices for the Bush Administration*, 2nd ed. (Washington, D.C.: Brookings Institution, 2002), p. 14; and see the U.S. Department of Defense press release regarding military spending for FY 2004 (www.defenselink.mil/news/Feb2003/b02032003_bt044–03.html). The figures cited above include defense-related expenditures by the U.S. Department of Energy, but do not include supplemental spending on military operations in Iraq and Afghanistan.

63. David Hendrickson, "Toward Universal Empire: The Dangerous Quest for Absolute Security," *World Policy Journal* 19, no. 3 (Fall 2002): 1–10; John Ikenberry, "America's Imperial Ambition," *Foreign Affairs* 81, no. 5 (September–October 2002): 44–60; Robert Litwak, "The New Calculus of Pre-emption," *Survival* 44, no. 4 (Winter 2002): 53–79; Jeffrey Record, "The Bush Doctrine and War with Iraq," *Parameters* 33, no. 1 (Spring 2003): 4–21; Jack Snyder, "Imperial Temptations," *National Interest* 71 (Spring 2003): 29–40.

64. Anja Manuel and Peter Singer, "A New Model Afghan Army," *Foreign Affairs* 81, no. 4 (July–August 2002): 44–59.

65. Anthony Cordesman, *The Iraq War: Strategy, Tactics, and Military Lessons* (Washington, D.C.: CSIS Press, 2003), pp. 493–516; Frederick Kagan, "War and Aftermath," *Policy Review*, no. 120 (August–September 2003): 3–27.

66. Frederick Barton and Bathsheba Crocker, "Winning the Peace in Iraq," *Washington Quarterly* 26, no. 2 (Spring 2003): 7–22; James Dobbins et al., *America's Role in Nation-Building: From Germany to Iraq* (Santa Monica: RAND, 2003); Robert Rotberg, "Failed States in a World of Terror," *Foreign Affairs* 81, no. 4 (July–August 2002): 127–40.

67. George Kennan, *American Diplomacy* (Chicago: University of Chicago Press, 1951), pp. 65–90; Hans Morgenthau, *Politics Among Nations: The Strug-*

gle for Power and Peace, abridged ed. (New York: McGraw Hill, 1993), pp. 148, 155–64.

68. Jeff Frieden, "Sectoral Conflict and U.S. Foreign Economic Policy," in John Ikenberry, ed., *American Foreign Policy: Theoretical Essays* (New York: Longman, 2002), pp. 138–67; Helen Milner, *Resisting Protectionism: Global Industries and the Politics of International Trade* (Princeton: Princeton University Press, 1988); Peter Trubowitz, *Defining the National Interest: Conflict and Change in American Foreign Policy* (Chicago: University of Chicago Press, 1998).

69. Michael Mandlebaum, *The Ideas that Conquered the World: Peace, Democracy, and Free Markets in the Twenty-First Century* (New York: Public Affairs, 2002); Tony Smith, *America's Mission: The United States and the Worldwide Struggle for Democracy in the Twentieth Century* (Princeton: Princeton University Press, 1994).

INDEX

Abrams, Elliot, 119, 150–51
Acheson, Dean, 102
Afghanistan, 153–56, 161–62
agenda setting: domestic, 1915–1919, 55–61; domestic, 1945–1946, 96–100; process of strategic adjustment, in the, 37–39, 41
Aideed, Mohamed, 138, 143
Albright, Madeleine, 129–30, 138, 142, 171, 207n.116
Allison, Graham, 121
Al Qaeda, 139, 154–55, 157
Ambrosius, Lloyd, 182n.1
American strategic adjustment: Cold War, following the (see Bush administration; Clinton administration; post-Cold War grand strategy); domestic policy adjustment, contrast with, 181n.43; domestic politics and, 37–42 (see also domestic politics); punctuated equilibrium as the pattern of, 38; World War One, following (see disengagement; post-World War One grand strategy); World War Two, following (see containment; post-World War Two grand strategy). See also grand strategy; strategic ideas
American strategic culture: elements of, 21; legacies of in American foreign policy, 4–5; liberalism in, 21–26 (see also liberal assumptions/ideas/vision; liberal internationalism); limited liability in, 26–30 (see also limited liability); sphere-of-influence arrangement with the Soviet Union complicated by, 87–88; subcultures of, 31–33; subcultures of, factors determining relative influence of, 33–36. See also culture*IL6*A National Security Strategy for a New Century, 131
Aristide, Jean-Bertrand, 138
Armitage, Richard, 150–51
arms control, 122–23
Asia-Pacific Economic Cooperation, 130
Aspin, Les, 129
Australia, 198n.119
"axis of evil," 158

Bacevich, Andrew, 140
Baker, Ray Stannard, 66
balance-of-power strategy: future unacceptability of, 170; military alliance as post-World War One option, 4, 48–49, 60, 68, 73–78, 80; as post-Cold War option, 115, 117–19; as post-Cold War option, Clinton administration rejection of, 132; as post-World War Two option (see mutual spheres of influence); realist supporters of, distinguished from primacists, 121
Bao Dai, 107
belief systems. See strategic ideas
Berger, Thomas, 14
Beveridge, Albert, 50–51, 69
bin Laden, Osama, 143, 155
blowback, 178n.13
Bohlen, Charles, 88
Bolton, John, 150–51
Boot, Max, 154
Borah, William, 50–51, 68, 70, 72–74, 76
Bosnia, 137–39, 142–43
Bradley, Omar, 94, 103
Britain: American commitment to Europe, desire to obtain, 54; concessions to at Versailles, 61–63; financial conditions in 1946–1947, 101; Iraq, support of the United States in, 157; League of Nations and, 47–48, 58–59; Middle East, waning of influence in the, 105–6; military alliance, opposition in the U.S. to, 50–51; military alliance, post-World War One proposal of, 44, 48–50
Bryce, Lord James, 77
Buchanan, Pat, 116, 134
Bullitt, William, 74, 188n.98
Burnham, James, 85
Bush, George H. W., 33, 128, 133, 138
Bush, George W.: initial realism of, 147–52; Iraq and, 157–58, 168; misinterpretation of, 1; on nation building, 161; preventive war, embrace of, 159–60; war on terror, launching of, 154–56; as Wilsonian classical liberal, 2, 162